The Big Bucks Guide to

Commercial Fishing in
Alaska

How to Run Away to Alaska,

Work Harder Than You Ever Thought Possible,

and Perhaps Even Get Paid

by

Capt. Jonathan Allen

Cover design: Rob Johnson, www.johnsondesign.org
Book design: Linda Morehouse, www.webuildbooks.com

Illustrations by Earl Douglas Allen
and by Shauna Crandall

Printed in the United States of America
First Edition
ISBN: 9780983907503

Published by
Prodigious Press
P. O. Box 537
Driggs, ID 83422

Dedication

To my lovely sister, Nancy Jo.

Acknowledgments

Ole Mogster, Wakiyamasan and Gaylord Clark are the three finest fishermen I was ever fortunate enough to work for. Without their example I would never have learned how to fish or how to conduct myself on fishing vessels. Thank you.

The self-publishing terrain is spotted with grifters and prevaricators, a mess for the first-time author. Without the help of Linda and Matt Morehouse, of Paradise Cay Publications, Inc., this book would never have been brought to press. Thank you.

Lastly, without the unlimited faith and support of my wife and partner, Tammy Allen, whom I take so utterly for granted, this book would never have been. Thank you, Baby. Clearly I could never have written it without you.

Table of Contents

Fishing Alaska!

Commercial fishing is an unusual occupation, one of the few where a young person without education can make an excellent living, provided he is capable of discipline, toughness, and ambition.

Alaskan fishing remains the single most dangerous occupation in America. It may also require the longest hours, be the most monotonous, and perhaps even be the most uncomfortable.

But in fishing it's the results that count, not family connections (except on small boats), or levels of education (of the formal kind), or even social skills (although they can come in handy).

The Bering Sea is arguably the richest fishing ground in the world. Most salt-water fish live in shallow water near the ocean bottom, where the food and hiding spots are.

The Bering Sea is very shallow, mostly continental shelf— so shallow my ancestors were able to walk across it a long time ago. The Bering Sea continental shelf supports the same fish density as the continental shelf waters off of the lower forty-eight, the difference being its width. The continental shelf off of most of Canada and the continental US averages twenty to thirty miles wide; in the Bering Sea it is hundreds of miles wide.

The Magnusson Act of 1977 protects the coastal waters 200 miles out from shore, which is good. Even better, the Pribilof Islands lie 400 miles off the coast of Alaska. That means, all together, 600 miles of incredibly rich fishing grounds, making the Pribilof Islands possibly the most valuable real estate on earth. That is some serious luck.

If you're an American you have access to these waters. You can join this lucrative industry, an industry where you can work outside, feed the world, and make good money without ever having to rip anyone off. I don't think too many Harvard graduates get opportunities like that.

The fishing industry has a very clear career path, whose entry-level positions are beginning processor and beginning deckhand. The next level is deck boss or processor foreman, then mate and engineer. Above them is the captain, and at the top is the vessel owner, who may or may not be the skipper.

Most fishing boats owners started at the bottom and worked their way up. If you apply yourself, work your way up the hierarchy, and take some risks, you may eventually even become rich.

But it will take time. To make good money fishing you must put in the time.

So let's get started.

What to Expect

Believe it or not, it is possible to have fun fishing commercially in Alaska. Not many people do it for fun, and it may not happen very often, but on those rare occasions when you pull up a stuffed crab pot worth $600 to each crewman, or when you and your buddies are whooping it up ashore in the sports bar at the Unisea Inn of Dutch Harbor, it can be fun.

But fishing is also uncomfortable, often painful. Expect to always be at least one, usually two, of the following: tired, hungry, or cold.

Fishing is an occupation to be proud of. Harvesting the sea and feeding the world is an honorable way to make a living, especially when compared to class action lawyers or congressmen. Fishing is also a very old profession, yet one that changes and evolves with spectacular speed. Fishing is often well-paid, usually demanding, occasionally exciting, frequently frustrating, and, to me, anyway, endlessly fascinating.

However, this is not an occupation for the soft. Everything you make, you will have earned. Even the least demanding shifts run twelve hours a day, seven days a week. The most demanding vessels (certain crab boats) work very nearly twenty hours a day for weeks at a time.

On most fishing boats you will be paid a percentage of vessel production, which means everyone's paycheck depends on the productivity of you and your shipmates. Understandably, this reduces shipboard tolerance of shirkers to zero. You either pull your weight or your fishing career will be quite short.

Before you seek a berth aboard a fishing vessel, a little honest self-evaluation is in order. Are you physically fit and capable of tough physical labor under rotten conditions for weeks or months at a time? Can you deal with rough, aggressive, perhaps even crude characters for the same extended time period? Most importantly, can you force yourself to carry out your responsibilities even though you are uncomfortable, tired, sick, bored, or unhappy?

If you can't, do yourself and the boat a favor and stay home. Fishing isn't for you.

There is one primary reason anyone goes to Alaska to fish: money. So, how much can you make? It ranges from nothing to hundreds of thousands of dollars a year. Many fishermen have paid for homes, businesses, advanced educations, or Harley Davidsons with a couple of good seasons. These successful fishermen had two things in common: they worked hard in a hot fishery, and they had enough discipline to save some of their money. I'm not sure which is more difficult.

Crew shares vary greatly from boat to boat. Obviously, income also depends on how many months a year one works. Experienced shipboard processors are seldom happy earning less than $5,000 a month during the high months, and deckhands expect even more. Quite a few young men and women earn between $50,000 and $100,000 a year. But it is not unusual to make a lot one year and considerably less the next.

Let me be clear about one thing, though: It's very possible to land a job fishing in Alaska, work harder than you've ever worked in your life, and if the fish are few, or the prices low, or the skipper unskilled, or the boat unlucky, you may make virtually nothing. Sometimes, it is way better to be lucky than highly skilled.

It happened to me. My first crabbing deck job was on a real dog of a boat. We crabbed Norwegian style (one crew working round the clock) with a short three-man deck crew. The boat hadn't crabbed for many years and it wasn't set up properly. She carried only old, worn, obsolete, orphaned gear the owner had bought from crab boats that had sunk.

We were crabbing for Bairdi crab, which were scarce that year and so thin the processing plants didn't really want them, so the price was lousy too. After a month of 23-hour work days in the middle of winter in the Bering Sea, I made $2,000 before taxes. Then the thief of a boat owner never sent me the final $500 settlement check he owed me. I made $2.17 an hour for the hardest work I have ever done in my life.

The story does have a happy ending, though. A month later I was hired aboard a top crab boat because I now had my new, hard-earned crabbing experience and a Coast Guard license. I was paid about $1,000 a day for almost six months.

America doesn't have much of a fishing tradition anymore, especially with the larger vessels that work the Bering Sea. This means there are many foreigners working aboard American fishing vessels. It also means most Americans seeking a berth aboard an Alaskan fishing vessel have never fished commercially before. So they'll be starting at the bottom, usually as a greenhorn processor at a shore plant or on a lesser boat.

That's how it works: sign on at an entry-level position on a mediocre boat, build experience, and complete your contract. Then take your experience and try for a better boat or a better job on the same boat. Poor vessels usually have vacancies, while the better vessels seldom have trouble crewing up with talented rehires.

There is nothing wrong with moving around, trying different fisheries and vessels, until you acquire a body of experience and find the right boat for you. But please, always complete your contract. Once you earn a reputation as a quitter, jobs will become few and far between.

There are three main methods of fishing in Alaska: nets, hooks, and pots. Generally it doesn't matter to a processor how the fish or crab are caught. It does matter how processors are paid. The shore-side factories pay by the hour, while the factory fishing boats usually pay a percentage of the catch, which is occasionally called a case price. Some of the factory boats only pay an hourly wage. Be sure to find out which system of payment your fishing boat uses before signing on, and keep, in a safe place, a copy of the contract that you sign.

Sometimes some of the less reputable companies will have you sign a contract and then whisk it away without giving you a copy. That way they can use it against you if you fail to perform. But a word to the wise: you will have a hard time enforcing your rights if the company falls short if you don't have a copy of your contract.

Usually, a percentage pays better than an hourly wage. Most processors take the first job offered to them and then try to gradually work into a deckhand job. Deck hands are paid at a higher rate and normally don't have to work on the slime line.

It might not be a bad idea to move around while you're still a processor and try different fisheries before getting locked into something that might not be your first choice. I've fished all three types of gear and wound up specializing in longlining because they were the first to offer me a captain's job. (In retrospect, maybe that wasn't such a good idea, since trawling, to me, is much more fun.)

I need to make one further vital point: working on a fishing boat is harder work than most people can imagine. Often the work goes on until it's done, no matter how long that may be.

It has to be that way. If the ice on the boat is building up to where the vessel is endangered, it has to be broken off, or the vessel and the crew will be lost. If a crewmember is seriously injured and is unable to work, the rest of the crew has to work harder to keep up production. If working at a nice comfortable speed doesn't get all the work done, you have to work faster—probably much faster. All experienced hands find it unremarkable to work 12 to 18 hours a day, seven days a week, for a month at a time.

This is a brutal schedule for most normal people, yet it has positive aspects as well. If you can work these hours cheerfully, it makes you quite valuable to the boat, and you won't have any problem keeping a job. You will also learn to work much faster and more efficiently than the vast majority of Americans.

Fishermen are usually successful when they eventually get a more normal job because they're used to working much harder and faster than most people. They have had to develop a very strong work ethic just to survive. Both of these attributes are invaluable, and will serve you well throughout your life.

I have several crab fishermen friends who crab ninety days a year, usually on the same boat, and then go home to the North Shore of Oahu, where they surf, smoke, and chase *wahines* for the other nine months. They have been doing it for years. Usually they gross about ninety thousand a year. That's not a bad lifestyle.

King Crab

Choosing a Fishery

Processing one kind of fish is not much different from processing another. There are some fish that processors dislike more than others, such as Pacific Ocean perch (with their many spines), or yellow-fin sole (which require a lot of work and usually aren't worth very much). But overall, cooking crab is the same mind-numbing, boring, uncomfortable work as driving pollock through a Baader fileting machine or pulling guts out of codfish.

First decide if your initial processing contract is a one-shot deal, perhaps to buy a car or finance a year of college. If so, take the first offer you get where the rough pay rate sounds acceptable. However, if you think you might want to make a career out of fishing, choose your fishery with more care.

While processing on one particular factory boat is more or less the same as any other, that isn't true of deck handing, the next step up the ladder. A deckhand job on a crab boat is very different than a deckhand job on a long liner or a trawler. The skills are different, the hours are different, the seasons are different, even the personalities of the fishermen are different.

Crabbing is brutal, dangerous—and usually well paid.

Longlining is a grind, every day is pretty similar, but if you're coordinated and apply yourself you can master it in less than a year. It's mostly setting the gear and retrieving and coiling the gear, with a little gaffing thrown in.

Trawling is different. The work isn't as hard, usually, but it takes years to master because there is a lot to learn about setting up, building, and repairing trawl nets.

Decide which fishery is most interesting to you and choose a processing job in that field. If you do an excellent job processing, that's the fishery where you'll get a shot at a deck job. We'll discuss the different fisheries in more depth a little later on.

If you're a college student looking for summer work, you need a different strategy. Most of the summer jobs are on salmon boats or in salmon canneries, so that's where you should concentrate your efforts. Happily, the salmon season starts around June and ends in late summer or early fall, which is perfect for a student's schedule.

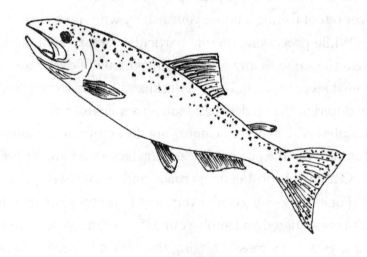

Chinook Salmon

Choosing a Boat

On the smaller catcher boats, which don't process on board, entry-level crew (or greenhorns), start out working on deck. Salmon boats, in particular, often hire a greenhorn deckhand or two. You'll find a list of thousands of current salmon fishing permit holders in the back of this book.

On the larger factory fishing boats, the entry-level position is fish processor. Fish processing is fish processing, so don't worry about the species too much, except for Pacific Ocean perch (POP).

I once worked on a head-and-gut boat harvesting a dozen types of fish. As the various seasons closed we worked our way down the list of available species. Finally we got to POP. The processors threatened to quit if we fished for Pacific Ocean perch, a small fish very similar to a bluegill except that it's bright red.

POP, similar to most perch, carries mild venom in its spines. The stabbings hurt after you've been stuck a couple of dozen times in a day, and it's hard not to start dreaming about going home. So (except for POP) the efficiency and safety of the vessel is far more important than the type of fish being processed.

Remember, though, jobs of any type are hard to come by on a top boat—especially for greenhorns. I suggest you take the first solid job offer you get, even if the boat is fishing for perch. If you think you can do better, you can always switch to a better boat after you complete your contract, and in the meantime you'll be earning money and gaining experience.

It is very difficult for a greenhorn to evaluate the difference between two vessels. Which boat is more lucrative?

Which boat is safer? Which boat is run most efficiently?

If I write that a particular fishing company is run by low-life scumbags who couldn't catch fish in an aquarium, I might get sued, and I might even be wrong if the vessel is under new management—so I can't do it.

But helping you evaluate vessels is pretty important, so I'll take a run at it. How does the vessel look? Squared away or dirty and disorganized? If there's a line of boats tied up together and the worst looking one has a lot of vacancies, guess what that means.

Keep in mind that a new paint job does not a good boat make: it's just a paint job. You must look deeper. The condition of a boat's fishing gear speaks loudly. So does the condition of the mooring lines. If they're worn out, the boat isn't being maintained.

Talk to the crew. A lot of returning crew who have worked aboard the same vessel for years is the best recommendation there is. Does the hiring seem well organized? Good organizations tend to operate good boats. Crew of other boats can sometimes bring you up to date on a particular boat's reputation. If you know someone who has fished recently, ask them for input. I've worked on good boats where much of the crew was either from the same small town on the other side of the country, or else related.

If, in the course of your job search, you get friendly with someone knowledgeable in the industry, run the name of a prospective fishing boat by them. The industry is smaller than you might think and people love to talk.

If you are ever fortunate enough to fish with someone talented who takes it upon himself to teach you a bit more about the trade than he has to, learn everything you can. There aren't great numbers of master fishermen around, and many of the experts aren't eager to share what they know. I once crabbed with a deck boss who would do his splices with his coat pulled over his head so no one could watch. What a jackass.

I would suggest remaining on a lower-paying boat where you are learning and progressing rapidly, rather than jumping to a slightly better boat where, after a couple of weeks, you may wind up stagnating. In the long run, knowledge is almost always more valuable than money.

In the past I've left higher paying jobs for lower paying vessels where I was doing more of the fishing (which is probably why it was lower paying). As a result, I picked up another fishery—trawling, my favorite. In the long run I came out ahead.

Once, I was looking for my first job on an albacore boat when a skipper with a full crew gave me his card and told me to call him if I found a job. He promised to let me know if my new skipper was a moron or a crook. That's a good man.

It illustrates the problem. In spite of a decade of fishing experience in Alaska, I still needed help evaluating tuna boats in Northern California. The first job in a particular fishery is always the riskiest one. After that, you'll have some experience and contacts to draw on.

Catcher Boats vs. Catcher Processors

There is a big difference between the two systems. Catcher boats catch their quarry and deliver it to shore-side or floating processing plants, and then return to the fishing grounds for another quick trip. Catcher processors (CPs) catch their fish or crab and process it right on board. They usually carry somewhere between 3 and 80 processors, depending on the boat size and the type of fishery.

CPs stay at sea for much longer trips than the catcher boats, since they don't have to worry about their crab dying or their fish spoiling. The fish is processed, cleaned, packed, and frozen onboard and is offloaded ashore in neat cardboard boxes or heavy paper bags. A catcher processor doesn't have to return to port until the freezer hold is filled or it runs out of food or fuel. I've seen them come in with just about all their food gone. The crew had been surviving on the same pollock (yuck!) they were processing—they were not happy campers!

Many fishermen prefer the catcher boats, with their quicker trips, fewer rules, smaller crew, and often higher pay. Other fishermen prefer the bigger, safer CPs, with their larger crews.

Summer salmon boats are the easiest catcher boats for a novice to find a berth on—more on that in the salmon fishing section. A catcher boat, with its crew of five or six, can't really afford more than one or two greenhorns, and often will carry only experienced fishermen. A catcher processor may carry as many as 10 or 20 new people each trip. There can be a lot of turnover. Many of the deckhands start out on the big boats and switch to the catchers as they gain experience.

The difference between the two systems is considerable, and you may have to make a choice between the two. Would you be happier in a large floating factory, one among many? Or would you prefer to work with a small, tight group, some of whom you might not particularly like? There is no right answer, but it's worth some thought.

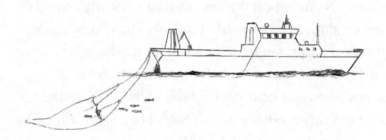

Factory Trawler

Processing at Sea

Processing fish at sea is factory work in a seagoing slaughter-house. There are a number of different jobs throughout the factory. All of them are repetitive, boring, and need to be done quickly.

On a pollock *surimi* boat many of the processors run auto-matic filet machines, such as Baaders or Toyos. This requires the processor to drop a single fish into a moving slot, head up and facing the correct way, one hundred and twenty-four times a minute. The machines have counters that record every missed slot. Some expert drivers can go a week without miss-ing a single slot. It takes youth, toughness, and thousands of milligrams of ibuprofen to drive a Baader machine for twelve hours a day, seven days a week, for a month straight.

A head-and-gut boat runs a "slime line," where the de-capitated fish ride down a conveyer belt until a processor grabs them, pulls out the guts, and drops them on another conveyer belt bound for the sorting and panning table.

On filet boats (head-and-gut boats with an additional filet line), cod are run through filet machines that carve both sides off the carcass. The filets then run down a candling line where they're inspected for flaws, such as worms and cancer, which are cut out. If you spend any time on a candling line you'll never eat cod again, which would be a shame because it's a superior tasting fish.

On pollock *surimi* boats the fish are ground into paste, mixed with sugar, extruded into 40-pound blocks, and frozen. On head-and-gut boats the fish are decapitated, their guts are removed, they're sorted by species and size, and then they're frozen into 40-pound blocks. These blocks must be broken from the plate freezer, bagged, and stored in the freezer hold.

On the larger vessels the freezer crew only freezes and stows the final product. On the smaller vessels the same crew does both the processing and the freezing. The point is there are a lot of different processing jobs on factory boats, depending on the fishery and the finished product.

Room and board is part of your pay aboard floating processors. The living conditions depend on the age of the vessel, the quality of the vessel management, company policy, and the fastidiousness of the captain.

Some of the big factory trawlers are almost comically comfortable. I was on one where the chief steward carved an ice sculpture for a Christmas dinner centerpiece.

I've been on others so filthy that I had to hold my breath when entering the berthing quarters.

Living Conditions

The range of living conditions on a fishing boat is all over the chart. The worst I ever saw was on a small freezer longliner owned by a bottom feeder of a fishing company. Both toilets (called a head on a boat) were misbehaving and the engineer was a bit of a minimalist. Rather than fix them, he removed them from the deck, leaving a four-inch hole to aim at. Hanging over the aft rail was the other option. I usually chose the aft rail, which became an adventure in thirty-foot seas, at night, in a snowstorm. Whoooh!

On that particular vessel the skipper and the engineer both had their own rooms, sharing a head—until it was removed. The other eleven crew members berthed in two rooms in two high bunk beds. The cook did most of the cleaning as time allowed, but the fishing boat was only thoroughly cleaned at the end of every trip, about every two or three weeks.

The living conditions on the big factory trawlers tend to be completely different. They usually carry a vessel housekeeper who does nothing but clean the living spaces. All of the senior management has a private room and head; middle management shares room and head with a roommate.

A common arrangement for the deckhands and processors is small two-man berthing areas not much bigger than a bunk bed that opens on to a larger day room and head, with usually four small berthing areas per day room. The *Alaska Ocean*, the fanciest factory trawler ever built, has two-man rooms for all the processors and deckhands, and telephones and piped-in music in every room as well.

On the mid-sized vessels—freezer longliners and head-and-gut trawlers—eight-man berthing areas are common, with a head for each large room. The smaller catcher boats have a private room for the skipper and one to three berthing areas for everyone else, with one or two heads on the boat.

If possible, women are berthed together. But if it is a choice between a female bunking with the guys or the captain bunking with the guys, well, it's not called the master's stateroom for nothing. Often a female federal fisheries observer will share a berthing area with a bunch of guys with no issues. The head will lock and she'll shower at off hours, or she'll share a more exclusive head. Fishermen are problem-solvers; this isn't a particularly difficult one.

There is also a wide range of general cleanliness on fishing boats. I've seen top crab boats that looked positively yacht-like. The crew hadn't changed in years and they had all made a fortune. They all took their boots off before entering the vessel's house, and even if it was mid-season, the respect they showed the boat and skipper was evident. Such boats have new paint, new gear, and are immaculate. They can hire anyone in the industry they want.

There is also the other extreme, where the skipper doesn't really care how the rest of the crew lives, where the general filth becomes a fire hazard as well as a health hazard. Try to walk through the vessel before signing on, to get an idea of the berthing and housekeeping conditions.

A professional fisherman may not always be clean, but he's always neat. After you've ridden out a few storms you'll see what I mean. All unsecured gear will work its way down to the lowest level possible, then slide back and forth with all the other debris. It's usually much easier to put things away securely in their place before the storm than to clean up afterwards.

I once ran a freezer longliner that held a large built-in safe in my stateroom. It wasn't secured properly and whenever the seas got really rough, the safe would hop out of its home and careen back and forth across the room. I was generally so tired only a direct hit on my bunk would wake me momentarily. I would remind myself not to roll out of bed in the dark, where a crushing blow from the safe would surely mash me like a bug, until it either calmed down or I really had to get up. Once the weather abated, I would shove the safe back into its hole, promising myself to secure it properly as soon as I got a chance, where it would stay until the next 25 degree roll.

This is not how you want to live. Keep things shipshape.

Shoreside Processing Plants

There are 19,000 shore-side processing jobs to be filled in Alaska each year. They seldom pay as well as the boats, but they don't sink very often either.

Unlike most fishing boats, processing plants will hire you sight unseen. They pay about $7.15 per hour for entry-level processors if room, board, and transportation are provided. But it's not unusual to work sixteen hours a day, seven days a week for a couple of months, with everything over 40 hours a week being overtime.

Many shore-side processing plants offer room and board or camping facilities. Others don't offer anything. For those that do offer room and board, sometimes it's free, other times it is five to ten dollars a day.

Salmon processing plants operate during the summer only and often provide camping spots rather than room and board. Most winter processing plants provide room and board. Make sure you discuss this with the cannery before you make a decision.

It is not uncommon for processors to make up to $3,000 a month, with a raise or two and overtime. Quite a few college students have paid their tuition working summers in the salmon canneries. Most importantly, they're a good source of initial experience, and occasionally it's possible to talk your way onto a shore-delivery fishing boat, or a tender, which may be the best reason of all for working at a shore plant.

Recorded information about currently recruiting companies can be heard at (907) 269-4770, ex. 7. Or try www. Jobs.

state.ak.us. Click on "Seafood Jobs" or "Alaska Job Bank". There is no fee for using this service of the Alaska Job Center Network. You have to be in Alaska, though, to be referred to one of these jobs.

There is even a "Traveling Seafood Workforce" program that offers extended work for shore-side processors. As the various seasons open and close, workers who have completed their contracts are moved from one plant to another. Most processing plants start recruiting in February and continue until the start of the season in June if need be. Some of the canneries hire through websites, but all hire walk-ups when they run short of labor.

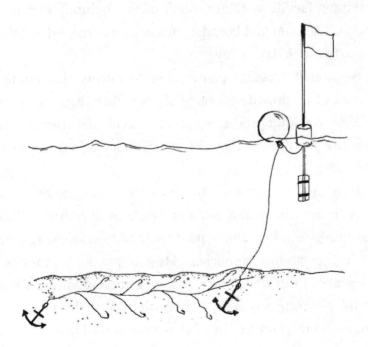

Longliner

Tendering

Tendering is a step up from working ashore in a cannery, but it isn't quite fishing. A tender boat goes out and meets the small salmon fishing boats, loads their catch aboard, and delivers the fish to the processing plant. This allows the fishing boats to keep catching.

The tender boats are usually crewed with a skipper and a deckhand or two. The skipper drives the boat, works the radio, and runs the operation. The deckhands pump the fish (the fish are usually transferred with a big slurry pump), maintain the boat, check the engine, cook, and all the rest.

Tenders usually anchor in some of the most beautiful bays in the world while they wait for their loads. Jobs can be had aboard these boats, particularly late in the season.

Most tender boats are large, out-of-season fishing boats, such as crab, longline, or trawl boats. The boats are often run by out-of-season fishermen, who are there only to protect their lucrative in-season berths.

If you find a job in a fish processing plant, maybe even unloading tender boats, you will meet a lot of tender boat operators and crew. If you work like an animal and let them know you're looking for a tender boat job, good things may happen. The job may last the entire summer, since some tender boats will move from one fishing area to another as the seasons open and close.

Tendering may not be fishing, but it's about as close as you can get.

Salmon Fishing

The Alaskan salmon fishery may be the best-managed fishery in the world. After being nearly destroyed in the 1960s by over-fishing and under-regulation, a limited entry permit system was introduced in 1973. New boats are prohibited from entering the fishery unless replacing an older boat. Only owners of limited entry permits, and their crew, are allowed to fish salmon commercially in Alaska.

The Alaskan Board of Fisheries insures enough salmon escape capture each year to sustain the stock. This is done by opening and closing the fisheries, sometimes daily, throughout the spawn. Alaska has funded hatcheries that release billions of young salmon each year. The state of Alaska is quite aware that commercial fishing remains its single biggest employer; consequently, the state of Alaska takes very good care of all commercial fishing.

But salmon fishing has its issues—farmed salmon, for one. At one time when salmon was scarce, its price would skyrocket. Now with a steady supply of farmed salmon available, the price of wild salmon can only rise so much before it is undercut by farmed salmon, even though wild salmon is a far superior product, free from all dyes, antibiotics, hormones, and genetic engineering.

Fishing wild Alaskan salmon used to pay very well. Not so much anymore. Over a good summer, a deck hand can expect to make $6,000 to $15,000 on a good boat. In the past it was a lot more.

Different types of salmon are worth different prices. This is important because when you're paid by share, your income is determined by price per pound, catch volume, and share size.

Here's a list of the types of salmon harvested in Alaska:

King Salmon

Also known as Chinook, it's a big, beautiful fish with a round body, black spots on its back, large scales, and a black mouth and tongue. They're hard to find, a high value fish. They're the most popular sport-caught salmon and can run well over 50 pounds. They get a premium price.

Sockeye Salmon

These are also known as red salmon. They feature a bright red filet and a sleek blue-green body. They feed on plankton filtered through their gill rakers, weigh up to 10 pounds, and command a premium price. If you ever try a fresh, in-season, Copper River Red at a good seafood restaurant, you will see why. Big Money.

Silver Salmon

Coho is their indigenous name. They have silver sides and a dark green back while at sea. When they enter fresh water to spawn, their sides turn red, their heads and back turn bluish green, and they develop a hooked jaw. Although not as valuable as the king and sockeye salmon, they taste nearly as good. Silvers usually run about ten pounds.

Chum Salmon

Some Alaskans say they're called dog salmon because they're only good for feeding your sled dogs. Others say it's because of the big, dog-like teeth they develop when they hit fresh water. I think they taste pretty good, so my guess is it's probably the teeth. They also develop big red stripes in fresh water, so maybe they should have been nicknamed tiger salmon. A mid-priced fish, the dog salmon is not terribly common.

Pink Salmon

These are also known as humpbacked salmon. They are the smallest and most common of the Pacific salmon. They are bright silver while at sea, and have a two-year life cycle. They develop a large hump and turn gray and white on contact with fresh water. They average a bit less than five pounds. Sometimes as many as 100 million are caught in a single season. They're not worth much, but you can catch a whole lot of them.

Salmon are caught four different ways: purse seine, gill net, troll, or set net. A purse seiner fishing boat works in tandem with a skiff that drags the free end of the net off the back deck of the seiner. The skiff and purse seiner separate, stretching out the quarter-mile-long net, then the skiff maneuvers quite close to the shore, where most of the migrating salmon congregate. The skiff and purse seiner circle around the fish and the free end of the net is passed back aboard the purse seiner. The net is then closed up at the bottom, or pursed, and the salmon are hauled aboard. Purse seiners usually carry a crew of five, counting the skipper.

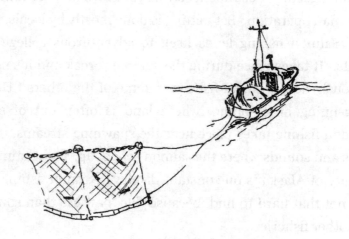

Gill Netter

A gill netter is a smaller operation, with a shorter boat and fewer crewmembers. The gill net is set off a reel over either the stern or bow of the gill netter, across the direction of travel of the migrating fish. The net carries floats on its head rope and weights on its foot rope, spreading it out like a fence in the water. The mesh size is selected to prevent the salmon from swimming through the net; their entangled gills prevent them from backing out. The net is retrieved by rolling it back on its reel. The fish are then plucked free as the net comes aboard and are tossed into the live tank.

Trolling for salmon uses even smaller fishing boats. A winter fishery, it consists of dragging baited hooks through feeding schools of fish. The crew often consists of a single fisherman, the boat owner, so we won't discuss it further.

Set netting is more of a shore-based fishery. The gill net

is dragged out from shore by a small, open boat. Once full, the net is cleaned of fish and reset. It's also a limited entry fishery, so don't get any ideas about setting your own net. It's kind of a one-man operation. Set netting is done mostly by locals.

Salmon fishing lends itself to adventurous college students. It takes place during the summer break and it's not as viciously demanding a fishery as some of the others. Unlike long-lining or crabbing, where land is often out of sight, salmon fishing takes place near the spawning streams, in the bays and sounds where the salmon school up, so the stunning beauty of Alaska is on constant display. Salmon fishing jobs are not that hard to find, because they pay less than some of the other fisheries.

Keep in mind that your first season, as with any fishery, probably won't pay very well. With no experience, you'll be expected to take a smaller share, possibly a half share. The job openings are usually on the new or less successful boats, and you will have almost no way of evaluating the boat's potential or the skipper's honesty. The first season, hope for the best and keep your eyes and ears open. Following seasons you'll be able to pick and choose.

The Easiest Way to Find a Summer Salmon Fishing Job

According to the State of Alaska, about 58 percent of Alaskan fishing jobs are in the salmon industry. The Alaska Department of Fish and Game keeps a list of commercial fishing permit holders at www.cfec.state.Ak.us/plook/ or you can just look in the back of this book, where you'll find a refined, sorted, current list of contact addresses of thousands of Alaskan fishing permit holders.

This salmon boat list is given as three appendices: purse seiner, gill netter, and combination seiner and gill netter. Seiners tend to be bigger, more capable boats that carry a larger crew than the gill netters and so are probably a better bet for the novice salmon fisherman. (Bristol Bay is the best place to fish on a gill netter because the fish volume is large and the fish value is high, making for a potentially lucrative summer, so I've included the Bristol Bay gill netters.)

A combination seiner/gill netter obviously has more than one permit. This can be quite valuable, because it may allow for extended fishing as the various seasons open and close, so they have their own list as well.

The best way to find a summer salmon fishing job is to contact some of the permit holders and ask. This is your chance to shine. All you have to do is put together a better resume and cover letter than anyone else. I've included a sample cover letter and resume to help you get started. (Look for them in the Appendix.)

Then you need to send off a number of well-put-together packages that demonstrate your attention to detail and care to permit holders in the fishing areas that are most interesting to you. Start early in the winter with a bulk mailing. Hopefully, you can schedule multiple interviews while in Washington, since you'll have to pay your own expenses.

Don't forget to visit all the Seattle-based factory boat companies while in town. (These are also listed in the back of this book.) You won't be successful if you're not persistent, so stick with it.

Make it easy for a skipper to hire you. Offer to come out early to help prep the boat. If the boat is leaving for Alaska earlier than you would like, alter your schedule, not the boat's. Often, if you need to leave school early to catch a fishing boat, your professors will make arrangements to help you. These are tough times and everyone needs a little assistance now and then, so don't be shy about asking for it.

Include in your package any letters of reference that you may have, including phone numbers. You have to stay positive, no matter what.

One of the marks of a true professional fisherman is that he never lets on when he's not feeling it. Emotional problems are not shared on a fishing boat, and problems back home are not shared on a fishing boat. If you can't maintain a façade of cheerfulness while searching for a job, you won't be able to maintain the façade when you're tired, hungry, and wet either. Your happiness doesn't have to be sincere, just reasonably convincing. Skippers hate whiners.

It really helps if you have some valuable life skills, such as cooking, mechanical, or sewing web. Welding is a skill in high demand. If you're strong or tough, that can be valuable.

Just got back from Afghanistan where you served as an infantryman? Mention it.

Grow up on a dairy farm where you had to get up at 4:15

AM every morning, including Christmas, to milk the cows? Hell, I'd hire you myself. Fishermen love farm boys. Let 'em know.

Were you a Sea Scout? Boat experience counts too.

The skipper does not want to sabotage his season by hiring a flake and then having to replace him in midseason when he doesn't work out. Lousy crew members can be unfit in so many ways: lazy, entitled, stupid, crazy, clueless, help-less, and on and on. Your resume and letter should reassure him that you know how to work, possess some toughness, are mentally and emotionally stable, and have something extra to offer.

Chances are you'll only make a half share your first season, especially on a good boat. Try for a full share, especially if you have something extra to offer—those cooking or diesel engi-neering skills we talked about.

But chances are you're going to have to work for half pay your first season in order to find a berth. From their point of view, greenhorns are surprisingly unhelpful until they learn some skills. So everyone else has to work harder to make the same money until the new guy can pull his own weight.

Still, some very good boats like to hire a greenhorn just to keep the crew shares down. Take the job at half share, work like hell, and convince them to hire you back for next season at full share and you'll be ahead of the game.

Crew share sizes can be a bit of a poker game. Don't forget half shares on a good boat often beat full shares on a lousy boat.

You'll have to show up in Seattle, or wherever the boat is tied up over the winter, a couple of weeks before getting under way for the fishing grounds. The boat and gear needs to be readied, and you don't get paid for this work. When you're paid by the share, your pay doesn't start until the fish start coming aboard. But you're still expected to prep the boat and ride it up to the fishing grounds. Usually the skipper will let you live on the boat while you're helping to get it ready to fish, but check with him before committing.

Just remember: when you catch a break, make the most of it. There are never enough really good crew to fill all of the jobs; there are, however, plenty of headaches out there looking for work.

When you find your spot, make it count.

Never complain. Even when the jellyfish stingers get in your eyes, just tie a bandanna over your face.

Think as much about the boat's needs as your own.

Be a good shipmate.

Leave your poor lifestyle choices at home unless the skipper is sitting on the next bar stool.

Learn as much as you can, as fast as you can.

Show up with a sea bag, rather than a suitcase.

Work harder and faster than you ever thought possible.

Be the first man on deck and the last man off the deck, unless you have to start cooking.

And never take the last pork chop.

Salmon Fishery Areas

False Pass

This fishery is located way out in the Aleutian Islands, a long way from anywhere. There are hardly any towns to speak of, a few villages and processing plants is all. Some people like it that way.

Even in the summer you can expect some awful weather here because the Aleutians are where the cold water out of the Arctic meets the much warmer Japan Current. Large temperature differentials make for high winds and bad weather. But you'll get some nice days during the summer too, even if the wind is usually blowing.

This might not be a bad place to fish for salmon if your plan is to move into some of the tougher winter fisheries, especially since the money tends to be good because of a lot of red salmon. The season starts in early June and runs until late August.

Chignik

This fishery is quite similar to the False Pass fishery, since it's located just to the east of the False Pass area. It also has the same long season, running from early June to late August. Most North Pacific storms travel west to east, so Chignik gets the same storms as False Pass, just a day later.

It is, however, a very good place to fish for salmon because there are even more red salmon to be caught and money to be made. Chignik is one of the highest paying areas in Alaska.

Kodiak

Kodiak is neck and neck with Dutch Harbor as the most productive fishing port in all of America. While Dutch Harbor mainly caters to the big catcher-processors who mostly fish the Bering Sea, Kodiak supports smaller catcher boats, including salmon boats, working the Gulf of Alaska. This makes it a good place to search for work.

Kodiak is actually a town, unlike many of the smaller communities that support the fishing fleet. This makes it easier to live here, should you choose to walk the docks looking for work. Kodiak, being just to the east of Chignik, enjoys many of the same storms as False Pass and Chignik—again, just a little later. It has an even longer season than Chignik, stretching well into September.

If you get established in Kodiak as a competent fisherman, you should do well. The smaller Kodiak catcher boats tend to pay better than the big Dutch Harbor vessels but often require more experience.

I know of a young hot-shot fishing skipper who filled his freezer longliner up with wormy fish that couldn't be sold. He was fired, flew to Kodiak, and found a job as a deck boss on a much smaller hand bait longliner. His new job wound up paying considerably better than his old captain's job.

Go figure.

Cook Inlet

Cook Inlet is a long bay with Anchorage lying at the head of it. It's a large body of water but still doesn't get the large seas and swells of some of the more exposed areas, even when the wind blows.

Most of the salmon boats fishing Cook Inlet are based out of Kenai or Homer. Locals claim that Homer is the Alaskan Riviera, but I have to admit that I have no idea what they're talking about. It does have a cool bar called the Salty Dawg Saloon in an old lighthouse, which is worth a visit and is a good place to buy a tee shirt.

The season runs from early June to late August and it can pay well, as most of the catch is red salmon.

Prince William Sound

In 1989 the Exxon *Valdez* ran aground on Bligh Reef in Prince William Sound, proving again the fallibility of man. It created the famous Valdez oil spill and made an ungodly mess.

The oil is mostly gone now and the salmon run has recovered. The salmon again return in great numbers but are mostly pinks, which aren't very valuable. I've seen pinks selling for as little as 12 cents a pound off the boat. What on earth sells for as little as 12 cents a pound?

You can make money, but you have to catch a lot of fish. Fortunately there are a lot of fish. Sometimes so many pink salmon are caught, the market is overwhelmed and all of the fish can't be sold.

The season runs from mid-June until late August. Cordova and Valdez are the main fishing ports in Prince William Sound. Valdez is also the southern end of the Alaskan pipeline and the ice-climbing capital of the world.

I only know that because when I told my brother that I had to go to Valdez for work he told me, "Dude, that is so chill, Valdez is so chill, it's like the ice-climbing capital of the world." I also know that it rains all summer long in Prince William Sound, 24 hours a day.

Southeast

The Southeast Alaskan salmon fishery has both its good and bad points. The fish caught are mostly pinks, so the money isn't great. It is also a good place to catch jellyfish, which means you spend a fair bit of your time trying to blink jellyfish stingers out of your eyes, which I count as a negative.

On the positive side, you're working in about the most beautiful place on earth. How would you like to fish in Glacier Bay National Park with glaciers calving and whales spouting? This is where all those fancy cruise ships sailing up the inside passage from the lower 48 are headed. Bring a camera—a waterproof camera.

The fishing is done in sheltered inside waters so calm seas are the norm. The season is only two months long, from late June until late August. There are more off days due to Department of Fish and Game fishing closures here than in any other area, giving you time to explore this lovely area.

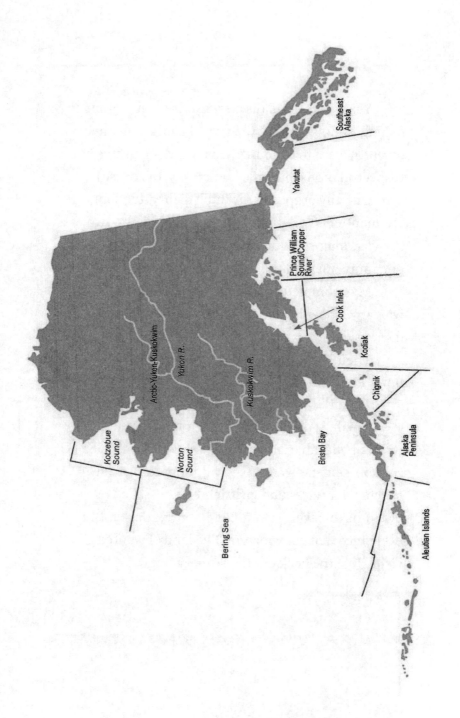

Southeast Alaska

Yakutat

Prince William Sound/Copper River

Cook Inlet

Kodiak

Chignik

Arctic-Yukon-Kuskokwim

Yukon R.

Kuskokwim R.

Bristol Bay

Alaska Peninsula

Kotzebue Sound

Norton Sound

Bering Sea

Aleutian Islands

Salmon Fishery Areas

Years ago I was discussing with some of my fishing buddies where the most beautiful women on earth were to be found (this was done in a very respectful, non-objectificational way, of course).

One guy proposed Air India flight attendants. He mentioned 1.2 billion people, divided by two, the vast majority quite poor and eager for an opportunity, makes for a massive pool to draw from.

My completely non-creative contribution was any Copenhagen Denmark park on a sunny day.

Then, from out of the blue came, "Petersburg, Alaska."

"What!"

"Yeah, I fished there all one summer, it was unbelievable. Petersburg is loaded with rich salmon seiner owners who all, apparently, have spectacular wives and girlfriends."

I have never been to Petersburg, Alaska. But ever since that conversation I've kind of wanted to visit. Just to check out the scenery.

Walking the Docks

I am not an advocate of walking the docks to find a fishing job—unless it's in Seattle. That may be because I've hired dozens of deckhands and processors off the docks, or on the side of the road, in Dutch Harbor, and it never quite worked out. I think that's because everyone I hired in Dutch Harbor had just been fired in Dutch Harbor. They brought their unacceptable work ethic with them, and invariably I had to send them on their way.

I never hired in Alaska unless I had no choice. Having said that, here's how you walk the docks looking for work on a salmon boat:

Try to look as responsible as possible (a shower and a shave sends an encouraging message). Try to be as sober as possible (yes, I've been approached by drunks looking for work—not a good look). A resume with a picture can be helpful, especially if you have something to brag about. Make sure it includes your cell phone number.

In March or April start walking the docks in and around Seattle: Anacortes, Bellingham, Everett, and Gig Harbor are all worth a look. Go down to the docks, talk to everyone; anyone may have a lead. Ask if you can talk to the skipper if you see someone working on a boat. Again, stay positive, friendly, and enthusiastic; make a good impression. Make sure you're signing on an *Alaskan* boat. West Coast salmon boats don't pay much.

Again, I don't recommend traveling to Alaska if you don't have a job lined up. But if you're determined and feel like driving up the Al-Can highway to Alaska, turn off at White Horse for Skagway and catch the ferry for Kodiak. Call the Alaskan Ferries ahead of time at (907) 465-3941 for scheduling information, because the ferries don't run every day.

Kodiak and Dutch Harbor are the two biggest fishing ports in America. Kodiak supports a large salmon fleet, Dutch Harbor does not. The Kodiak salmon season starts the second week of June, so if you don't find a job by then, head back to Cordova in the Prince William Sound.

During the last week of June try Petersburg, Sitka, and Ketchikan in Southeast Alaska.

By the Fourth of July you have a couple of choices. Either head back to Kodiak for the second time, since the season is about half over and there will be some openings, or take a shot at the Bristol Bay gill net fishery. Some of the ports harboring Bristol Bay gill netters include Dillingham, Togiak, and Naknek.

It might also be time to take a processing plant job. Sometimes, if you keep your eyes and ears open, you can land a fishing job while working at a processing plant.

People quit off of boats all the time. Except for logging, I've never found a line of work as physically difficult as fishing. People hire on unaware of how demanding the job can be; a lot of them quit as soon as they find out. Late in the season the skipper will be happy to hire a replacement locally. If you do well, you should then be set for the following year.

Trawling

Trawlers and trollers are often confused because they sound so similar; however, they are very different types of fishing boats. As we discussed before, trollers are a hook-and-line salmon fishing boat. (See illustration below.)

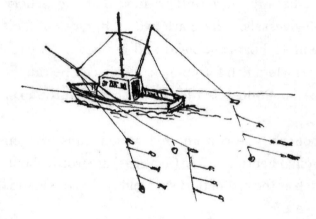

Troller towing lines

Trawlers are much larger vessels that due to their incredible fish-killing ability have about fished themselves out of existence a number of times. (See page 44 for illustration.)

The first factory trawler, indeed the first factory vessel of any type, was launched in Britain in 1954. Oddly enough, she carried all the components—plant freezers, automatic fish processing machines, and a fishmeal plant—that her most modern descendants carry today. One factory trawler I worked on, regularly caught over 800 tons of pollock a day. That is a heck of a lot of fish!

Today, with short seasons, numerous new target species, and worldwide fishing grounds, the big factory trawlers sail on into a murky future. Unfortunately, eventually trawling is probably doomed. It is a fun way to fish, but the Greenpeacers, crabbers, longliners, even the State of Alaska hate trawlers—especially the big factory trawlers. They tend to scoop up and destroy other types of fishing gear and the bottom of the ocean.

Somewhere over sixty factory trawlers work in Alaska. There won't be any more, either, now that the fishery is closed to new vessels. There are two main types of factory trawlers: pollock boats and head-and-gut boats. The really big factory trawlers fish for pollock, which can be caught in huge numbers. Pollock is fileted, minced, or ground into *surimi*.

The pollock A season, the roe season, runs from mid-January through February. Roe (fish eggs) are worth about six times as much as the rest of the fish, making the roe season the big money season.

The pollock B season runs from mid-August through September. Occasionally, if fish stocks are high, C and D seasons may be added as well.

Local villages around the Bering Sea receive about 7 percent of the total pollock allocation, which they often sell to some of the factory trawlers. Most of the big pollock boats extend their season by chasing hake (called Pacific whiting) off of the West Coast of the U.S. and Canada. Hake isn't much of a fish, making a lesser *surimi* and paying less than pollock. It does, however, extend the fishing season.

Back in the early 1990s there weren't enough American trawlers to catch all the pollock. New boats were entering the fishery every few months and fishing companies struggled to keep the vessels crewed.

This is no longer the case. Now much of the crew returns year after year to the same boat. However, with processing crews of 30 or 40 people there are bound to be openings, especially during the slower B season. Indeed, many processors work the B season only to protect their spot during the roe season.

Some trawlers do fish all summer long and could work out well for a college student. The trawlers expect a three- or four-month commitment and the big money is earned in the winter, during the spawn. The trawlers would prefer to hire processors interested in sticking with the industry for a while. You might keep that in mind during your interview.

Another type of factory trawler is the head-and-gut boat. They specialize in cutting the heads off and pulling the guts out of a whole range of different fish. Some of the fish they target include Atka mackerel, starry flounder, arrow tooth flounder, English and Rex sole, cod, Pacific Ocean perch, turbot, thorny heads, and red snapper.

These flexible trawlers tend to be smaller and carry fewer crew than the big pollock boats. They sometimes are granted a longer fishing season as well, because they can move from species to species as the various seasons are closed. Some are able to fish almost ten months out of the year. It's probably more interesting processing on a head-and-gut boat because you don't just work with one species.

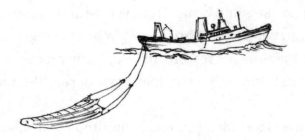

Trawler towing net

Trawling on either a pollock or head-and-gut boat consists of towing a large, semi-funnel shaped net behind the vessel. On the dragger's stern are two large main winches, each of which carries a stout wire, called a main wire. Each main wire is secured to a large metal wing, called a door, which flies through the water using the same principle as an airplane wing when towed at sufficient speed. From the doors run several wires, called bridles, which attach to the front of the net. The doors, which try to fly out perpendicular to the vessel, spread the net, while strategically placed floats and weights give the net its vertical opening.

The net can either be towed on the sea bottom or up in the water. Most fish live and feed on the bottom, making it the logical place to tow the net. Unfortunately, towing on the bottom tends to tear up the sea bottom and it catches and kills a lot of fish the fisherman can't keep, called by-catch. Those two problems are what make draggers so unpopular. They may prove to be insurmountable eventually.

At times, mid-water trawling can be extremely effective, especially at night when many bottom feeders tend to lift off the bottom and spread throughout the water column. Midwater nets are much larger, with a much bigger opening than bottom nets. When towed up off the bottom under the right conditions, they can fish incredibly clean, with virtually no unwanted by-catch, and of course, no bottom damage.

Trawlers can be divided into two other groups: factory trawlers and catcher boats. Trawler catcher boats usually pay better than the larger factory boats but are hard to get on if you are not experienced or related to the owner. They often carry only a few crew members. Factory trawlers carry between 25 and 130 people. They periodically hire novices, particularly during the slower seasons.

The entry-level position on a factory trawler is processor. The very best processors are allowed to work into a beginning deckhand position, called a combi. Or they can become factory foremen, unlicensed engineers, and (with sea time) mates. Processors and deckhands usually work 12 to 16 hours a day.

On the bright side, deck handing on a factory trawler is sort of fun. There's a lot to learn: splicing wire and line, repairing the net or sewing web, sorting fish and adjusting the gear, and so on. Trawlers carry the most complicated fishing gear of all. It takes a while to master it all.

The amount of hours a trawler deckhand works varies greatly, as well. When there's a lot of fish, deckhands are expected to help the processors catch up in the factory. When the vessel is bottom fishing on rough ground, the deckhands may have to work around the clock repairing nets. But when fishing slows a little, the tows become longer, and if the gear is in good shape, you may go hours without seeing a deckhand move, sort of like lions after a big meal.

Longlining

We'll discuss only the big freezer longliners for now. These big high-tech factory longliners have been around for a couple of decades. They prefer to be called freezer longliners rather than factory longliners as they don't much care for big factory trawlers and don't want to be confused with them. However, they both carry very similar fish processing factories aboard.

Longliners fish by laying a long line over the sea bottom for 2 to 15 miles. Every few feet a smaller, twine-like line called a ganglion is attached with a hook on one end. On each end of the long line is an anchor also connected to a line running to a set of floating buoys.

After the longline has been set on the bottom for a number of hours, the vessel grapples the buoys aboard and begins hauling the long line with a power block, called an offshore hauler. The longline itself is lifted off the bottom as the vessel runs slowly along in the same direction as the gear. As the longline comes aboard, the target fish are removed and processed, the by-catch is returned to the sea, and the longline is overhauled and coiled for reuse.

One of the deck hands, called a gaffer, stands next to the roller, where the longline comes aboard bearing cod and other fish. The gaffer sticks each target fish, usually Pacific gray cod, right in the forehead with his gaff and helps the fish up over the roller and onto the vessel. The gaffer "shakes" all the prohibited fish—salmon, crab, and halibut—that the large freezer longliners are prohibited from keeping.

Gaffing really gets exciting when the wind comes up and the seas build. The gaffer has to be able to gaff the cod in the head just as it comes out of the water, so he's standing in a hole in the side of the vessel about two feet above sea level. When the seas get rough, the skipper does his best to keep the wind on the other side of the bow, creating a lee, protecting his crewman, but ships don't run on rails and occasionally the gaffer gets blasted by a sea. This is how most longliners get hurt—well, that and getting snagged by a bare hook fluttering aboard.

> Once when we were hauling gear (bringing our gear back aboard and removing the fish), a rather large killer whale surfaced right alongside where the gaffer was working. We were fishing for gray cod, which orcas don't usually care for, so he wasn't causing any trouble, just checking things out. I called down to the gaffer, "Hey, Larry, take a pollock and hold it in your teeth and lean out over the water. Its OK, I seen 'em do it at Sea World. Wait, let me get my camera."
>
> Larry said something back to me I cannot repeat.

Freezer longliners usually fish for Pacific gray cod. Cod has been a food staple around the world for thousands of years. It is looking more and more likely that both the Vikings and the Basques fished the Grand Banks off of Canada hundreds of years before Columbus arrived. No good fisherman ever gives up his secret honey hole, so it's not surprising that the word never got out until a loud-mouthed Italian claimed to have discovered a new world. Cod remains one of the world's most important fish.

Processing on a longliner isn't much different than processing ashore or on a head-and-gut trawler, though the crew tends to be smaller and the hours longer. Some longliners work a fishing day, which means everyone works for 18 to 24 hours, and then all but one sleep for 6 or 7 hours. Longliners that work around the clock usually run three 16-hour shifts so everyone gets 8 hours off a day.

A deckhand's job on a longliner isn't as interesting as on a trawler. Most of the fishing tasks on a longliner—such as hand baiting hooks, coiling line, changing bad hooks, or tying ganglions—require speed and coordination but are really boring. However, longlining remains the fishery of the future, as it is tree-hugger approved. Far less by-catch is killed by longline fishing than bottom trawling. Halibut, or any other protected species, can be returned to the sea unharmed by shaking, a technique where the gaff is slid along the ganglion and the hook turned upside down, freeing the fish before it is brought on board.

Wages vary greatly from boat to boat because of the different skill levels of the skippers and crew. Luck also plays a significant role in determining the size of the catch, but that is true of any fishery. Longliners probably pay roughly the same as draggers.

Crabbing

Crabbing in the Bering Sea is by far the most dangerous fishing in Alaska. Some claim a crabber has only a seven-year life expectancy once he begins crabbing. It's a tough, brutal way to make a living.

The money can be unbelievable: crew shares of $40,000 for two weeks work, $1,000 daily earnings for months at a time. On the other hand, a crabber may risk his life daily, working around the clock for nothing.

All fishing is a gamble, but crabbing is the wildest gamble of them all.

Similar to the other fisheries, there are the same two classes of boats: catcher boats and catcher processor boats. Catcher boats are the more numerous and range in size from 80 to 150 feet in length. They usually carry a crew of about six and store the captured live crab in tanks of circulating seawater.

The crab is delivered to a crab processing plant weekly. They must be delivered alive; after seven days in a live tank they start to die. Only healthy crab are kept, because broken crab legs give off a chemical that poisons healthy crab.

The catcher processor crab boats tend to be bigger and carry more crew. They process the crab on board and offload processed frozen crab legs about once a month.

The main commercial species are red king crab, blue king crab, brown king crab, Opilio crab, and Bairdi crab. Hair crab and Dungeness are also pursued on a smaller scale.

Back in the 1970s, fortunes were made fishing red kings. Arctic Alaska Fishing Company (later sold to Tyson foods for over $200 million) was started with a single king crab boat, called the *Enterprise*, I believe.

Today the red king crabs are not nearly as numerous as they once were. No one really knows why, although changes in sea temperature and predators are suspected.

Presently the big money is being made in Opilio, seen in the store as snow crab and on TV in *The Deadliest Catch*. Opilio season runs from January 15th until mid-spring. The Opilios tend to be smaller than Bairdi, but far more numerous and far more lucrative to chase.

Legal snow crab run around two to four pounds and may not reach maturity for seven years. Some snow crab areas can be harvested from mid-November until the end of May.

Bairdi runs from mid-November into mid-winter. Bairdi crab is also referred to as tanner crab.

Red and blue king crab are fished in the fall for about a week each.

Brown king crab, harvested by only a few boats, is fished year-round.

Female crab are much smaller than the males and none are harvested commercially. They are incredibly fertile; each female may produce up to several hundred thousand eggs a year. I've read surveys where over two million immature Opilios were counted per square mile, with half expected to be eaten by cod each year.

Crabbing is a young man's gig. Strength and toughness are far more prized than brains. Eighteen to twenty-seven is about the right age for a deckhand on a crab boat. At twenty-seven or so, most crabbers start thinking about a new line of work or about moving into the wheelhouse.

Crab pots weigh about 800 pounds apiece and always seem to require pushing around a pitching, sometimes sub-merged deck. It takes a toll on a man. But if you really want to test yourself under extreme conditions, crabbing is a good way to do it.

Presently, most crab boats fish 250 traps. These square pots are baited with cod and herring, attached to a set of buoys, and launched individually in strings of about 30. After a couple of days soak time, the boat retrieves each pot by pull-ing the buoy line through a power block, removing the crab, re-baiting the pot, and if the area still looks promising, relaunch-ing the pot.

The more pots turned, the more crab caught. Slow boats may turn fewer than 10 pots an hour, average boats turn about 15 pots an hour, and very fast boats may turn as many as 25 pots an hour. That's an 800-pound crab pot lifted, dumped, re-baited, and launched every two and a half minutes for hours or days at a time.

Crabbers tend to be a tough bunch. Watching a crab boat crew and a boatload of Samoans interact in a Dutch Harbor bar can be very interesting; just don't let them get between you and the door. However, one has to respect anyone who can work as hard as a crabber. If you've ever read Jack London's *Sea Wolf*, he could have been describing a lot of modern-day crabbers.

During my first crab job, my deck boss told me I'd be back. He said I'd be on vacation and I'd wonder, "Was it as bad as I remember? Naah, nothing could be that bad." So I'd sign up again. But the second time around I'd decide, "This is even worse than I remember," and I'd retire from crabbing for good.

He was almost right. I've done it a couple of times since but I don't think I'll take any more crab deck jobs.

There is a lot of turnover in the crab fleet due to injury or exhaustion, and jobs can be found by walking the docks. A new man starts at half share and usually receives a remarkable amount of abuse from the rest of the crew. I think they want a mental toughness check before things hit the fan. Things get easier once you prove yourself.

Rationalization vs. Derby Crabbing

Prior to 2005 the crab fleet sailed out together at the start of the season, and the boat that caught the most crab by the end of the season made the most money. This derby style of crabbing made a dangerous fishery even more lethal as extra risks were taken and corners were cut. The boats were competing against each other until the quota was caught and the season was over, even if it only lasted a few days.

My very first night of crabbing was spent looking for a crew member of an adjacent crab boat who had been accidentally launched overboard in a pot he was baiting. There were several other crab boats setting gear in the area, but only the boat I was on quit setting gear to aid in the search.

Eight hours later, when there was no possibility of recovering the missing man alive, the boat with the missing man went back to crabbing, a man down. They had to be threatened by the Coast Guard before they stopped working and returned to Dutch Harbor for an investigation.

It wouldn't be handled the same way today.

Under the rationalization system, the Alaskan Board of Fisheries assigns a crab quota to each boat. The boats can take as much time as they need to catch their individual fishing quota (IFQ). If the weather turns bad they can stop crabbing. If a crew member is injured they can return to port without ruining the season.

With the present IFQ crabbing system each boat knows how much crab they'll be allowed to catch in a single season and the crew knows about how much they'll earn if they finish the season. That was not possible before. The disadvantage of the rationalization system is that the number of crab boats has shrunk from over 250 to 89 as IFQs have been consolidated. That's a lot of lost jobs.

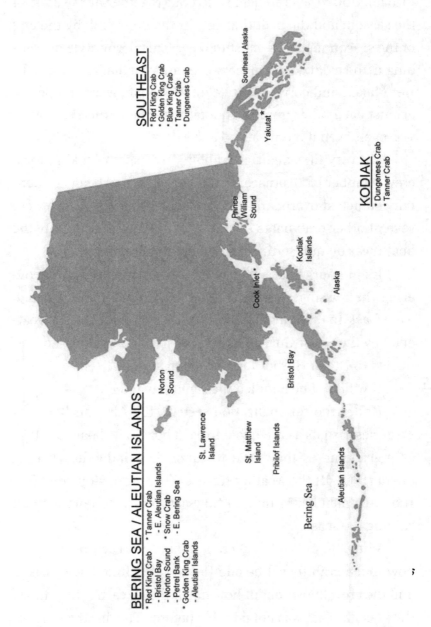

Finding a Crabbing Job

Finding a crabbing job is tough for a greenhorn. It is the most physically demanding and dangerous fishery, not a good fishery to break in on. Better to learn your way about a fishing boat before jumping into the fire of a crab fishery.

Probably the best way to find a berth on a crab boat, other than nepotism, is to do some work on the boat during the off-season, tendering or refitting work in the shipyard. Step up; make an impression. You don't have to be perfect—just better than everyone else. Simple.

There are plans to require all crabbers to take a two-day safety course prior to signing on; however, there are still a lot of details to work out so it's not a requirement yet. Presently the only safety requirement is that someone aboard has taken a course on how to conduct emergency drills.

To check the state of the regulations you can try www.amsea.org or call the Alaska Marine Safety Education Association at (907) 747-3287. They seem to be more on top of the Alaska marine safety training requirements than anyone.

However, having said the correct responsible thing, it is also true that sometimes new crew members are like cigarettes or bullets: when a skipper needs one, he needs one badly and right now. If a greenhorn crab fisherman is in the right place at the right time...

So we're back to walking the docks.

It's not much different from looking for a salmon fishing job. The principles are the same. Be friendly, respectful, helpful, clean, and sober. Never climb aboard a vessel without an invitation, any more than you would break into a potential employer's home.

Leave notes on bulletin boards all over town. Talk to everybody: harbor masters, waitresses, store clerks, priests—you're looking for leads. When you get one, move fast. Job openings don't last long on a good boat. Sometimes the boat will cast off as soon as they hire a last hand.

Be honest in your interview. If you can't deliver what you promise, it will cost you in ways you can't even imagine until it's too late. As on salmon boats, welders, mechanics, and cooks are valued. Don't forget to mention whatever other skills you possess.

Getting a chance to make a good impression is a lucky break; don't take it for granted. If you're unloading crab from a boat at a processing plant or delivering supplies or just taking the lines as the boat comes alongside, work harder, move faster, complain less than everyone else. They're all good habits to get into. A steady, good attitude indicates professionalism and can only help you in the long run.

Sometimes crabbing jobs are found in a tavern, but usually not by accident. If you're looking for a fishing job in a bar, have a soft drink: it's impressive. If you're there to drink, drink. If you're there to find a job, don't drink.

The very first time I tried to land a crabbing job was in Dutch Harbor in 1980, the last red king crab bonanza year. I had graduated from a maritime academy that year and had just completed my first contract on a research vessel. The first crab boat I approached was unloading live crab alongside a shore processing plant. The deckhand aboard told me, "Hell, yeah, the skipper's looking for a hand, we just lost someone to an injury. Stick around; the skipper will be back soon."

When the captain arrived, he asked me about my experience, age, and boat skills. I was 23 years old with a brand new third mate's license. He hired me.

"Grab your gear, we'll be done offloading in an hour, be back here by then."

When I returned in 45 minutes the boat was gone.

One of the dock workers told me, "They finished unloading early and couldn't wait. Too bad, the skipper said he really wanted to hire you, but he grabbed some other guy off the dock and left."

Disgusted, I walked to the airport and flew home to California, failing yet again to get rich.

Halibut Fishing

Halibut is always caught by longline, but only by a certain kind of longline fishing boat. Halibut boats are small, usually less than 60 feet. They can't process or freeze fish on board, only ice them down.

Before 1995 halibut was a derby fishery open to any small boat. It was a mess. You could always tell a halibut opening by all the yahoos on the radio and all the Maydays bouncing around.

Today it's individual fishing quota (IFQ) and a very professional, lucrative, small boat fishery indeed. The fishery is based primarily out of Sitka, but also out of Yakutat, Sand Point, Petersburg, Wrangle, Kodiak, and Homer. These boats fish their quotas in the spring and fall, keeping safely tied up in the winter and leaving the summer free for salmon tendering.

Hand baiting longline gear takes time to master and crew shares are so high that openings are few and far between on the good boats. But there are 3,500 boats in the fishery. If you get a chance to work on a halibut boat, take it, but you'll probably have to learn the trade on the larger freezer longliners out of Dutch Harbor, which means less money but more opportunities.

Halibut fishing is very political; at times it seems like all the fishing in the Bering Sea revolves around halibut. If too much halibut is caught accidentally by freezer longliners or factory trawlers, their season is ended. Halibut is the only fish in Alaska not regulated by either the state or federal government; instead it is regulated by the International Halibut Commission. Personally, I believe there is a whole lot more halibut swimming around than the International Halibut Commission does.

Herring Fishing

The herring fishery is an odd little fishery that can be quite lucrative. To put its size in perspective, about 80 million pounds of herring are caught annually, as opposed to 750 million pounds of salmon. A crew share can run from nothing to tens of thousands of dollars. Both purse seine and gill nets are used, but with smaller mesh size. Purse seine gear is used in the herring food and bait fisheries, while both are used in the sac roe fisheries. The value in the herring fishery is in the roe, which the Japanese prefer to caviar.

Herring schools are easily spotted by aircraft, making the fishery extremely efficient. Sometimes the entire harvest of a particular area can be caught in less than half an hour. I've heard of fishermen sinking their boats trying to corral a much bigger haul than their boats could handle. When rescue arrived, these fishermen insisted the catch—still in the pursed seine net—be saved, rather than the boat, as the herring were far more valuable than the fishing boat.

Many bays and sounds throughout Alaska have their own individual herring fishery, each requiring a specific limited-entry permit. Some boats have a number of permits and fish herring all summer, while others are more limited. Some boats fish a combination of salmon and herring.

Herring fishing is easy. It mostly consists of running between fishing areas and waiting for the herring to show up, with some gear and vessel maintenance thrown in. It's not a bad fishery to start on.

Ground Fish

These are the most diverse of Alaska's marine fisheries. They are found both in the Bering Sea (north of the Aleutians) and in the Gulf of Alaska (south of the Aleutians). We'll discuss some of the different types of ground fish, such as Pacific gray cod, walleyed pollock, Atka mackerel, sable fish, and rock fish.

Pacific Gray Cod

Cod is the oldest ground fishery in Alaska. Sailing ships used to sail north from the West Coast every summer to catch codfish. They are the main product of freezer longliners and a major product of head-and-gut factory trawlers. They can be sold as head-and-gut product or as filets. A lot of fishermen prefer cod to halibut.

Cod are opportunistic bottom feeders that grow to about 50 pounds and sport a single small whisker under their chin, a sort of piscine soul patch. Being bottom feeders, cod tend to carry a lot of worms and need candling to remove the worms if they're to be sold as filets.

Walleye Pollock

These are a bland, nondescript fish that were once used mainly for mink or fox food. Their main attractions are they can be found in vast numbers, they grow fast, they tend to school with other similar-sized pollock, and they don't have much flavor, making them perfect for industrial processing into *surimi*, a tasteless fish paste that can be flavored with anything, usually crab extract. Up to 85 percent of the entire biomass (all the fish in the sea) of the Bering Sea are pollock. They are smaller than, though related to, cod and can be harvested in three years.

Pollock roe is by far the most valuable part of pollock. Accordingly, the A pollock season takes place during the spawn when the roe is ripe.

Around 2.9 billion pounds of pollock are caught each year with pelagic trawls, meaning mid-water nets. Pollock is the most valuable Alaskan fishery, worth around $267 million a year.

Atka Mackerel

I've never seen Atka mackerel for sale in the U.S. They're mainly sold in the Far East. They're a smaller fish, not much bigger than your hand—an attractive light and dark green striped fish. Although found throughout Alaskan waters, they are most common along the Aleutian Islands where around 100 million pounds are caught each year by trawlers.

Sable Fish

These are a beautiful, black, muscular fish, as sleek as anything swimming in the sea. Also called black cod, they are worth more per pound than any other Alaskan fish—

black cod often sell for seven times the price of Pacific gray cod.

These fish are almost never sold in America; they're saved for the Japanese, where they have an almost crack cocaine-like addictive effect. They're an extremely oily fish, which apparently makes them both perfect for sushi and hard on the stomach. I once worked with a Japanese fish tech who loved to eat black cod every chance he got, even though he knew that all the oily flesh would make him sick for hours.

Like I said, Japanese crack.

Rock Fish

There are a lot of different kinds of fish lumped together under rock fish: Pacific Ocean perch, shortraker rockfish, rougheye rockfish, yelloweye rockfish, thornyhead rockfish, and dusky rockfish, to mention a few.

The most fun I ever had fishing was trawling for rockfish on cliffs, over rock piles, on top of almost any kind of rough ground. It takes a lot of skill and great concentration to fish rock fish successfully. The net gets torn up a lot, but the fish tend to be high value and good money can be made.

To protect the net on a rough sea bottom, the net sits up on ground gear made from steel balls or compressed tires. When the ground gear is dragged along the sea bottom, it forces everything up into the net, even coral and king crab, but it also grinds up the bottom pretty thoroughly. Rockfish don't move around much, and they are extremely slow growing. It takes Pacific Ocean perch 12 years to reach the size of a nice bluegill. Rougheyes have a life span of over 200 years.

Rockfish trawling requires very careful regulation. Most rockfish are caught with trawls, but longliners catch some too; about 100 million pounds are taken each year combined.

Flatfish

There are around 30 species of flat fish in Alaskan waters with about a third of that number fished commercially, including Greenland turbot; Alaska plaice; arrowtooth flounder; yellowfin; and rock, English, Dover, and flathead sole. Halibut has its own category and isn't considered a flat fish.

Arrowtooth flounder is one of the most common fish in Alaska, but unfortunately it's a soft, spongy mess that isn't worth much. I won't eat it.

There is a pretty big trawl fishery for yellowfin sole, but yellowfin isn't worth much and doesn't pay much. It is, however, easy to catch.

Turbot have their own longline season and can be very lucrative, but the killer whales love them and pick them off the longline gear as if they were eating grapes. I spent several turbot seasons trying desperately to outthink a pod of orcas, with an embarrassing lack of success.

Finding a Job on a Factory Boat

We've already discussed finding a job on a salmon boat, but it's a little different finding a job on a big catcher processor.

Don't try to walk the docks in Dutch Harbor. It's very expensive to get there, most of the cheap bunkhouses have closed, and a room at the Grand Aleutian runs $160 a night. I've heard of people moving into hidden World War II-era bunkers while walking the docks in Dutch Harbor. That's not a good idea—you'll freeze to death during the winter, and during the summer there just isn't that much fishing going on.

Most of the fishing companies hire through their main office, which is usually in Seattle. In the back of this book there is a well-scrubbed list that describes each company's hiring practices. The list is current, so use it.

Many of these companies will at least start the hiring process via telephone or Internet communications. Many have websites with online or downloadable applications. Others prefer you mail or fax your resume. Some even require that you apply in person and/or attend a company orientation before you'll be eligible for hire.

At some point you will likely find yourself in Seattle. Given the opportunity, drop by all the offices of the companies you're interested in. Fill out an application, be prepared to take a drug test, and have your resume ready.

What the personnel directors are looking for is manual labor experience or food processing experience, such as working in a slaughterhouse. If you have a high school diploma, military experience, or just look "squared away," so much the better.

It's not a bad idea to shave, get a haircut, and remove the nose stud prior to an interview, but it's not mandatory. You can visit every factory processor company in Seattle, all cleaned up and sober, in a day or two, impressing each human resources manager with your diligence and responsibility.

Be polite to everyone you talk to, drop off a resume, let them know you have a solid shot at passing a drug test, and hope for the best. Get a phone number where you can check in every couple of weeks and ask about the ship's departure date.

Another trick of the trade is to drop by a vessel tied up in Seattle, waiting for the next season, a couple of days before it is scheduled to depart. Talk with the factory foreman or manager and let him know you're packed and ready to roll at a moment's notice. Leave your cell phone number and you may get a call if someone no-shows.

Other Positions

The entry-level positions on fishing vessels are usually processor or deck hand. Two other possible entry positions are cook and federal fishery observer.

There are a number of different types of fishing boat cooking jobs. Some of the big factory boats with a hundred or more crew members have a steward's department of five or six people. The chief steward is a manager rather than just a cook. On a smaller boat with a six-man crew the cook may spend much of his time on deck fishing, as well as cooking and cleaning. Other small-boat cooks are paid a day rate by the crew; on still others, the new guy cooks or everyone takes a turn.

I once had to cook one day a week on a boat with a six-man crew. I probably knew less about cooking at the time than anyone who ever reads this book (that's probably not an exaggeration). But I bought a cookbook called *30-Minute Meals From the Academy* by the California Culinary Academy, and no one ever knew the extent of my ignorance, because before I got to the end of the book, I got a better job where I didn't have to cook.

30-Minute Meals From the Academy is a pretty handy cookbook and it might not be a bad idea to pick it up, or one like it, before heading north if you might be working on a small fishing boat. If you're an over-achiever you might even practice a little beforehand at home.

On some top boats a good, hardworking cook can make up to $10,000 a month. Even with that kind of pay, I've found it surprisingly difficult to hire a good cook. I've known of excellent boats that have been looking for a good relief cook, or even a good first cook, for years. If you're a good cook and are able prepare meals for 20 or 30 people and have documented experience, you should not have much trouble finding a job out of Seattle. Step on up, we need you!

Federal fishery observers are required on all fishing boats over 58 feet. They are (although they deny it) fish cops. They keep track of how many and what types of fish are caught, and insure that the fishery rules are followed. It's not a bad job; they don't usually work as hard as the fishermen and they make between $2,000 and $4,000 a month. If the fishing is really bad, that may make them the highest-paid person on the boat.

Some type of biological science degree is required, as well as the completion of a three-week training program. If you're interested, call the National Marine Fisheries Service at (206) 526-4191 for additional information. Most federal fishery observers that I've worked with were on their first job out of college and more often than not were female.

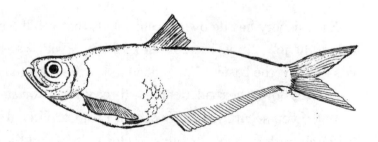

Herring

Knots and Knives

Do me one favor before you head north. Learn how to tie the following knots: clove hitch, bowline, and square knot. I drew you a picture, but ehow.com has a good one too. There is a saying, "If you can't tie a knot, tie a lot."

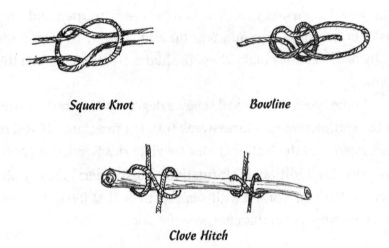

Square Knot   **Bowline**

Clove Hitch

Each fishery has its own specific skills that you'll have to learn on the job. Knots are not one of them. Every waterman needs to know the basics. You'll need to learn other knots and some splices down the road, but these three will get you started.

But if you secure the skiff with an East Carolina grocery store hitch, rather than a bowline or clove hitch, and the deck boss has to use a rope wrench (knife) to free it, you'll probably get yelled at. Do it twice and you'll *definitely* get yelled at.

Oh, and make sure you always carry a knife. Going knife-less is another sign of utter cluelessness. I once crabbed with a guy who never went on deck without at least a half dozen knives secreted about his person. He had a horror of being snagged in a buoy line and dragged overboard, so he made sure he could always reach something sharp if he was conscious, no matter the circumstances.

Most fishermen and processors carry a small, serrated steak knife-looking thing, called a Victorinox, at their waist. Use it for a week or so and when it gets dull, throw it away and drag out a new one.

There, I just saved you two ass-chewings.

Ten More Ways to Avoid Getting Yelled at, Fired, or Beat Up on a Fishing Boat

1. Don't claim to know how to cook if you can't.

2. Understand that you will be taunted, harassed, and tormented as a crab boat newbie. It's nothing personal. When you fall into the live tank hole in the foredeck and injure yourself, everyone will stop and laugh before helping you. Then they'll yell at you for slowing production. If you can't take that, you can't work on a crab boat.

3. Avoid talking about money—about how much you are or are not making. The skipper will think you care more about your own selfish needs than the boat's, which of course you do. We all do, we just shouldn't tell anyone.

4. If the skipper is having trouble finding fish, don't offer any advice, at least for the first month. I promise you he's more twisted up about it than you are.

5. Try to never say anything negative. I remember with awe, after a thirty-hour shift of poor crabbing in a driving blizzard on a crummy boat, the deck boss saying hopefully, "Just think, in less than 96 hours we'll be sitting in the Elbow Room." That's a pro.

6. Never, ever take or borrow someone else's things without permission.

I remember working on a large freezer long-liner as captain when my raingear never quite seemed to dry out. One night I got up in the middle of my sleep shift to check on things. I found the boat's biggest knucklehead wearing my raingear. I was not amused, and I believe I was able to convince him to leave my gear alone forever.

7. If you work on a boat with a federal fisheries observer, treat her carefully and with respect. Otherwise, you will create big problems for your company, your skipper, and yourself.

On second thought, treat all women aboard with the same care and respect, for the same reason.

8. Don't bring alcohol aboard the vessel without the skipper's permission. Some fishing boats allow their crewmembers to tie one on after offload in the delivery port. I don't know of any that allow alcohol to be brought aboard still in a bottle or can. If you don't get fired, you might very well get your share reduced.

9. Never whistle on the boat, expect to leave port on Friday, or request bananas on a fishing boat. All are considered bad luck.

Also, on a crab boat, all canned foods must be label out and right side up.

Honey bears are, of course, completely out of the question (a crab boat once sank and all the rescuers ever found was some floating honey bears).

10. Just because you're seasick or ill doesn't mean you don't have to go to work. You are expected to work through it. If you're injured, see if you can do some light duty, such as helping the cook. Fishing boats don't carry extra people, because that would reduce everyone's share. If there is any way you can continue to work, you must.

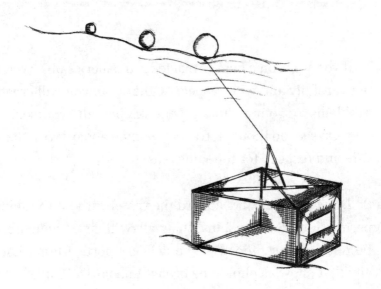

Crab Pot

Clothes

Pack your gear in a sea bag. Bring a sleeping bag, unless the company says not to. Don't try to save money with cheap raingear or boots. Buy the best. You can't go wrong with Grunden's rain gear and Extratuff boots. Most fishermen prefer sweat clothes to jeans and shirts. Loose sweat clothes are much more comfortable and warmer under raingear than conventional clothes.

There are good fishermen supply stores in Dutch Harbor; they're a bit more expensive than Seattle, but not unreasonably so. If you forget some of the more specialized personal gear, such as face shields or pile boot liners, you can usually get what you need in Dutch Harbor or Kodiak. Some of the fishing companies will take you to the fisherman supply store in Alaska as soon as you arrive. There you can pick out the gear you need and the cost will be deducted from your first check. Check with the company.

The following should see you through most of the fishing seasons:

- 4 heavy, hooded, sweatshirts
- 4 pairs of sweatpants
- 1 wool sweater
- 2 pairs felt boot liners. I put two in each boot, and it makes a huge difference.
- 6 pair Momoi rubber gloves
- 6 pairs cotton glove liners
- 10 pairs wool socks, some heavy, some light
- 10 pairs underwear
- 10 tee shirts, some long sleeved, some not

• 1 pair hiking boots. These are for when you are not working. You'll be wearing your Extratuffs when you are.

• 1 heavy jacket. You'll work in your sweat clothes and raingear. This is also for when you're not working.

• 1 wool watch cap. This is the best way to quickly regulate your body temperature. You lose most of your body heat through your head, so put it on or take it off as needed.

• 1 baseball cap. It keeps the water and jellyfish out of your eyes.

• 1 neoprene face shield or ski mask

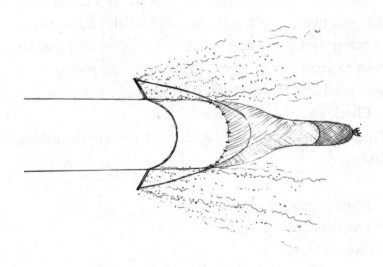

Bottom Trawl

Payment Issues

Usually this doesn't become an issue, but occasionally it does. Sometimes everything is on the up and up, but if you don't have much experience it may seem "fishy." I'll give you the benefit of my experience to help you judge for yourself. I'll start with a fish story that actually happens to be true, to illustrate just how badly things can go wrong.

There used to be a company fishing in Alaska that rumor insisted was owned by the Yakuza, the Japanese mafia. They flouted most of the fishing rules by fishing out of season, fishing closed areas, keeping the wrong species, and so on. When they were caught, they paid the fines and went right back to what they were doing.

The Coast Guard hated them. Instead of the usual polite, professional boardings, the Coast Guard used to board them like the marines hitting the beach at Tarawa, M-16s and 9mms all over the place.

One of their vessels, the *Northern Hero* I believe, had been fishing for over a month with a busy factory every day. Then word got out that crew share for the trip to date was about $65.00. They were working 16-hour days, mind you.

Things got dicey fast. The crew demanded to be returned to port immediately. The vessel management refused, whereupon many of the American crew began rioting. Some of the more abusive Japanese foremen were beaten down. The wheelhouse was stormed, where the American captain had barricaded himself inside.

It made for one of the most interesting single-side-band radio conversations I've eavesdropped on.

"Coast Guard, *Northern Hero*. I've got a problem here. The crew is demanding we return to Dutch Harbor immediately, and I've locked myself in the wheelhouse."

"*Northern Hero*, United States Coast Guard. Sir, are you saying the crew is mutinying?"

"Coast Guard, *Northern Hero*. Well, they're trying to break down the wheelhouse door and force us to return to Dutch Harbor. But hell, they just found out they've been working their asses off for over a month for less than a hundred bucks—

"They're in the wheelhouse, we're on our way back to Dutch."

"*Northern Hero*, United States Coast Guard. Are you safe?"

"Coast Guard, *Northern Hero*. Yes, I'm safe. We'll be back in Dutch in about a day."

A day later the *Northern Hero* was tied up in Dutch Harbor, where many of her crew were escorted by U.S. Marshals and FBI agents to jail. I don't know what happened to the crew, but I do know that getting charged with the federal crime of mutiny is something to be avoided at all costs.

Greenhorns.

The *Northern Hero* was tied up and soon out of business. I think it was that final fine of over $6,000,000 for continuing to ignore the fishing regulations that finally did it.

This story illustrates several important points. Bad boats have bad reputations. They can get in more trouble than you can imagine. If you hear a boat is badly run, skip it. You'll be better off in the long run, and it may even help you avoid a long stay in the federal pen.

The other point is if you're working for a crew share or percentage of the catch, rather than an hourly rate, it can be difficult to know how much you're making before you get your settlement check. If it's a single-product vessel such as a salmon or pollock boat, you can make a fair estimate:

If we have 10,000 cases of processed frozen cod aboard, the cases are 40 pounds each and we hope they will sell for an average of $1.20 a pound each. My share is 0.75%. My check is 10,000 x 40 x 1.20 x .0075 = $3600. Good for two weeks, not so good for a month.

See how important all those word problems were back in the sixth grade?

Remember that the size of the crew share doesn't always indicate the size of the payoff. One season I worked on a huge factory trawler where my crew share was, I believe, 0.0138%, which converted into about 15K a month. I then took a job on a crab catcher boat where my share was 7%, which earned me about 2K a month. Ten percent of nothing is still nothing and 0.0138% of $1,200,000 isn't bad. On average, I've found that smaller boats pay better than larger boats, but that is a generalization rather than an absolute.

Very often your share is broken into two parts: a guarantee and a bonus. If you quit or get fired you may only receive the guaranteed portion of your share.

Sometimes the captain is able to adjust the shares as he sees fit. This can be a good thing if you're doing more than your share of the work and the captain takes from the slackers and pays you more. It can also be a bad thing if the captain takes from your share and gives it to his idiot nephew.

Just something to be aware of: to protect yourself, make sure vessel management is happy with your work and hopes that you'll return the following year. You have very little leverage if everyone on board is hoping you'll just leave.

But we're not done yet; it gets still more complicated.

Your share is based on the total final price. That isn't a problem if your boat sells its catch to a local fish processing plant, because you'll know the value of the catch at every offload. Many small catcher boats will issue a single settlement check at the end of the season, with maybe a couple of draw checks along the way to help keep your bills current.

But often on catcher-processors many different types of fish and fish products are offloaded, some of which may be sold at the Tokyo fish auction, others of which may be sold to American or European buyers. Until all the transactions are complete, the final value of the load is unknown.

This issue is dealt with by issuing two checks. The first, called a draw check, is about 80 percent of the best estimate of the value of the catch. The settlement check is issued after the last of the fish is sold, usually a few months after it is caught. Sometimes, if there is a market glut, the product will be held in refrigerated storage until the price moves up; that really slows down your settlement check, and the storage charges will be deducted from the sale amount. Great.

Some boats pay a larger percentage to the crew, but only after fuel, food, bait, and excessive gear losses are deducted from the gross. For example: The boat catches $120,000 worth of fish. Expenses are $30,000, leaving a net of $90,000. A 10 percent crew share would then be $9,000.

Personally, I'd rather have a smaller total crew share with no expenses taken out, because boat owners sometimes can get a little creative. But you usually don't get a choice. I'm just giving you my preference.

The next question is who pays for your transportation from Seattle to Alaska? If you ride the boat both ways, obviously it's not a problem. Generally the boat will buy your air ticket from Seattle to Alaska. If you quit or get fired before your contract is up (usually 2 to 4 months), your plane ticket will be deducted from your earnings. If you complete your contract, the company generally pays for the ticket and you will likely be invited back.

WARNING: If you quit before you've earned enough to pay for a return plane ticket, you may be put off the boat in a small Alaskan town with no way to get home.

Alaskan state law specifies that this isn't legal, as a number of fired ex-crew members have pointed out to me. However, the law has a number of loopholes, such as fired for fighting, or drugs, or my favorite, failure to obey a direct order, that kind of negate the law.

I once asked one of my owners (who had worked his way up from deck hand to billionaire) about the issue of plane tickets for quick quitters.

He said, "Tell them to hire the very best attorney they can afford, our company will hire the very best attorney we can afford, and we'll see who runs out of money first."

Quitters put the boat in a real bind, so they're not treated well on Alaskan fishing boats. Don't do it if there is any way you can avoid it. If you are on a real rough boat, just dig a little deeper, concentrate on getting through one day at a time, and you'll be proud of yourself for the rest of your life.

Once I worked on a boat with a lazy screw-up who eventually got fired. A year later, walking through Pike's Place Market in Seattle, I saw him with his girlfriend decked out in matching American Dynasty jackets. What a poseur. If you can't complete your contract on a fishing boat, you shouldn't rock its colors. I should have tried to kick his ass.

Halibut

The Good Parts...

I look back on what I've just written with some trepidation. Would I take a fishing job after a discussion of not getting paid, of mutinies on board, of being cheated on your crew share? Maybe not. Probably not. So I'd better go over what else you get out of the deal.

Any fisherman will tell you he fishes for the money. However, it is much more than that. It is one hell of an experience, especially once you get out of the factory onto the deck. I worked as a Merchant Marine officer for ten years all over the world prior to fishing commercially. I got more sea stories out of my first year of fishing than in my previous ten years working on merchant ships.

Things just happen on a fishing boat. They anchor in small bays in the Aleutian Islands to wait out monster storms, dragging and resetting their anchor all night. Sometimes everyone else is so exhausted you're left alone in the wheelhouse to keep watch and everyone is sleeping safe. Except that all you know about watch-standing is a spacy, disjointed five-minute lecture from the skipper before he stumbles off to bed.

Longline fishermen struggle to outwit orcas, luring them to other nearby boats to protect their own catch, which leads to a later dockside brawl.

Sometimes the fish are so thick in the factory they spill off the conveyor belt and pile on the deck thigh deep and still they come pouring aboard. The captain, chief engineer, and cook all come running into the factory to turn on the slime line to help catch up.

I've seen doomed, frantic sea lions trying to scramble up

the sheer side of an anchored processing ship to escape a pod of rapacious orcas bent on slaughtering them. I've looked out the wheelhouse window and seen frisky black and white Dall porpoises playing just inside the face of a wave above my eye level.

You ain't gonna see that working at Wal-Mart.

You'll meet some fascinating people, mostly in a good way, others not so much. I've worked for captains as bad as Jack London's character Wolf Larson in his book *The Sea Witch*; indeed, he would fit right in the crab fleet today. However, the finest human beings I've ever met, I met fishing.

America today, for the most part, is a soft country, filled with soft people. Just because you've figured out how to enrich yourself at the expense of the rest of the country doesn't make you tough. It makes you slimy.

I suspect there are very few people I would admire working on Wall Street, but I admire every competent fisherman and processor working in Alaska. They earn everything they make, solve their own problems, and ask only to be treated fairly by their government and their employers. These people, along with the men and women fighting in Iraq and Afghanistan, are my guys, my heroes, the real Americans who give this country its value.

They are the best this country has to offer, even if they sometimes drink a little too much.

Fishing is a challenge. Most people aren't tough enough to be successful at fishing. I once won a bar bet on how many at the bar had wrestled in high school. I don't remember how many of the fishermen at the bar had wrestled, but it was more than the guy who bought the next round guessed.

If you're tough enough to wrestle or run cross-country in

high school, you should be able to fish or process. The toughness takes place between your ears. Can you keep doing something you don't want to do anymore? How about when you're
tired, hungry, or sick? Some of the best processors I know
are women about 5'2" and 115 pounds. Want to find out how
tough you are without having to shoot anyone? Try fishing.

Alaska is a spectacularly beautiful place. If the Aleutian
Islands weren't so remote, they would be world famous for
their wild, savage beauty; imagine the Alps rising directly from
the sea. There are islands in the Aleutian chain that probably
have not been landed on in decades. I've been told that on
the south side of Unalaska Island is a WWII-era ghost town
that can only be approached from the sea—though no one ever
does—still with dishes on the tables in the abandoned build-
ings.

The inside passage between Seattle and Alaska is a gor-
geous place. Tourists pay big money to make the trip. For
some fishermen that's their commute. If they get the urge,
they can stop at one of the small towns along the way and take
a soak in one of the local hot springs, especially if they're ahead
of schedule. Alaska is a special place; it's just cold, dark, and
hard to get to.

Other Expenses

There are some other expenses you should be aware of. Every Alaska State resident has to pay $60 for a commercial fishing license; for nonresidents it is $125. Usually the company will pay for it and deduct it from your settlement.

Don't underestimate the cost of the raingear you'll be wearing when you work. A set of Grundens raingear, top and bottom, runs around $200. But you don't want anything cheaper; it will just fall apart. Extratuff boots run around $70 a pair, so with gloves figure around $300 just for your outer layer.

Taxes

A word of caution about taxes: PAY THEM.

On smaller boats, with crews of 12 or fewer, fishermen are sometimes considered independent contractors and taxes are not withheld. You will be given a 1099 form. A surprising number of fishermen never file a tax return and never pay income taxes. The amounts can add up fast.

It is amazing the number of fishermen who make serious money and yet wind up bankrupt. Usually there are taxes, ex-wives, drugs, or a boat involved, often all four. The IRS has been known to meet fishing boats as they drop off their catch to check the social security numbers and federal tax status of the crew members. If you cheat, they'll probably catch you eventually and you'll owe them forever.

If you're fortunate enough to land on a good boat in a strong fishery and make some excellent cash, hire a financial planner or a tax accountant. They'll find you a few loopholes, but figure about a third will go to the government. Be sure to budget for this huge outlay if you're on a boat that doesn't withhold. A number of my friends have lost ten years of their lives after a small dispute with the IRS.

Health

Fishing demands good health. If your body can't handle ridiculously long hours and freezing conditions, don't go fishing. Fishing vessels don't carry spare labor. You will be expected to continue working while sick for as long as physically possible.

Don't report aboard ship flabby and out of shape, especially if you're going crabbing. First of all, they probably won't hire you, and secondly, you probably won't be able to do the work. You have to be able to work full speed from day one. A learning curve is expected—a conditioning curve isn't. Personally, I run five miles a day for at least a month prior to going crabbing, and I still lose about 20 pounds my first month of work, so don't take it lightly.

It is a good idea to have your teeth checked prior to heading north. Dental care is extremely limited in the Bering Sea. If you suddenly need a root canal in the middle of a fishing trip, it may very well develop into the most painful experience of your life. When medical emergencies require a cessation of fishing and return to port, it can cost the company and crew hundreds of thousands of dollars. Everyone accepts this for real emergencies, but preventable emergencies, such as most tooth problems, are not appreciated by anyone. An intelligent person would also have a physical checkup.

Be very, very careful of even small cuts and scratches. Most fish are covered in a slime that protects them from bacteria; the slime is loaded with friendly bacteria that can explode if it finds a break in human skin. I have seen some spectacular infections, called fish poisoning, where the swelling was so great that the skin looked about to burst. It takes only the slightest break in the skin, to take hold. Treat all cuts and scratches quickly, and get help if you need it—for even the smallest of wounds.

Seasickness

Unfortunately, most fishing, except for salmon, takes place in the winter when the weather is at its worst. Forty-foot waves are not uncommon, particularly in the Gulf of Alaska. Seasickness can be a real problem. Most people who get seasick in rough weather get over it within a week or so, but it is a miserable week. Try to just keep working through it. Eating soda crackers and drinking 7-Up sometimes works.

I used to encourage my new processors by telling them that no one ever dies of seasickness. Since then I've found that may not be entirely true; some bodies never acclimatize, even with meds. If you are unable to keep down food and, more importantly, water, you can really get into trouble. Let someone know if you don't seem to be getting over the normal seasickness. Marizine and Dramamine tablets both help but will make you drowsy, especially Dramamine.

The best seasickness medicine is the Transderm Scop patch. It requires a prescription, but if you can get some it sure works. Put it on several hours before putting to sea; it lasts for about three days, by the end of which you should be adjusted to the vessel thrashing about. Don't try to wear one all the time, though, because it has some hazardous side effects.

Emergency Drills

The death toll on sunken Alaskan fishing boats is shocking. Between 1991 and 1998, 239 fishing boats sank in Alaskan waters, with 97 lives lost. 1981 was the deadliest year of all, with 39 vessels sunk; six sank in a single storm within a few hours of each other. The deadliest sinking was the *Arctic Rose* in 2001 with 15 souls lost.

The *American No 1* was the most encouraging sinking. She carried a crew of 33, with no fatalities. Apparently she had held an abandon-ship drill only hours before the actual sinking.

Roughly the same numbers of vessels are lost each year, but the death rate has been steadily declining. There are a couple of factors in play here: First, individual fishing quotas (IFQ) for fishing and crabbing are certainly safer than derby fishing and crabbing. Secondly, the industry stakeholders (captains, engineers, and owners) are becoming more safety conscious, and that is to their credit.

I think every fishing boat should have a fire drill, abandon-ship drill, and man-overboard drill at least once a month, preferably on the first day after leaving port, particularly if new crew members have just joined the vessel. If it's a small fishing boat with a small, steady crew, they should at least talk about it over lunch now and then.

There was a time when fishermen almost prided themselves on not preparing for disasters, but after all the carnage I don't think that is still the case. Unfortunately, we are not all the way there yet; there are still boats where safety is not treated as respectfully as it should be.

So to ease my conscience, I'm going to give you an emergency drill right now. You are more responsible for your own safety than anyone. After all, who's more motivated?

• Your first day aboard, find your survival suit; this is your most important life-saving device. It's a red neoprene suit that you climb into and zip up to your face. It will be stored in a large orange or white bag.

Forget the life jackets. What is the point of floating if you freeze to death? You can't wear both, so go for the survival suit; it will keep you warm *and* afloat. Pay special attention to getting the hood and face flap secured properly. Studies have shown this is the main cause of heat loss and survival suit failure.

These suits may be stowed in your stateroom, in the factory, or in lockers on deck. Find them. Work out the best route from your workstation and your bunk to where the survival suits are stowed. If the emergency lights fail, can you find them in the dark? How about with a 20-degree list?

You do not want to jump into Alaskan waters without your suit. The water is so cold that in about ten percent of the time it will stop your heart and you're done. Even if your heart keeps working, you'll be dead of hyperthermia in less than an hour, unless you're wearing your survival suit.

Take one out of its bag and put it on. If you can't put it on, start to finish, hood on, all zipped up in less than a minute, keep practicing. One trick is to keep your right arm out of the suit until the hood is on and the suit is partly zipped. If the zipper sticks, ask the skipper for some wax; he should have some.

Don't let anyone cover up the survival suits locker with gear. It shouldn't happen, but it does.

If you're a very large person you won't fit into an Adult-sized survival suit, you are going to need a Jumbo. Find it now, before the boat starts filling with water.

Never put the suit on inside the vessel. Survival suits are extremely buoyant, and if the boat fills with water they will trap you. A remarkable number of skippers have been found dead in their survival suits, starfished against the overhead of the wheelhouse of their sunken fishing boats. Occasionally fishermen are found dead in their survival suits, but not very often. It's like having a heart attack in the lobby of the Mayo Clinic: you may still die, but you got to like your odds of survival.

• Next, find the life rafts, your second most important lifesaving device. They'll be located on deck in a white canister stowed in a cradle designed to allow the raft to float free and inflate automatically should the vessel sink. There should be some launch instructions on the raft or on a nearby sign. If there isn't, you can also launch the raft by lifting it over the rail and dropping it into the sea.

The line leading out of the canister is called the painter. If the slack in the painter is taken up and a sharp jerk is administered, the canister will pop open and the raft will inflate. If there is more than one life raft, tie the rafts together. They're easier to spot that way.

• Never abandon ship until the captain passes the word.

• Another automatically deployed device is the EPIRB, Emergency Position-Indicating Beacon. It is designed to float free and begin transmitting a distress message. The rescue will be directed to the location of the EPIRB, so take it with you, tie it to the raft, and wait. Someone will be along shortly.

• Stowed in the raft should be some seasickness pills. Take them. The raft will bounce around like a cork in the big seas; somebody is going to get sick, causing a chain reaction. Even if you don't get seasick, you may change your mind once you've been basted in a moderate coating of vomit. Most people who don't survive in a life raft are done in by dehydration and loss of electrolytes.

That's your abandon ship drill. If you find all the equipment I've mentioned and understand what I've written, you should be able to survive a sinking.

Now for a man overboard drill.

If someone is washed over the side in your presence, throw a life ring over immediately; in fact, throw them all over. Notify the wheelhouse immediately and try not to lose sight of the head bobbing in the seas. I think you should point at the man as long as you can see him so the skipper or anyone else helping with the spotting knows where to look.

You'll probably lose sight of the man before the vessel can be turned around, so everyone on board needs to be up and looking from all points of the vessel, the higher the better.

Standing on top of the wheelhouse is my favorite spot to search from.

If a crewman is lost over the side without anyone seeing it happen, he may not be missed for hours. The boat will go back and look for him, but he won't be found. So remember the old sailing ship adage, "One hand for the ship, one hand for yourself."

As for a fire drill, there isn't much I can tell you, as they tend to be specific to the vessel. However, it is imperative that you do some studying before the fire.

• What kind of fire extinguishers do you have on board? There are instructions on the canisters.

• Where are they located? Again, know the location of the fire extinguishers nearest to your work station and your bunk. Remember, a full fire extinguisher only lasts for a minute or two. So don't wade into a burning mess spraying your ass off and expect to make it out the other side before you're running on empty. It's nice to have someone behind you feeding you full ones as you need them.

• Remember to notify the wheelhouse before fighting the fire, or better yet, send someone to call the bridge while you fight the fire. You want to get on the fire fast, since given un-limited fuel, air, and heat, the fire will double in size every four minutes. Good luck.

Don't let these drills scare you; you'll do fine. Just start your emergency thinking ahead of time rather than mid-emergency. Don't think that none of this can happen to you, because I promise you it can. You just need to be prepared and rely on your shipmates.

In *Working on the Edge* by Spike Walker, my favorite crabbing book of all time, one of the characters manages to grab one of his shipmates who's been washed over the side and he tells him, "I've got you, Mike, and I'm not going to let you go."

It gets me every time.

Survival Suit

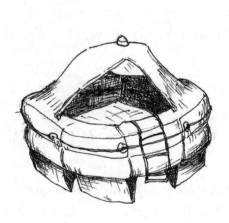

Life Raft

Sea Time Documentation

The Coast Guard is requiring more and more marine licenses and seaman papers. To get either one requires documented sea time and a test. Worry about the test in about three years, but ask for a sea-time documentation letter from the skipper or company as soon as you complete your first deckhand job. You don't get sea time for processing jobs, but try to document deck or engine jobs as carefully as possible, because you'll need three years worth before you can sit for a Mate's or Assistant Engineer's license.

Even if you don't think you'll ever sit for a Coast Guard license (required of captains, mates, and engineers on many fishing boats), get the sea-time letter after every contract. Circumstances change and you may someday decide to sit for a license. It's very difficult to go back years later and get sea time letters out of defunct companies or retired skippers.

You'll find a sample Coast Guard sea time sample letter in the Appendix. Study it. Be sure your employer writes you something similar.

Age

Fishing is a young man's game. Most fishermen and processors are between 18 and 25 when they start. Some crab boats won't hire anyone over 27 to work on deck.

Older workers seem to suffer more sore backs, stiffer

joints, and take longer to recover from injuries. And frankly, once the mid-twenties are reached, it becomes harder to train and brainwash the new crewman.

There are, however, people in their forties working on some of the processor boats.

But by the time they hit their 30s, most deckhands and processors either move into vessel or factory management or retire.

Discrimination

There are a few women working as deckhands, usually on draggers. Women are widely used as cooks, processors, and factory foremen. Some of the most respected factory foremen are women. As stated earlier, results are what matter. If you're good, you will be appreciated; if not, you'll be gone.

There are many different types of people fishing in Alaska: Mexican, Black, Polish, Korean, and on and on. There are also more jobs available than good people to fill them.

If you're good, you'll be welcome. If you find a boat where you're discriminated against in spite of doing a great job, move on, you're working for an idiot. Good workers are too valuable to hassle, except by a fool.

Drugs and Booze

Every boat and every company has its own policy, and every year there is less tolerance. Most of the better-managed companies insist on a pre-hire drug test. Many of the larger companies do not allow any drinking from the time the crew members leave Seattle until they return to Seattle.

Drunken fishermen create so many problems, such as missed flights and boats or falling overboard, that eventually all the larger companies will ban drinking. It may not be such a bad thing, as it is remarkable how many inebriated fishermen are found dead in Dutch Harbor bay each year, arms locked around a piling, after failing to clamber aboard their vessel nested three boats out from the dock.

There are some boats that *will* employ serious drinkers, because they have little choice. The worst fishing boat I ever worked on had a truly skilled deck gang. They were all master longline hand baiters—tough, skilled, expert gaffers. The vessel was awful: small, slow, poorly maintained, owned by one of the worst fishing companies in Alaska. It took me a Dutch Harbor offload to understand why such a terrible vessel carried such a talented crew. Once the product was offloaded, the crew immediately began drinking and didn't sober up until we were two days out of port.

The deck boss asked me to fire Bobby, the slowest deck hand aboard.

"Sure, I'll fire him if you want," I told the deck boss, "but leaving Dutch he was the only crewmember sober enough to get up and let the lines go. I can't get under way by myself, so if you promise to get up the next time we leave Dutch Harbor, I'll get rid of Bobby."

"He's not that slow, I guess. Maybe we better keep him," said the deck boss.

So we kept Bobby. He wasn't much of a fisherman, but he was a fully functional human being. On leaving Dutch Harbor, he and I were usually the only two relatively sober fishermen on board for a day or two, and neither of us possessed the skills of the rest of the crew, once they sobered up.

If you have lifestyle issues, you may still be able to find a boat—it just won't be a good one.

Drugs are mostly a problem when applying for a job. A drug screening test is often required, and often the companies won't hire you if you come up positive.

I worked for a company once that was having trouble finding competent crew members. During the hiring process they would ask, "Are you ready for your drug test? Or would you like to wait a month or so?"

I doubt very many companies are quite so understanding

I doubt very many companies are quite so understanding today. Federal regulations require drug tests all around whenever there is a marine casualty or a serious injury. If you're using, even if you had nothing to do with the problem but get caught up in the dragnet, you will go down hard. You'll lose your job, most of your pay, and may get put off the vessel in some funky little town on the Alaskan coast you've never heard of, with no money to get home. I've seen it happen.

I'm not saying drug use never happens on a fishing boat; I'm just saying it's high risk. If there's no way you can clean up for a few months, I'd concentrate on the smaller boats. They tend to be more informal. Who knows, you may find one where the skipper smokes more than you!

Airline Tickets

Once you're hired by a fishing company, they will supply you with an airline ticket from Seattle to the fishing vessel. The company will have you sign a contract that obligates you to work aboard their vessel from one to four months. If you complete your contract, the company pays for your round-trip ticket. If you fail to complete the contract, the cost of the round-trip ticket is deducted from your earnings.

Some of the tougher companies will not supply you with a return ticket if you quit before earning enough to cover its cost. The State of Alaska requires that they supply you with a return ticket under most circumstances. But if you're fired for cause (drugs, stealing, refusal to work, etc.), the ship could put you off in Dutch Harbor without a return ticket—just something to keep in mind.

A few companies, usually crabbers, will advance you a ticket, but deduct it from your check—even if you complete your contract. Ask about the company's ticket policy before you fly north. In any case, it is your responsibility to get yourself to Seattle.

Passport

It is a good idea to get a passport prior to going fishing. They don't cost much and they are good for ten years. The big trawlers, especially, are starting to fish all over the world in an effort to stay busy once the Alaskan season ends. American boats have fished off New Zealand, Russia, Indonesia, and Argentina, with additional areas opening all the time.

When big boats go foreign, there is always a scramble for passports. If you have yours already when you begin your job search, you just may get snapped up overnight.

Fishing Magazines

There are a couple of excellent commercial fishing magazines on the market. Read them carefully for several months and they will fill you in on the hot fisheries and where they're occurring. You might even pick up the odd practical fishing tip. *National Fisherman* is the largest and oldest commercial fishing magazine, and it is quite good. Its address is: Journal of Publications, 120 Tillson Ave., Suite 201, P.O. Box 908, Rockland, Main 04841-0908. Its website is: nationalfisherman.com. However, it covers the entire national fishing scene, so there are lots to articles on East Coast Fishing, even in the West Coast edition.

Pacific Fishing is excellent and deals solely with the West Coast. Its address is: Salmon Bay Communications, 1515 N.W. 51st, Seattle, WA 98107. Its website is: pacificfishing.com. Anyone interested in a career in commercial fishing should subscribe to at least one of these magazines. I like *Pacific Fishing*.

Schools

There are a number of courses offered that might help the novice, or even the experienced fisherman. Courses in firefighting, first aid, metal shop, math, and net mending can only help. Fishing schools are located on the coasts. Many of the coastal community colleges have fishing departments, especially in the Northwest.

If you're still in high school, load up on metalworking and math classes. As you move up, you'll need those skills: metal shop for the engine room and factory, math for working in the wheelhouse.

Another possibility, that I hesitate to suggest because it is so time-consuming, is a four-year maritime academy. These schools train young men and women to work as merchant ship officers. At last count there was one academy in California, one in Texas, and four on the East Coast.

Academy boys are not always popular with "real" fishermen, because they usually start in the wheelhouse rather than the factory or the back deck, and occasionally they let their egos run wild and free. But they can usually find a job and perhaps they do learn something of value at the academy. At the very least they're usually faster than anyone else at computing their daily share.

And perhaps it's not such a bad thing to have a college degree, a U.S. Coast Guard Third Mate's Unlimited License, and possibly even a Naval Reserve Commission. But four years (three with previous college experience) is a very long time.

Employment Paperwork

Be sure to have the proper paperwork together to prove your citizenship before you begin your job search. Most people use their driver's license and their original social security card. A passport, birth certificate, or certificate of naturalization will also do the trick.

If you're not an American citizen you'll need a Green Card and a valid INS authorization to work, or at least some fairly high quality fakes (that's a joke, not a legal opinion).

Make it as easy as possible for potential employers to hire you by having all the needed documents ready to go.

Getting Ahead

So, how do you move up in your chosen fishery? Well, brown-nosing has its proponents, but I would recommend the more honorable method of doing more than your share of work without complaint.

What you do is this (and I've seen it work many times): You make yourself the best processor in the factory. You watch the more experienced guys very carefully and learn as much as quickly as possible. Volunteer for the harder tasks and master them. Come to work early, stay late, don't complain, and don't cause trouble. Try to build a reputation as one of the hardest workers aboard ship.

Then approach the deck boss and tell him you're interested in working on deck. After every shift, or once a day if you have two shifts a day, instead of going to bed, go out on deck and help the deckhands for a couple of hours. If there isn't much going on, see if someone will teach you a needed skill: knots, splicing, welding, or sewing web. I know it's a lot of work. You may only get 5 or 6 hours of sleep a day. But it's the best way to move up and it's still probably easier than law school.

As for the next step – deckhand to deck boss – by the time you're ready for that promotion, you'll know what you have to do. But when all else fails, just do more than your share, and be the best on the boat at what you do. At least on a good boat, the people who matter will notice.

Never forget that a boat is not a democracy. Captains don't normally enjoy arguing or negotiating with their crew. What the captain says goes, with a very few exceptions usually involving life or death or criminal sanctions.

If you have trouble with authority, you'll have trouble on a fishing boat. Do as the captain asks quickly and cheerfully and you should be fine. On the bigger boats there is a chain of command. Try very hard to stay on good terms with your supervisor. Going over her head never works out very well.

Foreign-Owned Fishing Boats

Up until the mid-1970s, when the Magnuson Act extended America's control of its fisheries from 3 miles offshore to 200 miles offshore, there weren't any large American vessels fishing the North Pacific. The Japanese had been fishing this area for many years, but the Magnuson Act drove out the foreign-owned and operated fishing boats. So the Japanese companies built their own onshore fish processing plants. They built large American-flagged draggers and longliners that carried the required number of American crew and officers, but were owned, run, and fished by Japanese.

The Norwegians did the same with their big pollock draggers. They carry the required American flag (only American flag vessels can fish in U.S. waters), and they carry the required American licensed officers, but they also carry a Norwegian or Japanese fishing master, who does the fishing.

It's hard to blame the foreigners who have chosen to invest in American fishing. Americans could have done the same, but instead many chose to invest in collateralized debt obligations. Now it's too late; the fisheries are closed to new boats. Some of the best Alaskan fishing vessels are owned and operated by the Japanese and Norwegians—as well as some of the worst. There's nothing wrong with working on a foreign-owned boat. Who knows, perhaps as we acquire the required skills, Americans can take more of a leadership role on these vessels fishing in our waters.

I've worked with and for Norwegians, Japanese, and Americans. I advise you to work where you can learn the most. If the foreigners will train you, great; if they won't, you're wasting your time. Move on.

Alaskan Fishing Outlook

It doesn't look like there are any more under-exploited fisheries left in Alaska, with the possible exception of arrowtooth flounder and clams. Any new growth in fishing can only come from a corresponding growth in the biomass or by finding new fisheries around the world to exploit. Presently there are American boats fishing from the Falklands to Siberia. Perhaps someday the Americans will join the Japanese and Norwegians as the world's preeminent distant water fishermen. But for now, Alaska remains the bread and butter of the big American factory boats.

Fish populations in Alaska, as well as the rest of the world, go through cycles. Some historically great Alaskan fisheries, such as shrimp and red Alaskan king crab, have almost disappeared, while other traditional Alaskan fisheries such as Opilio crab have recently exploded beyond all expectation.

Species rise and fall. A successful long-term processor should be able to process many different types of fish and crab. The successful long-term deckhand should know to fish with nets, hook and line, and crab pots. The successful long-term boat owner should be able to rig his vessels for several different types of fishing. Flexibility is becoming the key to success.

The move away from derby fishing to IFQ fishing has reduced the number of jobs significantly. It has probably reduced the chances of making a really big score as well. It has, however, minimized the chances of being skunked completely. It has also made these most dangerous fisheries safer as well.

It is hard for me to say if it has helped or hurt the average fisherman in Alaska. I guess it depends on if he is able to find a good boat or not. But I think the IFQ style fishery will in the long run benefit the fisheries themselves as the fishermen with individual fishing quotas have a long-term vested interest in protecting the fish stock, rather than just trying to catch more fish or crab than anyone else.

The Bering Sea is the richest fishing ground left on Earth, and with proper fishery management it should continue to thrive, even as individual fisheries rise and fall.

Worst Day of Fishing Ever

In the interest of full disclosure I feel that I should relate a final sea story, so you can appreciate just how bad things can get on a fishing boat.

A processor, who shall remain nameless only because I can't remember his name, was breaking a freezer, when a 40-pound block of frozen fish slid out and hit him in the head, knocking him silly. The foreman suggested he take a break up on deck, in the fresh air, to gather his wits.

Longliners, in particular, often haul their gear running into the wind for hours at a time, allowing thousands of seabirds to hover just to the side of the vessel, feeding on the fish parts discharged to the sea during processing. When eating well, sea bird flocks void themselves a lot, almost in a steady, white, chalky, rain, which our processor soon discovered.

He ran for cover, flattening himself alongside the fishing boat's house, considering his next move.

It began to rain, or so it seemed, though it was one of those rare Bering Sea sunny days. The skipper was hauling gear in hand steering, alone, with no one to relieve him, when he suddenly had to relieve himself. So he threw open the door just behind his steering station, dashed out, and let fly, completely unaware of the dazed processor huddled one deck below.

So in the space of less than half an hour the poor processor was knocked unconscious, crapped on, and, well, you get the picture . . . .

True story. You have been warned.

Glossary

Auto Baiter: A machine that automatically baits longline hooks as they're set out the stern of the vessel.

Baader: Type of processing machine.

Baiter: Crew member on a crab boat who prepares the crab bait and then puts it in the pot about to be launched.

Berth: Place to sleep or place to tie up boat.

Bleed: Stab codfish in heart to drain blood.

Bleeder: A senior processor who directs the catch to different parts of the factory as needed, or a crew member responsible for bleeding and sorting the catch.

Bottom Gear: Steel balls (spindles) or compressed tires (tire gear) that the bottom nets sit on to keep the web off of rough ground.

Bottom Net: Trawl net designed to be fished by dragging along the sea bottom.

Bow: Front of boat.

Brailer: Web-covered basket used with a crane to transfer fish or crab.

Bridge: Also known as the wheelhouse. Vessel nerve center, where navigation takes place.

By-catch: Unintended catch.

Carpal Tunnel Syndrome: Inflammation of wrist tendon sheaths caused by repetitive motion.

Circle hook: A round hook used in longlining that is very hard for a fish to free itself from.

Cork Line: Top of the net, a line supported by floats.

Crab Pot: Steel and web trap used to catch crab and occasionally cod.

Catcher Processor: A fishing boat that processes the fish it catches in its onboard factory.

Catcher Boat: Fishing boat that delivers its catch ashore to be processed. It can be a salmon boat, longliner, crab boat, or trawler.

Cod End: The very back of the trawl net where the catch is contained.

Cork Piler: Crew member who piles the corks on the deck of a salmon seiner as the net is retrieved.

Crew Share: The percentage of the catch the crew is paid.

Deck: Floor of the boat.

Deck Boss: Senior member of the deck hands. His job is to make sure the skipper's orders are carried out.

Deck Hands: Crew who work on deck and handle the fishing gear.

Derby Fishing: A type of fishing season where all boats start out even and compete to catch the most fish until all the allowable biomass is caught.

Doors: Heavy, rectangular, wing-like devices towed behind the trawler to spead the net perpendicularly to the direction of the vessel's movement.

Dragger: Trawler.

Engineer: Officer responsible for the vessel's engines. Usually believes himself to be the smartest person aboard; occasionally correct.

Factory Trawler: A trawler that processes the fish it catches in an onboard fish processing factory. It is often very large, with some well over 300 feet in length.

Farmer: Derogatory term used to describe an unskilled deck hand.

Fathom: Six feet.

Fishing License: License required by the State of Alaska of all members of the deck department. Processors are exempt.

Fish Poisoning: An infection caused by a marine bacteria entering a break in the skin. Can be very serious if untreated.

Fishmeal: After the meat is carved off the fish, the leftovers are cooked, ground up, and sifted, creating fishmeal, which is almost pure protein. Fishmeal plants can be smelled a mile away.

Floating Processor: A large vessel, often a retired merchant ship, that processes fish and crab that are delivered to it from smaller catcher boats.

Fish Slime: A yucky coating that protects the fish. It contains a lot of bacteria that can cause fish poisoning.

Full Share: The share of a completely competent fisherman.

Gaff: A big hook about 20 inches long used to bring fish aboard a longliner.

Gaffer: Deckhand who hooks each fish caught on the longline gear that the boat wants to keep and helps it aboard. He also "shakes" all prohibited species, returning them to the sea.

Ganglions: twine used to connect hooks to the longline, usually about 18 inches long.

Galley: Kitchen and dining room on a boat.

Gill net: A net that works by snagging fish that attempt to swim through it.

Gilson wire: The heavy wires on the trawlers used to drag the loaded cod ends up trawl ramp and aboard.

Greenhorn: New guy on his first boat.

Handcuffs: Bracelets that prevent injury when running certain types of headers.

Half Share: What most greenhorns earn. Can be half, or a little more than half, of what a full-share deck hand earns.

Hatch: Horizontal opening in the boat.

Hatchery: Plant where salmon eggs are hatched to be returned to the wild.

Haul: To bring the fishing gear and hopefully some of the targeted fish aboard the fishing vessel.

Header: Machine that cuts the head off of fish. Can be very dangerous to the processor running it.

Hold: Area under the hatch where the product is often stored.

Individual Fishing Quota (IFQ): A given amount of fish a particular boat is allowed to harvest.

Knot: Nautical mile per hour, just over one MPH.

Lead Line: The bottom of the purse net that is weighted.

Lead Piler: Crew member who piles the lead line on a seiner.

Live Tank: The cargo hold of the crab vessel filled with recirculating sea water to keep the catch alive.

Longline: A fishing style using hooks attached to a very long line, often over ten miles. The longline is retrieved and fish removed from the hooks. Not as productive as trawling but far less wasteful.

Mate: Deck officer, who works below the skipper, runs the show when the captain is asleep or too drunk.

Offshore Hauler: Hydraulic device used to recover the longline and all the attached fish.

Permit Holder: The rich guy who owns the fishing permit that the boat fishes under.

Pew: A spike on the end of a long handle used to move fish about.

Pelagic: Means up in the water. Pelagic fish spend most of their time in mid water.

Plunger Pole: Looks like a long toilet plunger, used on seine boats to scare fish into the net.

Port: Where the ship ties up, or the ship's left side.

Power Block: A hydraulic wheel used to retrieve all sorts of fishing gear such as longlines, crab pot buoys, and seine nets.

Processor: Crew member who converts the whole fish into frozen product.

Purse Line: Line used to cinch up the bottom of the purse seine net.

Purse Seining: A fishing method used to catch salmon and herring where the school of fish is surrounded by the net, the net is pursed closed, and most of the net is drawn aboard. The fish is then transferred to the fish hold.

Roe: Fish eggs, harvested from herring, salmon, cod, and pollock for the Japanese market.

Rules of the Road: Ship handling rules concerning collision avoidance.

Scopolamine: A seasickness patch placed behind the ear that releases medication for three days.

Skate: Ray or a unit of longline gear.

Skiff: Small boat carried on fishing boats, on seiners used to maneuver the net.

Skipper: Captain (often believe themselves to be divine).

Slime Line: Where the target fish are first processed on any type of fish factory.

Splice: To join a rope or a wire together.

Starboard: Right.

Stern: Back of boat.

Surimi: A Japanese invention. Ground up fish paste, can be flavored many different ways.

Survival Suit: A neoprene suit used by crew members to abandon ship, can keep them alive for hours. Know where yours is located on the vessel. Coast Guard requirement.

Tender: Boat that transports fish from the catcher boat to the shore processor.

Toyo: Processing machine.

Trawl: Funnel-shaped net dragged behind the fishing vessel. Some of the largest have forward opening circumference of about a mile.

Troll: Commercial fishing method involving towing baited hooks behind the vessel. Used in salmon fishing.

Wahine: Hawaiian term for babe.

Wheelhouse: Where the vessel is steered from; vessel nerve center.

Web: The mesh of a net.

Web Piler: Crew member who piles the web of the seine net on the deck.

Zipper: line laced through the aft end of the cod end that must be removed before the cod end is dumped.

Date

SAMPLE General Sea Service Letter
Company's/Ships Letter Head

From: (See: 46 CFR 11.211 for specific information)

To: United States Coast Guard
National Maritime Center (NMC)
100 Forbes Drive
Martinsburg, WV 25404

Subject: ACCUMULATION OF <EMPLOYEE'S> SEA SERVICE

Dear NMC:

Please be advised that <employee name> <mariner identification number> is/was employed by our company as a <position>. The following is an accumulation of <employee name>'s sea time.

Vessel Name	Official Number	Vessel Type	Propulsion	GRT	HP	Position	Route	Begin Date	End Date	Days Underway

Days Underway in the past 3 years: _____ Days Underway in the past 5 years: _____.
Total Days Underway: _____. The listed sea service consists of <8 OR 12> hour days underway. By documenting 12 hour day service, I am attesting that 12 hour days have been authorized by the United States Coast Guard, per each vessel's manning requirements.

Whoever, in any matter within the jurisdiction of any department or agency of the United States knowingly and willfully falsifies, conceals, or covers up by any trick, scheme, or device a material fact, or makes any false, fictitious, or fraudulent statement or entry, shall be fined not more than $10,000 or imprisoned for not more than 5 years or both (18 U.S.C. 1001).

I certify that this statement is true and correct to the best of my knowledge and is in accordance with the warning notice listed above (18 U.S.C. 1001).

<SIGNATURE BY AUTHORIZED COMPANY REPRESENTATIVE>
<PRINTED NAME OF AUTHORIZED COMPANY REPRESENTATIVE>
<CONTACT NUMBER IF DIFFERS FROM LETTERHEAD>

John Newbie
100000 Main Street
Wanta Job, CA 00000
Phone: 123-345-5678

February 28. 2011
Captain Skip Workaholic
Back Breaker Lane
Never Ending Bay, WA 00000

Dear Captain Workaholic:

I am very interested in working for you this summer on the Salty Lady. I have wanted to fish in Alaska for as long as I can remember, and I am doing everything I can possibly think of to land a summer job. I am a sophomore at Cal Poly and I am looking to work hard over the summers and put my earnings toward my hefty tuition until I'm finished with graduate school.

While I am lacking fishing experience, I grew up on a potato farm in Driggs, Idaho and I am accustom to performing under extreme conditions; hard work and long hours, usually while cold, hungry or both. I can fix just about any farming equipment that needs attention. During the off season, I worked for Grand Targhee Ski Resort as an avalanche rescue crew-member. This required the ability to work hard and fast, under an extreme sense of urgency. For this, I am CPR and First Aid certified.

The most satisfying work I have done has been some of the toughest. I've gone deep sea fishing with my relatives on the Washington coast many times so I know I have no seasickness problems. To sum things up, the good news is that you would not need to teach me how to work. My parents already did that for us. I would love to show you that my deal is to work harder than anyone else, that I am a quick learner and I know how to follow directions under pressure. I'd love the opportunity to prove it.

I look forward to hearing from you soon.

Sincerely,

John Newbie

John Newbie
100000 Main Street
Wanta Job, CA 00000
Phone: 123-345-5678

SKILLS:

Accomplished Rescue Worker; Grand Targhee Avalanche Rescue Team
Great Team Player
Able to work long hours, under extreme conditions, while maintaining quality
Mechanically skilled
Experienced with boats and navigation

ACHIEVEMENTS:

Completely restored and rebuilt John Deere combine in time for potato season
Won "Best Barbeque" three years and running, at Teton Valley County Fair
Rowed on Cal Poly on Freshman Eight Man Shell – 2010-2011
Took Pope and Young Archery record for Elk - 2009
Raised $4,300 in pledge monies for "Running Long for the Cure" 27 mile marathon - 2010

WORK EXPERIENCE:

2000 to Present: Newbie Potato Farming

Ran all heavy equipment farming implements during potato growing and harvest season. Learned all about diesel repair of all farming equipment. Planted, maintained, harvested, loaded and hauled potato's for 10 seasons. Managed 500 acre Irrigation system, including irrigation repairs and operations.

2008 to Present: Grand Targhee Ski Resort Fire and Rescue

Worked with Targhee Fire and Rescue as Avalanche rescue crewmember. This entailed working with rescue dogs to recover avalanche victims, recover injured skiers and snowboarders and transporting to safety. Administer First Aide and CPR when necessary. I also maintained radio contact with medics and doctors at nearby hospital. Scheduled airlift rescues when necessary. Maintained CPR and First Aid certifications

EDUCATION:
Currently pursuing Horticulturist & Agriculture Masters Degree at Cal Polytechnic in San Luis Obispo, CA
High school diploma at Teton Valley High school, Driggs, ID in 2008

INTERESTS:
Cooking, skiing, snowboarding, mountain biking, big game hunting & fishing .

PHYSICAL STATISTICS:
Height: 6' 2"   Weight: 200 Birth date: 11/30/1991

10th & M Seafoods
1020 M ST
Anchorage, AK 99501
Phone: (907) 272-3474
Fax: (907) 272-1685
Website:
Email: tenmsea@alaska.net
Job applications: email resume

10th & M Seafoods
1304 Laona Cir
Anchorage, AK 99518
Phone: (907) 561-5160
Fax: (907) 561-5191
Website:
Email: tenmsea@alaska.net
Job applications: email resume

Absolute Fresh Seafoods Inc
504 Front St
Craig, AK 99921
Phone: (907) 738-0134
Fax: (907) 747-7577
Website:
Email:
Job applications:
    apply by mail or in person

Alaska Coho Girl Smoked Fish LLC
1900 Meander Cir
Anchorage, AK 99516
Phone:
Fax: (907) 344-8250
Website:
Email:
Job applications: fax resume

Alaska Fresh Seafoods Inc
105 Marine Way
Kodiak, AK 99615
Phone: (907) 486-5749
Fax: (907) 486-6417
Website:
Email:
Job applications: apply by mail or fax

Alaska Sausage Company Inc
2914 Arctic Blvd
Anchorage, AK 99503
Phone: (907) 562-3636
Fax: (907) 562-7343
Website:
Email:
Job applications: apply in person

Alaska Seafood Systems
420 Marine Way
Kodiak, AK 99615
Phone: (907) 486-2053
Fax: (907) 486-2052
Website:
Email:
Job applications: apply by mail or fax

Alsek Fish
PO BOX 202
Yakatat, AK 99689
Phone: (254) 204-2443
Fax:
Website:
Email: alsekfish@gmail.com
Job applications: mail or email resume

Alyeska Seafoods Inc
551 W Broadway
Unalaska, AK 99685
Phone: (907) 581-1211
Fax: (907) 581-1695
Website:
Email:
Job applications: mail or fax resume

Annette Island Packing Company
PO Box 10
Metlakatla, AK 99926
Phone: (907) 886-4661
Fax: (907) 886-4660
Website:
Email:
Job applications: "job line" (907)
    866-5627

Aqua Tech
6221 Petersburg St
Anchorage, AK 99507
Phone: (907) 563-1387
Fax: (907) 563-1852
Website:
Email: aqua@alaska.net
Job applications: apply by mail or
    email

Belt Freezer Facility
Shakes St
Wrangell, AK 99929
Phone: (907) 874-3346
Fax: (907) 874-3035
Website:
Email:
Job applications: apply by mail or fax

Bering Fisheries
146 Gilman Rd
Unalaska, AK 99692
Phone: (907) 947-8697
Fax:
Website: iberingstarfisheries.com
Email: info@beringstarfisheries.info
Job applications: mail or fax resume

Coastal Cold Storage Inc
PO Box 307
Petersburg, AK 99833
Phone: (907) 772-4172
Fax: (907) 772-4176
Website: costalcoldstoragealaska.com
Email: via "contact us" on website
Job Applications: Contact Greg, Kim or Doug
    toll free at (877) 257-4746

Candysmoke
PO Box 765
Delta Junction, AK 99737
Phone: (907) 895-4071
Fax: (907) 895-4944
Website:
Email:
Job applications: apply by mail or fax

Coffee Point Seafoods
PO Box 230
King Salmon, AK 99613
Apply to Double E Foods
3625 1st Avenue South
Seattle, WA
Phone: (907) 424-3721
Fax: (206) 768-8985
Website: eefoods.com
Email: via "contact us" on website
Job applications: downloadable applica-
    tion to fax

Copper River Seafood - Anchorage
1400 East Ave
Anchorage, AK 99501
Phone: (907) 424-3721
Fax: (907) 222-0348
Website: copperriverseafood.com
Email: info@crsalaska.com
Job applications: online application

Copper River Seafoods- Retail LLC
8430 Laviento Dr
Anchorage, AK 99515
Phone: (907) 349-8234
Fax:
Website: copperriverseafood.com
Email: info@crsalaska.com
Job applications: online application

Craig Fisheries
PO Box 88
Craig, AK 99921
Phone: (907) 826-3241
Fax: (907) 826-3801
Website:
Email:
Job applications: apply by mail

Custom Seafood Processors Inc
35722 Kenai Spur Hwy
Soldotna, AK 99669
Phone: (907) 262-9691
Fax: (907) 262-3110
Website: seafoods-direct.com
Email: asd@alaska.net
Job applications: mail, email, or fax
    resume

Dejon Delights LTD
PO BOX 712
Haines, AK 99827
Phone: (800) 539-3608
Fax: (907) 766-2505
Website: dejondelights.com
Email: dejon@dejondelights.com
Job applications: mail or fax resume

E C Phillips & Son - Ketchikan Facility
1775 Tongass Avenue
Ketchikan, AK 99901
Phone: (907) 247-7975
Fax: (907) 225-7250
Website: ecphillipsalaska.com
Email: humanresources@ecphillipsalaska.com
Job applications: download application and mail, email, or fax back

Favco Inc
PO Box 190968
Anchorage, AK 99519
Phone: (907) 278-1525
Fax: (907) 276-6626
Website: favcoinc.com
Email: favco@favco.net
Job applications: mail, fax, or email

Fee's Custom Seafoods
PO Box 790
Whittier, AK 99693
Phone: (907) 472-5055
Fax: (907) 472-5055
Website: feescustomseafood.com
Email: feescustomseafood@yahoo.com
Job applications: email

Fisherman's Express LLC - Plant 1
1350 East Ave
Anchorage, AK 99501
Phone: (907) 884-4976
Fax: (907) 569-3476
Website: fishex.com
Email:
Job applications: mail or fax resume

Global Seafoods North American- Kodiak
Facility
800 Marine Way E
Kodiak, AK 99615
Phone: (425) 223-3116
Fax:
Website: globalseafoods.com
Email: info@globalseafoods.com
Job applications: mail or fax resume

International Seafoods of Alaska, Plant 2
517 Shelikof St
Kodiak, AK 99615
Phone: (907) 486-4768
Fax: (907) 486-4885
Website: sea-world.com
Email: via "contact us" on website
Job applications: mail or fax resume

Jerrys Meats & Seafoods
5165 Glacier Hwy Ste B
Juneau, AK 99801
Phone: (907) 789-5142
Fax: (907) 789-3306
Website: jerrysmeats.com
Email: via "contact us" on website
Job applications: mail or fax resume

Juneau Alaskan & Proud Market
615 Willoughby Ave
Juneau, AK 99801
Phone: (907) 586-3101
Fax: (907) 225-0614
Website:
Email:
Job applications: mail or fax resume

Kachemak Bay Seafoods- Homer Facility
4470 Homer Spit Rd
Homer, AK 99603
Phone: (907) 229-1551
Fax: (907) 235-2799
Website:
Email:
Job applications: Mail or fax resume

Kenai Landing- Egg House
2101 Bowpicker Ln
Kenai, AK 99611
Phone: (907) 563-3474
Fax: (907) 563-3442
Website:
Email:
Job applications: mail or fax resume

Kodiak Smoking
420 Marine Way
Kodiak, AK 99615
Phone: (907) 539-5411
Fax: (907) 486-0600
Website: Kodiaksmoking.com
Email:
Job applications: mail or fax resume

Leonard's Landing Lodge
PO Box 282
Yakutat, AK 99689
Phone: (907) 784-3245
Fax: (907) 784-3591
Website: Leonardslanding.com
Email: via "contact us" on website
Job applications: mail or fax resume

N SE RAA - Hidden Falls Hatchery
1308 Sawmill Creek RD
Sitka, AK 99835
Phone: (907) 747-6850
Fax: (907) 747-1470
Website: nsraa.org
Email: via "contact us" on website
Job applications: availability posted on
    website; call, fax, or mail

North Pacific Seafoods
4 Nickerson Ste #400
Seattle, WA 98109
Phone: (206) 726-9900
Fax: (206) 726-1667
Website: northpacificseafoods.com
Email: Info@npsi.us
Job applications: downloadable online

Northern Lights Smokeries LLC
PO BOX 848
Petersburg, AK 99833
Phone: (907) 772-4608
Fax:
Website: nlsmokeries.com
Email: wildsalmon@nlsmokeries.com
Job applications: email or mail resume

Norton Sound Seafood - Savoonga Plant
PO Box 906
Nome, AK 99762
Phone: (907) 443-2304
Fax: (907) 443-2457
Website: nortonsoundseafoodproducts.
    com
Email: nss@nsedc.com
Job applications: email, fax, or mail
resume

Noyes Island Smokehouse LLC
PO BOX 314
Craig, AK 99921
Phone: (907) 826-2596
Fax: (907) 826-2447
Website:
Email:
Job applications: mail or fax resume

Pacific Seafood
317 Shelikof Ave
Kodiak, AK 99615
Phone: (907) 486-8575
Fax: (907) 486-3007
Website: pacseafoods.com
Email:
Job applications: job postings online.
    Call or mail resume

Pacific Star Seafoods Inc
PO Box 190
Kenai, AK 99661
Phone: (907) 283-7787
Fax: (907) 283-9485
Apply to Double E Foods
3625 1st Avenue South
Seattle, WA

Pacific Star Seafoods (cont'd)
Phone: (907) 439-5876
Fax: (206) 768-8985
Website: eefoods.com
Email: via "contact us" on website
Job applications: downloadable application to fax

Pacific Sun Products LLC
638 Stedman St
Ketchikan, AK 99901
Phone: (907) 225-1786
Fax:
Website:
Email:
Job applications: mail resume

Peninsula Processing & Smokehouse
LLC
720 Kalifonsky Beach Rd
Soldotna, AK 99669
Phone: (907) 262-8846
Fax: (907) 262-0827
Website: great-alaska-seafood.com
Email: seafood@great-alaska-seafood.com
Job applications: mail, fax, or email

Peter Pan Seafoods – Multiple locations
The Tenth Floor
2200 Sixth Avenue
Seattle, WA 98121
Phone: (206) 728-6000
Fax: (206) 441-9090
Website: ppsf.com
Email:
Job applications: online or downloadable application to be mailed in

Petersburg Community Cold Storage
5700 Nordic Dr
Petersburg, AK 99833
Phone: (907) 772-4001
Fax: (907) 772-4032
Website:
Email:
Job applications: mail or fax resume

Polar Seafoods- Seward Facility
PO Box 570
Seward, AK 99664
Phone: (907) 224-7066
Fax: (907) 224-8748
Website:
Email:
Job applications: mail or fax resume

Prime Select Seafoods Inc
PO Box 846
Cordova, AK 99574
Phone: (907) 424-7750
Fax: (907) 424-7751
Website: pssifish.com
Email: salmon@pssifish.com
Job applications: mail or email resume

Resurrection Bay Seafoods
PO Box 1710
Seward, AK 99664
Phone: (907) 224-3366
Fax: (907) 224-3723
Website:
Email:
Job applications: mail or fax resume

Roys Select Alaskan Catch
PO Box 20481
Juneau, AK 99801
Phone: (907) 209-9120
Fax: (907) 582-2308
Website:
Email:
Job applications: mail or fax resume

Sagaya Corporation - Whitney Road
    Facility
1101 Whitney Rd
Anchorage, AK 99501
Phone: (907) 830-3630
Fax: (907) 279-2042
Website:
Email:
Job applications: mail or fax resume

Salamatof Seafoods Inc
PO Box 1450
Kenai, AK 99611
Phone: (907) 283-7000
Fax: (907) 283-8499
Website:
Email:
Job applications: mail or fax resume

Sea Level Seafoods LLC
PO Box 2085
Wrangell, AK 99929
Phone: (907) 874-2401
Fax: (907) 874-2158
Website:
Email:
Job applications: mail or fax resume

Seafood Producers Cooperative
507 Katlian Dr
Sitka, AK 99835
Phone: (907) 747-5811
Fax: (907) 747-3206
Website: spcsales.com
Email: tiffany-spcak@gci.net
Job applications: online application or
    email resume

Taku Smokeries
550 S Franklin St
Juneau, AK 99801
Phone: (907) 463-4617
Fax: (907) 463-5312
Website:
Email:
Job applications: mail or fax resume

The Auction Block Co
4501 Ice Dock Rd
Homer, AK 99603
Phone: (907) 235-7267
Fax: (907) 235-4833
Website:
Email:
Job applications: mail or fax resume

The Fish Factory LLC
800 Fish Dock Rd
Homer, AK 99603
Phone: (907) 235-1300
Fax: (907) 235-1350
Website: thefishfactory.net
Email: mikema@thefishfactory.net
Job applications: mail or fax resume

Trappers Creek Inc
5650 B St
Anchorage, AK 99518
Phone: (907) 561-8088
Fax: (907) 561-8389
Website:
Email:
Job applications: mail or fax resume

Trident Seafoods Corporation – Multi
   Facilities
5303 Shilshole Avenue, NW
Seattle, WA 98107
Phone: (206) 783-3818
Fax: (206) 782-7195
Website: tridentseafoods.com
Email: hr@tridentseafoods.com
Job applications: apply online via

Western Alaska Fisheries
521 Shelikof Ln
Kodiak, AK 99615
Phone: (907) 486-4112
Fax: (907) 486-5588
Website:
Email:
Job applications: mail or fax resume

Westward Seafoods Inc
2101 4th Avenue Ste 1700
Seattle, WA
Phone: (206) 682-5949
Fax: (2067) 682-1825
Website: westwoodseafoods.com
Email:
Job applications: online profile and ap-
   plications

Wild Alaska Salmon Products
PO Box 521131
Big Lake, AK 99652
Phone: (907) 892-5479
Fax: (907) 892-5479
Website:
Email:
Job applications: mail or fax resume

Yakutat Seafoods LLC
532 Max Italio Dr
Yakutat, AK 99689
Apply to Double E Foods
3625 1st Avenue South
Seattle, WA
Phone: (907) 439-5876
Fax: (206) 768-8985
Website: eefoods.com
Email: via "contact us" on website
Job applications: downloadable appli-
   cation to fax

Yamaya Seafoods
100 E 54th Ave
Anchorage, AK 99518
Phone: (907) 563-5588
Fax: (907) 561-8310
Website:
Email:
Job applications: Mail or fax resume

Aleutian Spray Fisheries, Inc
5470 Shilshole Ave., NW, #300
Seattle, WA 98107
Phone: (206) 784-5000
Fax: (206) 784-5500
Website: www.Starboats.com
Email: Personnel@starboats.com
Job applications: available online
Vessels: C/P Starbound, F/V Path
    finder, F/V Siberian Sea, F/V US
    Liberator, F/V Starfish
Product: pollock, ground fish

Glacier Fish Company
1200 Westlake Ave. North, AGC building
    Ste 900
Seattle, WA 98109
Phone: (206) 298-3120
Fax: (206) 298-4750
Website: www.glacierfish.com
Email: jobs@glacierfish.com
Job applications: available online
Vessels: F/T Alaska Ocean, F/T Pacific
    Glacier, F/T Northern Glacier.
Product: pollock

Alaska Leader Fisheries, Inc.
P.O. Box 569
Kodiak, AK 99615
Phone: (360) 318-1280
Fax: (866) 649-2675
Website: www.alaskanleaderfisheries.com
Email: via "contact us" on website
Job applications: available online
Vessels: *longliners;* F/T Alaskan Leader,
    F/V Bristol Leader, F/V Bering Leader
Product: Pacific cod

American Seafood Company
Market Place Tower
2025 First Ave., #900
Seattle, WA 98121
Phone: (206) 448-0300
Fax: (206) 448-4867
Website: www.americanseafoods.com
Email: sally.walker@americanseafoods.com
Job applications: downloadable form; email,
    fax or mail
Vessels: F/T American Dynasty, F/T Ameri-
    can Triumph, F/T Northern Jaeger, F/T
    Northern Eagle, F/T Northern Hawk, F/T
    Ocean Rover, F/T Katie Ann
Product: pollock

Arctic Storm Management Group, LLC
2727 Alaskan Way, Pier 69
Seattle, WA 98121
Phone: (206) 448-0300
Fax: (206) 547-3165
Website: www.arcticstorm.com
Email: hr@arcticstorm.com
Job applications: online application or mail
    resume
Vessels: C/P Arctic Fjord, C/P Arctic Storm
Product: pollock, cod

Blue North Fisheries
2930 Westlake Ave., N #300
Seattle, WA 98109
Phone: (206) 352-9252
Fax: (206) 352-9380
Website: www.bluenorthfisheries.com
Email: bluenorth@bluenorthfisheries.com
Job applications: downloadable form; email,
    fax or mail back

Blue North Fisheries (cont'd)
Vessels: *freezer/longliners & 1 crab catcher*; Blue North, Blue Pacific, Blue Gadus, Blue Ace, Blue Pearl, Blue Ballard, Free Ballard, Blue Star, Blue Attu
Product: Pacific cod, crab

Bering Select Seafood Company/ Clipper Seafoods Ltd.
641 W. Ewing Street
Seattle, WA 98119
Phone: (206) 284-1162
Fax: (206) 283-5089
Website: www.beringselect.com
Email: none
Job applications: phone to obtain application and mail back w/ resume
Vessels: *freezer longliners*; Clipper Endeavor, Clipper Epic, Clipper Surprise, Frontier Spirit, Frontier Explorer, Frontier Mariner
Product: cod, Pacific halibut

Deep Sea Fisheries
3900 Railway Avenue
Everett, WA 98201
Phone: (425) 742-8609
Fax: (425) 742-8699
Website: www.deepseafisheries.com
Email: hr@deepseafisheries.com
Job applications: downloadable form; email, fax or mail back
Vessels: F/V Alaska Mist, F/V Ambassador, F/V Alaskan Enterprise, F/V Pavlof

Deep Sea Fisheries (cont'd)
Product: Pacific cod, black cod, Greenland turbot and various ground fish

Fishermen's Finest
1532 N.W. 56th Street
Seattle, WA 98107
Phone: (206) 789-1137
Fax: (206) 281-8681
Website: www.fishermensfinests.com
Email: aheyano@fishermentsfinest.com
Job applications: downloadable form; email, fax or mail back
Vessels: *head-and-gut factory trawlers operate 10 mo. out of year;* F/V American No. 1, F/V U.S. Intrepid
Product: ground fish

Fishing Company of Alaska
200 West Tomas Street, #440
Seattle, WA 98119
Phone: (206) 284-1559
Fax:
Website: None
Email:
Job applications: must visit office and attend orientation before hiring
Vessels: *head-and-gut and pollock factory trawlers;* Alaska Warrior, Alaska Victory, Alaska Juris, Alaska Spirit
Product: pollock and ground fish

Golden Alaska Seafoods, LLC
2200 6th Avenue, #707
Seattle, WA 98121
Phone: (206) 441-1990
Fax: (206) 441-8112

Golden Alaska Seafoods (cont'd)
Website: www.goldenalaska.com
Email: via "contact us" on website
Job applications: apply online via website
Vessels: *processing ship only*; M/V Golden Alaska
Product: pollock

Icicle Seafoods, Inc.
4019 21st Avenue W #300
Seattle, WA 98199
Phone: (206) 282-0988
Fax: (206) 282-7222
Website: www.icicleseafoods.com
Email: Kara Winger of H/R at karaw@ icicleseafoods.com
Job applications: apply online via website
Vessels: *processing ships only;* Arctic Star, R.M. Thorstenson, Northern Victor
Product: pollock, salmon, crab, ground fish, herring

Iquique U.S., LLC
Seattle, WA 98199
Phone: (206) 286-1661 (x210)
Fax: (206) 957-4663
Website: None
Email: awegner@iquiqueus.com
Job applications: Write or phone for application
Vessels: *head & gut factory trawlers;* Eureka, Cape Horn, Rebecca Irene, Unimack
Product: ground fish

M/V Salvage/Cascade Fishing, Inc.
4215 21st Avenue West
Seattle, WA 98119
Phone: (206) 282-3277
Fax:
Website: none
Email:
Job applications: write or call
Vessels: *head-and-gut factory trawler;* Sea Fisher
Product: ground fish

Trident Seafoods Corporation
5303 Shilshole Avenue, NW
Seattle, WA 98107
Phone: (206) 783-3818
Fax: (206) 782-7195
Website: www.tridentseafoods.com
Email: hr@tridentseafoods.com
Job applications: apply online via website
Vessels: F/T Island Enterprise, Kodiak Enterprise, Seattle Enterprise
Product: salmon, crab, pollock, ground fish
The three factory trawlers pay a share price; Trident has other processors that pay by the hour

O'Hara Corporation
7017 15th Avenue N.W.
Seattle, WA 98117
Phone: (206) 706-4166
Fax: (206) 706-4165
Website: www.oharacorporation.com
Email: "contact us" via website
Job applications: MUST APPLY IN PERSON

O'Hara Corp. (cont'd)
Vessels: C/P Defender, C/P Constellation
Product: Alaska ground fish

Premier Pacific Seafoods, Inc.
111 W. Harrison
Seattle, WA 98119
Phone: (206) 286-8584
Fax: (206) 286-8810
Website: www.prempac.com
Email: resumes@prempac.com
Job applications: online
Vessels: *processing ships;* Ocean Phoenix, Excellence
Product: pollock

Prowler Fisheries/Alaska Longline Company
P.O. Box 1989
Petersburg, AK 99833
Phone: (907) 772-4835
Fax: (907) 772-9385
Website: www.alaskalongline.com
Email: via "contact us" on website
Job applications: online application and printable download to be faxed to above
Vessels: P/V Prowler, Bering Prowler, Kjevolja, Zenith
Product: Pacific cod, black cod, and turbot

Baranof/Courageous Fisheries
4502 14th Avenue NW
Seattle, WA 98107
Phone: (206) 545-9501
Fax: (206) 545-9536
Website: www.baranofcouragous.com
Email: via info@baranofcourage.com

Baranof/Courageous Fisheries (cont'd)
Job applications: online
Vessels: *crab and longline boats;* Baranof, Courageous
Product: crab, Pacific cod, black cod

Beauty Bay of Washington LLC
84 Las Queradas Lane
Alamo, CA 94507
Phone: 925-820-8068
Fax:
Website: none
Email:
Job applications: send resume
Vessels: freezer longliner
Products: Pacific cod

Signature Seafoods, Inc., Regal Fish LTD
4257 24th Avenue, W.
Seattle, WA 98199
Phone: (206) 285-2815
Fax: (206) 282-5938
Website: www.signatureseafoods.com
Email: via "contact us" on website
Job applications: online application and downloadable application to be mailed or faxed
Vessels: *processing vessels;* The Lucky Buck, M/V Ocean Fresh
Products: salmon

SnoPac Products, Inc
5053 E. Marginal Way South
Seattle, WA 98134
Phone: (206) 764-9230
Fax: (206) 282-5938
Website: www.snopac.net

SnoPac Products, Inc (cont'd)
Email: via "contact us" on website
Job applications: accepts *ONLY* signed, original applications, *In Person*, at above address. Application forms are downloadable from website.
Vessels: *processing ship*; Snopac Innovator
Products: Pacific cod, yellow fin sole, herring, salmon, and crab

Yardarm Knot Fisheries, LLC
2440 West Commodore Way, Suite 200
Seattle, WA
Phone: (425) 881-8181
Fax: (425) 861-5249
Website: www.unisea.com
Email: info@unisea.com
Job applications: online application and "job-line" (425) 861-5330
Vessels: *processing ship*; Yardarm Knot
Products: crab, cod, pollock

Coastal Villages Longline, LLC
711 H Street, Suite 200
Anchorage, AK 99501
Phone: 907-278-5151
Fax:
Website: www.Coastalvillages.org
Email:
Job applications: downloadable application to be mailed in
Vessels: *freezer longliners*; Deep Pacific, Lilli Ann, North Cape
Product: Pacific cod

Gulf Mist – Management Company
Deep See Fisheries
3900 Railway Avenue
Everett, WA 98201
Phone: (425) 742-8609
Fax:
Website: www.deepseafisheries.com
Email:
Job applications:
Vessels: *freezer longliners*; Alaska Mist, Pavloff
Product: Pacific cod

Shelford's Boat Ltd
P.O. Box 12946
Mill Creek, WA 98082
Phone: (425) 787-2576
Fax: (425) 742-8222
Website:
Email:
Job applications:
Vessels: *freezer longliner;* Aleutian Lady
Product: Pacific cod

Vessel	Owner	Address	City	State	Zip	Area
3 SISTERS	LUDWIG STEVEN	BOX 328	SILVANA	WA	98287	Bristol Bay
7 Z.S	JOHNSON MICHAEL	BOX 70032	SOUTH NAKNEK	AK	99670	Bristol Bay
ABBONDANZA	BROWN LARRY	BOX 054	EEK	AK	99578	Bristol Bay
ABEREE	OMAN PHILIP	BOX 1494	LONG BEACH	WA	98631	Bristol Bay
ABLE MABEL	MCCLAIN STEVEN	BOX 305	UNALASKA	AK	99685	Bristol Bay
ABUNDANCE	SCHOLLENBERG EDWARD	2650 E TUOLUMNE	TURLOCK	CA	95382	Bristol Bay
ADELHEID RENEE	WASSILLIE NATHAN	BOX 156	TOGIAK	AK	99678	Bristol Bay
ADIE	AMES STEVEN	BOX 2724	KODIAK	AK	99615	Bristol Bay
ADRENALINE FORCE FV	ADRENALINE FORCE LLC	205 CREGO HILL RD	CHEHALIS	WA	98532	Bristol Bay
AGNESIA	HIRATSUKA LOUIS	901 WILDROSE CT	ANCHORAGE	AK	99518	Bristol Bay
ALACRITY	GUGEL SAMUEL	1911 DOLLY VARDEN CIR	ANCHORAGE	AK	99516	Bristol Bay
ALASKALOU	HAGLUND ROCK	37759 LIBERTY LN	ASTORIA	OR	97103	Bristol Bay
ALAVIA	SKRIVANICH MARTIN	3911 VERN HARDSON	GIG HARBOR	WA	98332	Bristol Bay
ALBATROSS	TUFTE PAUL	7529 BOWSER CT	CRANE LAKE	MN	55725	Bristol Bay
ALEUTIAN	HEIL ERIC	2717 W 65TH AVE	ANCHORAGE	AK	99502	Bristol Bay
ALEUTIAN PRIBILOF 4	BOTHE WILLIAM	1104 STILLWATER DR	JUPITER	FL	33458	Bristol Bay
ALEX H	MIKKELSEN GLENN	2 PARK PL	EDMONDS	WA	98026	Bristol Bay
ALGONA	PARKER JAMES	1717 1ST ST	MARYSVILLE	WA	98270	Bristol Bay
ALIA	VANDERLIND LARRY	353 COURTNEY ST	ASHLAND	OR	97520	Bristol Bay
ALICIA	ELLIOTT PAUL	15891 E CRESTMONT	ROSEVILLE	MI	48066	Bristol Bay
ALICIA DAWN	KANULIE WALTER	BOX 133	TOGIAK	AK	99678	Bristol Bay
ALPHA	BAKK DONALD	BOX 8315	NIKISKI	AK	99635	Bristol Bay
ALPHA I	BRIGGS ROLAND	UGASHIK VIA	KING SALMON	AK	99613	Bristol Bay
ALPINE	BASARGIN SAFRON	BOX 1764	HOMER	AK	99603	Bristol Bay

Vessel	Owner	Address	City	State	Zip	Area
AMBER J	PAPETTI SAVIOR	2005 RED ROCK DR	MCKINNEY	TX	75070	Bristol Bay
AMBER SKY	JOHNSON CHARLIE	1331 W 82ND	ANCHORAGE	AK	99518	Bristol Bay
AMIGOS	NELSON ANDREW	8333 WILCOX ST	ANCHORAGE	AK	99502	Bristol Bay
AMPLE	ABALAMA CHARLES	BOX 3	EGEGIK	AK	99579	Bristol Bay
AMY MARIE	KNUTSEN FRED	BOX 187	DILLINGHAM	AK	99576	Bristol Bay
AMY NICOLE	CHRISTENSEN MACARLO	413 HAINES AVE	FAIRBANKS	AK	99701	Bristol Bay
ANDREW B	BERNTSEN ROBERT	4315 SW HOLGATE	SEATTLE	WA	98116	Bristol Bay
ANDY O	NIELSEN FREDERICK	BOX 86	DILLINGHAM	AK	99576	Bristol Bay
ANGEL BABETTE	AYOJIAK MARTIN	BOX 132	TOGIAK	AK	99678	Bristol Bay
ANGELA	AYOJIAK HOWARD	BOX 122	MANOKOTAK	AK	99628	Bristol Bay
ANGIE	CNUCON SERVICES INC	2430 HWY 20 E	COLVILLE	WA	99114	Bristol Bay
ANN LOUISE	PEITSCH ANDREW	43234 PENTTILA LN	ASTORIA	OR	97103	Bristol Bay
ANNA ROSE	CHUKWAK SERGIE	BOX 338	NAKNEK	AK	99633	Bristol Bay
ANNE MARTHA	FISHN B SEAFOODS INC	201 1/2 S FEDERAL BLVD	RIVERTON	WY	82501	Bristol Bay
ANNIE	KOGER WILL	3840 RAILWAY AVE	EVERETT	WA	98201	Bristol Bay
ANNIE K	PEARSON JAY	75 HYLAND STRINGER RD	RAYMOND	WA	98577	Bristol Bay
ANNIE K	ROSS JEFFERSON	4137 FALLICITY CARNATION RD SE	FALL CITY	WA	98024	Bristol Bay
ANNIE LOU	CHUNAK WASSILLIE	BOX 16	NEW STUYAHOK	AK	99636	Bristol Bay
ANNY JOY	KVINGE JORN	2321 WINDJAMMER CT NW	OLYMPIA	WA	98502	Bristol Bay
ANTHONY BOY	CROMOSINI CESARE	4 GALE RD	GLOUCESTER	MA	1930	Bristol Bay
ANUSKA	EVANS W LYNN	9025 116TH ST NE	ARLINGTON	WA	98223	Bristol Bay
ARCTIC OSPREY	MANCHESTER INTERNAT'L LLC	18022 17TH AVE NW	SHORELINE	WA	98177	Bristol Bay
ARCTIC TERN	REEL SHAUN	BOX 7115	SPOKANE	WA	99207	Bristol Bay
ARCTIC WIND	ROBERTS KENT	550 S 100TH W	AMERICAN FORK	UT	84003	Bristol Bay
ARGENT	DOTY MARK	16221 BIRCH WAY E	GREENWATER	WA	98022	Bristol Bay
ARIEL ROCHELLE	MOORE LESTER	BOX 88	MANOKOTAK	AK	99628	Bristol Bay

Vessel	Owner	Address	City	State	Zip	Area
ARIES	HANSEN, OLAF & TANYA	BOX 3	NAKNEK	AK	99633	Bristol Bay
ARIES	PRIMOZICH BRYCE	4781 N VANDERBILT ST	PORTLAND	OR	97203	Bristol Bay
ARLINE	DYE CHARLES	1645 E ZINNIA ST	CASA GRANDE	AZ	85122	Bristol Bay
ARTHUR	GRAY ROBERT	BOX 28595	BELLINGHAM	WA	98228	Bristol Bay
ASHLYN K	NICHOLAI GARY	BOX 87	TOGIAK	AK	99678	Bristol Bay
ASTREA	MARTIN TIMOTHY	BOX 1912	VALDEZ	AK	99686	Bristol Bay
AURORA ANNE	GEORGE MORRIS	BOX 41	CLARKS POINT	AK	99569	Bristol Bay
AVENTURA	OHLSEN ERIC	18 NEWELL ST	SEATTLE	WA	98109	Bristol Bay
BABE & GENEVIEV	TUNGUING GUST	BOX 5040	KOLIGANEK	AK	99576	Bristol Bay
BABY BLUE	FORBES MARY	BOX 141	TOGIAK	AK	99678	Bristol Bay
BABY LOU	ANELON TIM	BOX 167	ILIAMNA	AK	99606	Bristol Bay
BABY-FRANCES	ALIOTTI JOSEPH	8 CARIBOU CT	MONTEREY	CA	93940	Bristol Bay
BALROG	GOLDEN VIEW FISHERIES INC	2054 ARLINGTON	ANCHORAGE	AK	99517	Bristol Bay
BANDIT	MANOR DARRIN	868 CHERRY AVE	BAINBRIDGE ISLAND	WA	98110	Bristol Bay
BAR MAID	KORTHUIS DAN	782 1600 RD	DELTA	CO	71416	Bristol Bay
BARBARA J	HOLMES JEFFREY	973 GRAYS CREEK RD	INDIAN VALLEY	ID	83632	Bristol Bay
BARBARIAN	DIDRICKSEN MARIE	BOX 124	CATHLAMET	WA	98612	Bristol Bay
BAY TRIPPER	ANDERSON JOHN	BOX 1264	GRAND MARAIS	MN	55604	Bristol Bay
BAZE	KAYOUKLUK LARRY	BOX 5026	KOLIGANEK	AK	99576	Bristol Bay
BB 40	CHATONEY HENRY	BOX 683	HAINES	AK	99827	Bristol Bay
BB II	MERSHON PHILIP	BOX 536	COLLEGE PLACE	WA	99324	Bristol Bay
BEAGLE	TILLY JAMES	BOX PVY	ILIAMNA	AK	99606	Bristol Bay
BELAIR	MACKENZIE JOE	4118 CHERRY LN	ANACORTES	WA	98221	Bristol Bay
BELLA DONNA	WALDRON KYLE	1721 SW WATERSIDE CT	OAK HARBOR	WA	98277	Bristol Bay
BELLATRIX	ATKINSON ROBERT	900 BROWN ST	ANCHORAGE	AK	99501	Bristol Bay
BELLICOSE	STEVENS MARTIN	15823 WILDAIRE DR SE	YELM	WA	98597	Bristol Bay

Vessel	Owner	Address	City	State	Zip	Area
BELLWETHER	LANDRUD TAYLOR	1409 TACOMA POINT DR E	LAKE TAPPS	WA	98391	Bristol Bay
BELLWETHER	PRIES ROBERT	1089 LAKE WASHINGTON BLVD N #A209	RENTON	WA	98056	Bristol Bay
BEN SEA	CAIN KENNETH	BOX 1805	BELLINGHAM	WA	98227	Bristol Bay
BENJIMAN	MAUD WILLIAM	BOX 146	MANOKOTAK	AK	99628	Bristol Bay
BERING BAY	MIRKOVICH ANTHONY	2213 DAVIS DR	BURLINGAME	CA	94010	Bristol Bay
BERING GALE	DUNPHY RONALD	1935 KAREN RD	OAK HARBOR	WA	98277	Bristol Bay
BERNICE II	LUNDGREN JOHN	921 AUTUMN LN #243	BELLINGHAM	WA	98229	Bristol Bay
BERTHA B II	LUDWIG MARK	16300 38TH AVE NW	STANWOOD	WA	98292	Bristol Bay
BESSIE JEAN	PANRUK DAVID	BOX 41	CHEFORNAK	AK	99561	Bristol Bay
BETTY G	NAYLOR JAMES	697 SUMMER LN	WHITESALMON	WA	98672	Bristol Bay
BETTY JEAN	BND LLC	716 GRANDVIEW AVE	COLLEGE PLACE	WA	99324	Bristol Bay
BEV'S	PETERSON BEVERLY	BOX 55	EGEGIK	AK	99579	Bristol Bay
BIG DIPPER	LIBBY JAMES	11680 CANGE ST	ANCHORAGE	AK	99516	Bristol Bay
BIG DOGGER	CARSCALLEN CAREY	3007 E SNOW RD	BERRIEN SPRINGS	MI	49103	Bristol Bay
BIG RED	CARLSON ROBERT	5923 E HWY 61	HOVLAND	MN	55606	Bristol Bay
BIGFOOT	HALL RAYMOND	84654 TELEPHONE POLE RD	MILTON FREEWATER	OR	97862	Bristol Bay
BILLY AARON	BLUE BERTHA	BOX 135	TOGIAK	AK	99678	Bristol Bay
BJ	BONIN, F & VERVOORT, J	BOX 183	NAKNEK	AK	99633	Bristol Bay
BLAKE B	BAXTER GARY	318 BAYSIDE RD	BELLINGHAM	WA	98225	Bristol Bay
BLUE ADRIATIC	KERSHNER DIANA	16310 DENSMORE AVE N	SHORELINE	WA	98133	Bristol Bay
BLUE ANGEL	TOLSMA RUSSELL	2887 ALDERGROVE RD	FERNDALE	WA	98248	Bristol Bay
BLUE FALCON	DORIO GLORIA	1111 W 14TH ST #7	SAN PEDRO	CA	90731	Bristol Bay
BLUE FOX	ASPELUND RYAN	2891 S LAKESHORE LP	PALMER	AK	99645	Bristol Bay
BLUE SKY	ARNESTAD RYAN	17330 43 DR NW	STANWOOD	WA	98292	Bristol Bay
BLUE SWAN	STRAUB KERRY	BOX 56650	NORTH POLE	AK	99705	Bristol Bay
BLUE THUNDER	WALLONA PHILLIP	BOX 62	TALKEETNA	AK	99676	Bristol Bay

Vessel	Owner	Address	City	State	Zip	Area
BLUEWATER	CHUCKWUK JEREMIAH	BOX 22	ALEKNAGIK	AK	99555	Bristol Bay
BONZAI	LIBBY JAMES	11680 CANGE ST	ANCHORAGE	AK	99516	Bristol Bay
BOO BOY	NANALOOK MAURICE	BOX 2763	BETHEL	AK	99559	Bristol Bay
BOSS	BASARGIN FEODOT	BOX 3535	HOMER	AK	99603	Bristol Bay
BOYA	JOHN NATHAN	1320 DENALI ST #5	ANCHORAGE	AK	99501	Bristol Bay
BRACOR BAY	BOONE DAVID W	BOX 396	HOMER	AK	99603	Bristol Bay
BRANDO	BACKMAN GARY	301 E BIRNIE SLOUGH RD	CATHLAMET	WA	98612	Bristol Bay
BRAVE ULYSSES	DRAPER, CLINTON & DARIAN	5030 SE MONTEGO ST	HILLSBORO	OR	97123	Bristol Bay
BRAVO	MONTECUCCO TOM	5017 W HOUSTON	SPOKANE	WA	99208	Bristol Bay
BRENDA A	ANDREWS SASSA	BOX 6	ALEKNAGIK	AK	99555	Bristol Bay
BRIAN H	HAMMER KENNETH	2464 NW 198TH ST	SHORELINE	WA	98177	Bristol Bay
BRIANNA CRIS	APOKEDAK BRIAN	BOX 11	LEVELOCK	AK	99625	Bristol Bay
BRIANNE LYNN	NEHUS ZACHARY	BOX 1334	UNALASKA	AK	99685	Bristol Bay
BRINY	HILL CHARLES	BOX 2872	HOMER	AK	99603	Bristol Bay
BRISTOL DAWN	SOUTHLAND PAUL	BOX 257	WRANGELL	AK	99929	Bristol Bay
BRISTOL FURY	K 8 CORPORATION	2211 NE 217TH AVE	BATTLEGROUND	WA	98604	Bristol Bay
BRISTOL K	KALLSTROM M.BLANCHE	BOX 550	DILLINGHAM	AK	99576	Bristol Bay
BRISTOL NYMPH	CURCURU SALINA	6 APPLE ST	GLOUCESTER	MA	1930	Bristol Bay
BRISTOL PRINCESS	FORD JAMES	6720 SAMUEL CT	ANCHORAGE	AK	99516	Bristol Bay
BRISTOL SYNERGY	DUTTON ROBERT	1801 GRAND AVE	EVERETT	WA	98201	Bristol Bay
BRISTOL TIDE	BANNISH & FOURTNER FISHERIES	BOX 361	NAPAVINE	WA	98565	Bristol Bay
BRISTOL WEIR	BRISTOL WEIR INC	19618 61ST AVE SE	SNOHOMISH	WA	98296	Bristol Bay
BRISTOLIZER	CASTO MARK A	2225 SW LK ROESIGER RD	SNOHOMISH	WA	98290	Bristol Bay
BRISTOLOU	HAGLUND ROCK	37759 LIBERTY LN	ASTORIA	OR	97103	Bristol Bay
BRITANY MICHELLE	WELSH ALAN	13020 FOSTER RD	ANCHORAGE	AK	99516	Bristol Bay
BROWN BEAR	WALL RANDALL	92416 SVENSEN MKT RD	ASTORIA	OR	97103	Bristol Bay
BRUTUS	BENNER JASON	BOX 3027	PALMER	AK	99645	Bristol Bay

Vessel	Owner	Address	City	State	Zip	Area
BUZZARD	PIERCEY FISHERIES INC	720 CEDAR	EDMONDS	WA	98201	Bristol Bay
BW-1	BRIGGS ROLAND	UGASHIK VIA	KING SALMON	AK	99613	Bristol Bay
BYRD	WALATKA FRED	3107 W 29TH AVE	ANCHORAGE	AK	99517	Bristol Bay
C QUEST	DESJARLAIS EUGENE	6550 LIMESTONE CIR	ANCHORAGE	AK	99507	Bristol Bay
CADENZA	MARINKOVICH FRANK	2901 WHITE CLOUD AVE NW	GIG HARBOR	WA	98335	Bristol Bay
CALAHAAN	CARDOSO FLAVIO	2910 W 32ND #2	ANCHORAGE	AK	99517	Bristol Bay
CALLIE ANN	RIDDLE CALVIN	BOX 203	NAKNEK	AK	99633	Bristol Bay
CALLISTO	SABOL ANDREW	11710 PACIFIC VIEW RD	MALIBU	CA	90265	Bristol Bay
CAMILLA	NYHAMMER SVEIN	18504 RIDGEFIELD RD NW	SHORELINE	WA	98177	Bristol Bay
CAPE CLEAR	BLOOM ARTHUR	BOX 42	TENAKEE	AK	99841	Bristol Bay
CAPT GREG	SWAB DANIEL	901 S GRAY RD	MERRITT	MI	49667	Bristol Bay
CAPT SLACK	THORSON MATTHEW	BOX 455	DILLINGHAM	AK	99576	Bristol Bay
CAPTAIN CHRIS	OLSON PETE	BOX 813	DILLINGHAM	AK	99576	Bristol Bay
CAPTAIN HOOK	JEFFERIES WILLIAM	4703 SR 4 W	ROSBURG	WA	98643	Bristol Bay
CAPTAIN K	JOHNSON RONALD	BOX 1174	DILLINGHAM	AK	99576	Bristol Bay
CARALYN	BENEDICT DAVID	17099 W SHADY POOL CT	SURPRISE	AZ	85387	Bristol Bay
CAROL JEAN	AKELKOK LUKI	BOX 1245	DILLINGHAM	AK	99576	Bristol Bay
CAROL SUSAN	RICE CODY	BOX 1315	GIRDWOOD	AK	99587	Bristol Bay
CASCADIA	CARPENTER LANNY	4210 SHINCKE RD	OLYMPIA	WA	98506	Bristol Bay
CASEY	COOK HAROLD	11021 WING POINT WY NE	BAINBRIDGE ISLAND	WA	98110	Bristol Bay
CASPER BAY	NIELSEN GARITH	BOX 1089	KOKHANOK	AK	99606	Bristol Bay
CASSIE MARIE	NASH PATRICK	193 SALMONBERRY LN	FRIDAY HARBOR	WA	98250	Bristol Bay
CASSIOPEIA	STADEM RONALD	825 S BEGICH DR	WASILLA	AK	99654	Bristol Bay
CATCHPEN	JENNINGS LEO	500 LOCHER RD	TOUCHET	WA	99360	Bristol Bay
CATHRYN LEE	STIER KELLY	2183 SKYLINE DR	HOMER	AK	99603	Bristol Bay
CATHY LYNN	HUBBARD DAVID	35297 CONIFER LANE	ASTORIA	OR	97103	Bristol Bay

Vessel	Owner	Address	City	State	Zip	Area
CAT'S PAW	COFFEEN JON	317 OHIMA DR	WALLA WALLA	WA	99362	Bristol Bay
CAYUSE	WALKER MACGREGOR	5615 N DELAWARE AVE	PORTLAND	OR	97217	Bristol Bay
CEE DUST	WILSON CHESTER	BOX 234	NAKNEK	AK	99633	Bristol Bay
CENTAUR	MCTAGGART STUART	420 E HOWELL	SEATTLE	WA	98122	Bristol Bay
CENTAURUS	STADEM BROS. PARTNERSHIP	1826 E 26TH AVE	ANCHORAGE	AK	99508	Bristol Bay
CESCA MARIE	ALIOTTI SALVATORE	1238 BUENA VISTA AVE	PACIFIC GROVE	CA	93950	Bristol Bay
CHALLENGER	HOLLINGSWORTH DAVID	7910 KIANA CIR	ANCHORAGE	AK	99507	Bristol Bay
CHALOUPE	MISTY FJORD SEAFOOD INC	2450 TONGASS AVE #225	KETCHIKAN	AK	99901	Bristol Bay
CHARISMA	NEWFOUND ENTERPRISES	BOX 914	PLYMOUTH	NH	3264	Bristol Bay
CHARITY	RESETARITS CHRISTIAN	BOX 3063	HOMER	AK	99603	Bristol Bay
CHARLIE-MAGGIE	KARL EVAN	BOX 8	DEERING	AK	99736	Bristol Bay
CHELSEA MARIE	SHADE STEVEN	BOX 872	DILLINGHAM	AK	99576	Bristol Bay
CHENANN	MCMAHAN CHARLES	BOX 110	GAKONA	AK	99586	Bristol Bay
CHERI LYNN	GREER THOMAS	BOX 1366	PETERSBURG	AK	99833	Bristol Bay
CHERILYN S	TIKIUN JAMES	BOX 131	NUNAPITCHUK	AK	99641	Bristol Bay
CHEROKEE	PULLEY MARC	10112 226TH AVE CT E	BUCKLEY	WA	98321	Bristol Bay
CHERYL LYNN	KRAMER PETER	BOX 374	COPPER CENTER	AK	99573	Bristol Bay
CHERYL'S SONG	NELSON W. DAVID	BOX 724	CATHLAMET	WA	98612	Bristol Bay
CHILKAT	BATTREAL TRAVIS	3838 N 183RD	EARLY	TX	76802	Bristol Bay
CHRIS R	SMITH JAMES	4136 MERIDIAN N	SEATTLE	WA	98103	Bristol Bay
CHRISTIANA	FRIENDLY LEROY	BOX 8017	TUNTUTULIAK	AK	99680	Bristol Bay
CHRISTINE JANE	CANNON PETER	BOX 4471	BREMERTON	WA	98312	Bristol Bay
CINNAMON GIRL	BELT PATRICK	BOX 1696	MARYSVILLE	WA	98252	Bristol Bay
CLARA JOAN II	JIMMY JOHN	BOX 32	CHEFORNAK	AK	99561	Bristol Bay
CLARE-ANN	VEAL TIM	47113 STEVEN ST	KENAI	AK	99611	Bristol Bay
CLARE-ANN B	MERRINER JAMES	8600 SHEBANOF AVE	ANCHORAGE	AK	99507	Bristol Bay

Vessel	Owner	Address	City	State	Zip	Area
CLEAN SWEEP	WHITAKER ERIC	BOX 1323	WOODINVILLE	WA	98072	Bristol Bay
CLOUD 9	TEMPLE THOMAS	488 ELDERBERRY	HOMER	AK	99603	Bristol Bay
CLYDE	WORHATCH ANDY	BOX 614	PETERSBURG	AK	99833	Bristol Bay
COACHMAN II	URE JOHN	1324 ISMAILOV	KODIAK	AK	99615	Bristol Bay
CODY BOY	BAXTER DAVID	4455 MORESBY WY	FERNDALE	WA	98248	Bristol Bay
COHO TOO	COHO INC	BOX 645	WARRENTON	OR	97146	Bristol Bay
CONNIE GEE	GROAT KENNETH	462 KLONDIKE	HOMER	AK	99603	Bristol Bay
CONRADO JUAN	SMEATON NICK	BOX 1205	DILLINGHAM	AK	99576	Bristol Bay
CORDOVA	RADON MICHAEL	RURAL BAY 406	WHELEN	VI		Bristol Bay
CORMORANT	HOOVER MARY	841 E STADIUM BEACH RD W	GRAPEVIEW	WA	98546	Bristol Bay
CORVUS	THOR & SCHULZ ENTERPRISES INC	24121 SW NEWLAND RD	WILSONVILLE	OR	97070	Bristol Bay
COTTONWOOD	LARSEN CURT	777 SCENIC DR	TWO HARBORS	MN	55616	Bristol Bay
COURAGEOUS	HUSE DON	BOX 373	PETERSBURG	AK	99833	Bristol Bay
COWBOY	ALBERT DENNIS	2831 WILEY POST	ANCHORAGE	AK	99517	Bristol Bay
CRAWDAD	CRAWFORD THOMAS	5051 WEAVER RD	ELLENSBURG	WA	98926	Bristol Bay
CREWCUT	FLYNN BRENDAN	371 SCHOOL RD	LOPEZ	WA	98261	Bristol Bay
CRUSER	EROFEEFF FEODOR	BOX 937	WOODBURN	OR	97071	Bristol Bay
CRYSTAL MARIE	KROEZE RANDELL	924 DOUBLEVIEW DR	CAMANO ISLAND	WA	98282	Bristol Bay
CURRAGH	BLAKEY DANIEL	15890 EUCLID AVE	BAINBRIDGE ISLAND	WA	98110	Bristol Bay
CYDFOD	THOREEN BRYCE	2442 NW MARKET ST #403	SEATTLE	WA	98107	Bristol Bay
DAKOTA	MALSBURY, DORWIN & ROBIN	535 SPRING HAVEN DR	OLDTOWN	ID	83822	Bristol Bay
DANIELLE	SENER FISHERIES LTD	2610 FRANKLIN ST	BELLINGHAM	WA	98225	Bristol Bay
DARCI J	JOHN THOMAS	BOX 95	KIPNUK	AK	99614	Bristol Bay
DARLENE	STENSLAND DUANE	817 NW 107TH ST	SEATTLE	WA	98177	Bristol Bay
DARLENE LIZ	KASAK ROY	BOX 16	DILLINGHAM	AK	99576	Bristol Bay
DASHAR	MAIJALA WENDALL	5570 WILLIAMS RD	MAKINEN	MN	55763	Bristol Bay
DAUNTLESS	SALTWATER ALASKA LLC	12821 HACE ST	ANCHORAGE	AK	99515	Bristol Bay

Vessel	Owner	Address	City	State	Zip	Area
DEACON	SABO ERICK	3123 N SHIRLEY	TACOMA	WA	98407	Bristol Bay
DEAD RED	TREFON EDWARD	BOX 39273	NINILCHIK	AK	99639	Bristol Bay
DEBORAH	CURRIER KEVIN	12020 CROSS ST	JUNEAU	AK	99801	Bristol Bay
DEBORAH R	MOLISKY CHARLES	2495 CAPE GEORGE RD	PORT TOWNSEND	WA	98368	Bristol Bay
DEBORAH RENEE	FERRIGNO LEONARD	2387 ROLLING HILLS DR	CLARKSTON	WA	99403	Bristol Bay
DEE LAURALEE	SHOSTAD JEFFREY	36008 49TH AVE S	AUBURN	WA	98001	Bristol Bay
DELUXER	HENDRICKSON PAUL	7019 LILLOOET LP	ABERDEEN	WA	98520	Bristol Bay
DEM BOYS	WASSILY JIMMY	BOX 3	CLARKS POINT	AK	99569	Bristol Bay
DENISE N	LARSON PHILLIP	BOX 1201	DILLINGHAM	AK	99576	Bristol Bay
DERICK	BAVILLA ALBERT	BOX 71	TOGIAK	AK	99678	Bristol Bay
DESCENDANT	POZDEEV MAXIMILIAN	BOX 3010	HOMER	AK	99603	Bristol Bay
DESERAE LEIGH	WASSILLIE SAMMY	BOX 45	LEVELOCK	AK	99625	Bristol Bay
DESIREE MARIE III	LOGUSAK FRANK	BOX 278	TOGIAK	AK	99678	Bristol Bay
DESPERADO	BRASWELL JERROLD	BOX 138	DILLINGHAM	AK	99576	Bristol Bay
DIAMOND J	SPENCER JERRY	2142 N TREAT AVE	TUCSON	AZ	85716	Bristol Bay
DIAMOND STAR	DAVI THOMAS	19530 REDDING DR	SALINAS	CA	98908	Bristol Bay
DIAMOND V	HANSEN JOHN	BOX 101182	ANCHORAGE	AK	99510	Bristol Bay
DIANA	NEHUS ROBERT	210 W BAYVIEW	HOMER	AK	99603	Bristol Bay
DIANA D	CARNEY DANIEL	BOX 871210	WASILLA	AK	99687	Bristol Bay
DIANA RUTH	THERCHIK RAYMOND	BOX 37111	TOKSOOK BAY	AK	99637	Bristol Bay
DIANE CHRIS	WALVATNE JEFF	3738 MUD BAY RD	LOPEZ	WA	98261	Bristol Bay
DICTATOR	KALUGIN ILESAY	BOX 2727	HOMER	AK	99603	Bristol Bay
DIRE STRAITS	CRANE VERNON	2300 BLACK SPRUCE CT	FAIRBANKS	AK	99709	Bristol Bay
DIXIE B	PULLEY DONALD	10112 226TH AVE CT E	BUCKLEY	WA	98321	Bristol Bay
DOMINIQUE	SPINALE DOMINIC	4445 ROCK ISLAND DR	ANTIOCH	CA	94509	Bristol Bay
DONNA MARIE	DELGROSSO RUSSELL	4653 E VIA DONA RD	CAVE CREEK	AZ	85331	Bristol Bay
DONOVAN	GLOKO NORMAN	BOX 71	MANOKOTAK	AK	99628	Bristol Bay

Vessel	Owner	Address	City	State	Zip	Area
DORINDA LEE	RIVERA CHRISTOPHER	BOX 250	WARNER SPRINGS	CA	92086	Bristol Bay
DORIS MARIE	BECK THOMAS	2102 32ND ST	ANACORTES	WA	98221	Bristol Bay
DORLEEN	MARTIN KENT	BOX 83	SKAMOKAWA	WA	98647	Bristol Bay
DOROTHY B	KOHLWES GARY	5960 CEDAR ST	FREELAND	WA	98249	Bristol Bay
DOROTHY PEARL	NORDIC MARINE INC	200 W 34TH AVE #981	ANCHORAGE	AK	99503	Bristol Bay
DOUBLE D	MILLER AARON	BOX 334	NASELLE	WA	98638	Bristol Bay
DOUBLE DIPPIN'	WALTON INDY	38725 GAVIN CIR	SOLDOTNA	AK	99669	Bristol Bay
DOUBLE EAGLE	JOHNSON WILLIAM	BOX 193	DILLINGHAM	AK	99576	Bristol Bay
DOUBLE SHOT	HAVENS DENNIS	1049 COLUMBIA ST	CATHLAMET	WA	98612	Bristol Bay
DRIFTER III	NIEMELA KENNETH	BOX 342	RAINIER	OR	97048	Bristol Bay
DUEL	PENALOZA JUAN CARLOS	3155 SPRUCE CAPE RD	KODIAK	AK	99615	Bristol Bay
DYNAMIC	PETIT NORRIS	BOX 811	SOUTH BEND	WA	98586	Bristol Bay
E.G.	RILEY WALTER	10320 COMPASS CIR	ANCHORAGE	AK	99515	Bristol Bay
EAGER BEAVER	ANTHONY PHILLIP	2803 LEONARD DR	EVERETT	WA	98201	Bristol Bay
EAGLE	MATSON JOHN	BOX 49001	PORT HEIDEN	AK	99549	Bristol Bay
EAGLE CLAW	FLORA JONATHAN	34710 MOONRISE ST	HOMER	AK	99603	Bristol Bay
EAGLE ONE	TUKAYA WASSILLIE	BOX 165	TOGIAK	AK	99678	Bristol Bay
EARLY TIMES	SMITH GARTH	2498 PIEDMONT AVE	BERKELEY	CA	94704	Bristol Bay
EARNESTLY	KUNZ ERNEST	418 SR #105	RAYMOND	WA	98577	Bristol Bay
ECHO II	MUTE DAVID	BOX 2267	BETHEL	AK	99559	Bristol Bay
ECOLA ANNE	LEWIS CLIFF	BOX 1095	CANNON BEACH	OR	97110	Bristol Bay
EDA F	STAMMERJOHAN BEN	BOX 2127	KINGSTON	WA	98346	Bristol Bay
EDDIE JR	GENOVESE EDMOND	1681 VIA ISOLA	MONTEREY	CA	93940	Bristol Bay
EFTHAGEA	ANELON GREGORY	BOX 246	NEWHALEN	AK	99606	Bristol Bay
EILEEN J II	JENKINS PAUL	BOX 366	BETHEL	AK	99559	Bristol Bay
ELAINE CHRISTINE	WILSON GEORGE	BOX 8	LEVELOCK	AK	99625	Bristol Bay
ELDORADO	GREENFIELD	BOX 237	CHINOOK	WA	98614	Bristol Bay

Vessel	Owner	Address	City	State	Zip	Area
ELEMENT	BASARGIN IVAN	BOX 3495	HOMER	AK	99603	Bristol Bay
ELIZABETH ANN	HENDRICKS JEFF	5930 LAUREL SHAW CT	FERNDALE	WA	98248	Bristol Bay
ELIZABETH M	MUSTOLA RONALD	79519 BLACKFORD RD	CLATSKANIE	OR	97016	Bristol Bay
ELMA J	LYON, MEGAN & YAKOBI	50884 MOUNTAIN GLACIER CT	HOMER	AK	99603	Bristol Bay
ELSIE LYNN	REEL WILBUR	7316 238TH AVE	REDMOND	WA	98053	Bristol Bay
ELUSIVE	ELUSIVE LLC	2021 4TH AVE N #9	SEATTLE	WA	98109	Bristol Bay
ELUSIVE	HEDLUND THOMAS	BOX 186	ILIAMNA	AK	99606	Bristol Bay
EMIL	FERKINGSTAD ROBERT	817 NW 107TH ST	SEATTLE	WA	98177	Bristol Bay
EMORY JAMES	MCMAHAN JOHNNY	BOX 184	GAKONA	AK	99586	Bristol Bay
ENDEAVOR	SMITH MARK	11200 JEROME ST	ANCHORAGE	AK	99516	Bristol Bay
ENDURANCE	CHELEDINAS SCOTT	BOX 6424	BOZEMAN	MT	59771	Bristol Bay
ENERGIZER	FLETCHER DAVID	860 53RD ST	PORT TOWNSEND	WA	98368	Bristol Bay
ENTERPRISE	WEAVER SANDERS	4110 DEBARR RD #G-9	ANCHORAGE	AK	99501	Bristol Bay
ENTROPY	STRONG CLINTON	BOX 571	PAHALA	HI	96777	Bristol Bay
ERIC THE RED	LIBOFF JERRY	BOX 646	DILLINGHAM	AK	99576	Bristol Bay
ERICA C	HANSON GLENN	309 BIRCH ST	KENAI	AK	99611	Bristol Bay
ERICK ALLEN	AYOJIAK PHYLLIS	BOX 96	TOGIAK	AK	99678	Bristol Bay
ERIKA LEIGH	BLOOM ARTHUR	BOX 42	TENAKEE	AK	99841	Bristol Bay
ERIKA LYNN	FOLLMAN HARRY	12656 LAKE DR E	SEDRO WOOLLEY	WA	98284	Bristol Bay
ERIN K	SCHWARTZ JAMES	BOX 1506	PETERSBURG	AK	99833	Bristol Bay
ERIN L	JOHNSON WARREN	23231 32ND AVE NE	ARLINGTON	WA	98223	Bristol Bay
ERIN LEE ANN	SCHMELZENBAC EVERT	920 REZANOF #B	KODIAK	AK	99615	Bristol Bay
ERIN N	NESS MIKE	14419 GREENWOOD AVE N #A	SEATTLE	WA	98133	Bristol Bay
ERIN RAE	WILLIS TIM	2995 WASHINGTON ST	EUGENE	OR	97405	Bristol Bay
ERLIJO	PATTON DARRELL	33 STEPHENS RD	ELMA	WA	98541	Bristol Bay
ESCULENT	NEWSON DAVID	217 141ST AVE NE	BELLEVUE	WA	98007	Bristol Bay
ESKIMO VIKING	HANSEN DAVID	BOX 1043	BELLINGHAM	WA	98227	Bristol Bay

Vessel	Owner	Address	City	State	Zip	Area
ESPRESSO	EWERS KIM	615 E WELLS FARGO DR	BROOKSIDE	UT	84782	Bristol Bay
ESTHER C	CUBERT DAVID	BOX 261	BEAVER	WA	98305	Bristol Bay
ETERNITY	GUGEL, GEROLD & KRISTINE	1911 DOLLY VARDEN CIR	ANCHORAGE	AK	99516	Bristol Bay
ETHAN	PETERS DEBRA	BOX 359	NAKNEK	AK	99633	Bristol Bay
EUFEMIA II	NEVOLOSO GIOVANNI	1514 KIMBALL AVE	SEASIDE	CA	93955	Bristol Bay
EVA	UPTON HERBERT C3	BOX 2854	HOMER	AK	99603	Bristol Bay
EVA C	CHARLIE MICHAEL	BOX 1704	BETHEL	AK	99559	Bristol Bay
F/V KUKAK	JOHNSON DAVID	1242 A FREEMONT AVE N	SEATTLE	WA	98133	Bristol Bay
FAIRISLE	GIRVAN PETE	1242 MARILYN DR	OGDEN	UT	84403	Bristol Bay
FAITH	CARDINALLI STEPHEN	800 DRY CREEK RD	MONTEREY	CA	93940	Bristol Bay
FALCON	FALK TAD	940 W CLATSOP AVE	ASTORIA	OR	97103	Bristol Bay
FALCON	WISENOR MELVIN	BOX 277	WHITE BIRD	ID	83554	Bristol Bay
FANTASEA	KALLSTROM TED	7146 RD 8 NW	EPHRATA	WA	98823	Bristol Bay
FANTASEA II	MATTSON CRAIG	BOX 530	NASELLE	WA	98638	Bristol Bay
FAR AND AWAY	OKSVOLD OLE	2601 NW 86TH	SEATTLE	WA	98117	Bristol Bay
FARALLON	ANGASAN FRED	BOX 70069	SOUTH NAKNEK	AK	99670	Bristol Bay
FAST BREAK	DODGE RANDY	8524 NE 176TH ST	BOTHELL	WA	98011	Bristol Bay
FAT CAT	CHRISTENSEN STAN	2095 STOVALL RD	WALLA WALLA	WA	99362	Bristol Bay
FAT CAT	STAGE TIMOTHY	BOX 1970	HOMER	AK	99603	Bristol Bay
FAT CHANCE	PEPER DEAN	1406 19TH AVE	SEATTLE	WA	98122	Bristol Bay
FERKING	DUNLAP HEIDI	26 YOUNG ST	ASHEVILLE	NC	28801	Bristol Bay
FERKING II	CROZIER RANDY	4311 212 ST CT E	SPANAWAY	WA	98387	Bristol Bay
FIASCO	MYERS JEFFERY	2950 W TELEQUANA DR	WASILLA	AK	99654	Bristol Bay
FIDDLER II	COFFEEN JON	317 OHIMA DR	WALLA WALLA	WA	99362	Bristol Bay
FINAL SET	BASARGIN NIKOLAI	BOX 1145	HOMER	AK	99603	Bristol Bay
FINMARK	NEWMAN KEANE CHAVIS	2214 CANDY PL #3	ANCHORAGE	AK	99508	Bristol Bay
FIRDA	ISAKSEN KARL	1 LAS OLAS CR #110	FORT LAUDERDALE	FL	33316	Bristol Bay

Appendix 5
Gill Netters, Salmon

Vessel	Owner	Address	City	State	Zip	Area
FISCHER	KASS KELLY	1044 GOODNEWS CIR	ANCHORAGE	AK	99515	Bristol Bay
FISH N CHICKS	TENNYSON RICHARD	BOX 167	DILLINGHAM	AK	99576	Bristol Bay
FISH TRAP	FARREN DANIEL	4970 TUNDRA ROSE	HOMER	AK	99603	Bristol Bay
FISHALOT	PIKE JEFFERY	BOX 2293	BELLINGHAM	WA	98227	Bristol Bay
FISHIN' FOOL	BINGMAN JAMES	BOX 82	DILLINGHAM	AK	99576	Bristol Bay
FLOOD TIDE	BRILL RONALD	8775 46TH PL W	MUKILTEO	WA	98275	Bristol Bay
FLYIN LION	BRITO ANGELO	BOX 1006	DILLINGHAM	AK	99576	Bristol Bay
FLYIN TIGER	HILLEY DAVID	BOX 1411	DILLINGHAM	AK	99576	Bristol Bay
FLYING LADY	PAPETTI SALVATORE	BOX T	BELLINGHAM	WA	98227	Bristol Bay
FOR GET ME KNOT	ASPELUND ALVIN	BOX 430	NAKNEK	AK	99633	Bristol Bay
FORCE FIVE	HEUKER BROS INC	BOX 98	CASCADE LOCKS	OR	97014	Bristol Bay
FORCE FIVE II	HEUKER TIMOTHY	BOX 98	CASCADE LOCKS	OR	97014	Bristol Bay
FORCE FIVE V	HEUKER DAN	BOX 98	CASCADE LOCKS	OR	97014	Bristol Bay
FORESIGHT	NOSTE JOHN	121 WOODGROVE LN	CAMANO ISLAND	WA	98282	Bristol Bay
FOUR D S	BURNFIELD SCOTT	561 E EAGLE RIDGE DR	SHELTON	WA	98584	Bristol Bay
FOX TROTT	TROTT GEORGE	308 E LITTLE ISLAND RD	CATHLAMET	WA	98612	Bristol Bay
FOXY LADY	CRANE VERNON	2300 BLACK SPRUCE CT	FAIRBANKS	AK	99709	Bristol Bay
FRANCES A	ADAMS ENTERPRISES INC	2055 SARATOGA AVE	ANCHORAGE	AK	99517	Bristol Bay
FRANCESCA J	SUTTON THEODORE	BOX 52	TOGIAK	AK	99678	Bristol Bay
FREELANCER	ALIOTTI ROBERT	462 JACKSON ST	MONTEREY	CA	93940	Bristol Bay
FRIENDSHIP SEVEN	FOX MORGAN	BOX 49069	PORT HEIDEN	AK	99549	Bristol Bay
FV LEWIS & CLARK	CHARLES BRUCE	BOX 6037	BOZEMAN	MT	59771	Bristol Bay
FV NOMADA	OKSVOLD OLE	2601 NW 86TH	SEATTLE	WA	98117	Bristol Bay
G. G.	GRILLO JACK	1118 SHELL AVE	PACIFIC GROVE	CA	93950	Bristol Bay
GABI V	PRIMOZICH JON	BOX 1733	ANACORTES	WA	98221	Bristol Bay
GAIL S II	MUTE JOSEPH	BOX 5026	KONGIGANAK	AK	99559	Bristol Bay
GALE	BUCHANAN JANET	BOX 70094	SOUTH NAKNEK	AK	99670	Bristol Bay

Vessel	Owner	Address	City	State	Zip	Area
GEMINI	OLYMPIC HENRY	BOX 35	ILIAMNA	AK	99606	Bristol Bay
GENTLE BEN	BEAMER ERIC	1000 WEST CASCADE LN	LYNDEN	WA	98264	Bristol Bay
GEORGETTE ROSE	WILSON GEORGE	BOX 8	LEVELOCK	AK	99625	Bristol Bay
GHOST	GUMLICKPUK WILLIAM	BOX 71	NEW STUYAHOK	AK	99636	Bristol Bay
GHOSTRIDER	SCHONBERG KRISTIAN	BOX 993	ALLYN	WA	98524	Bristol Bay
GINA LISA	DAVI FRANCESCO	746 NEWTON ST	MONTEREY	CA	93940	Bristol Bay
GINNEY G	HUNSINGER WILLIAM	BOX 1237	ASTORIA	OR	97103	Bristol Bay
GIRLA	KAPATAK EDWARD	BOX 5002	KOLIGANEK	AK	99576	Bristol Bay
GK	GADAMUS JACK UAF	BOX 751139	FAIRBANKS	AK	99701	Bristol Bay
GLACIER BAY	MILLER THOMAS	BOX 1931	KODIAK	AK	99615	Bristol Bay
GIYAN	SHUGHART FRANK	301 E TORRANCE LN	OAK HARBOR	WA	98277	Bristol Bay
GOAT ROPER	SMITH LANSING FISHERIES LLC	743 SANTA PAULA CT	BOISE	ID	83712	Bristol Bay
GOLD DIGGER	CARR MICHAEL	BOX 804	PORT TOWNSEND	WA	98368	Bristol Bay
GOLD DIGGER	GOLD DIGGER FISHERIES LLC	4461 OLD GARDINER RD	PORT TOWNSEND	WA	98368	Bristol Bay
GOLD RIVER	MITCHELL JASON	41 STRAWBERRY PT RD	BELLINGHAM	WA	98229	Bristol Bay
GOLDEN GREEK	KOURIS NIKOLAS	2101 W 29TH AVE #25	ANCHORAGE	AK	99517	Bristol Bay
GOLDEN HUE	MCINTYRE MONTY	585 PLEASANT BAY	BELLINGHAM	WA	98229	Bristol Bay
GONE FISHEN	LIBERATI JACK	BOX 524	KING SALMON	AK	99613	Bristol Bay
GOOD FORTUNE	ANELON JERROLD	BOX 002	ILIAMNA	AK	99606	Bristol Bay
GOOD HOPE II	IVANOFF ALVIN	BOX 7	NAKNEK	AK	99633	Bristol Bay
GRACE	RESETARITS DOUGLAS	BOX 3063	HOMER	AK	99603	Bristol Bay
GRAMMA DOLLIE	FV MANZANITA INC	14928 180TH AVE SE	MONROE	WA	98272	Bristol Bay
GRAMMY	LARSON BOICE	BOX 112	DILLINGHAM	AK	99576	Bristol Bay
GRAY GHOST	MERSHON PHILIP	BOX 536	COLLEGE PLACE	WA	99324	Bristol Bay
GRAYLING	KINIKALK EVAN	BOX 11	TOGIAK	AK	99678	Bristol Bay
GUERIE MARIE	MILLETT CHESTER	6960 VIBURNUM DR	ANCHORAGE	AK	99507	Bristol Bay
GUNSLINGER	TORMALA THOMAS	BOX 1254	KODIAK	AK	99615	Bristol Bay

Vessel	Owner	Address	City	State	Zip	Area
GUNS-N-ROSES	GARDNER LUKE	BOX 62	NASELLE	WA	98638	Bristol Bay
GYRE	ANDERSON STOSH	BOX 310	KODIAK	AK	99615	Bristol Bay
GYRFALCON	VENEROSO GEORGE	BOX 83	WHITE HAVEN	PA	18661	Bristol Bay
HALEIGH C	SEE ALAN	BOX 99	NASELLE	WA	98638	Bristol Bay
HALL PT	MUNHOVEN DONALD	BOX 6335	KETCHIKAN	AK	99901	Bristol Bay
HALO	SMITH DAVID	BOX 1790	DILLINGHAM	AK	99576	Bristol Bay
HAPPY HOOKER	KINGMA KEN	22774 BUCHANAN ST	MOUNT VERNON	WA	98273	Bristol Bay
HARLEQUIN	KING EIDER FISHERIES LLC	BOX 446	NAKNEK	AK	99633	Bristol Bay
HARVEST MOON	HOFF FRANK	45157 218TH ST	OLDHAM	SD	57051	Bristol Bay
HARVESTER	SMITH ALEXANDER	11200 JEROME ST	ANCHORAGE	AK	99516	Bristol Bay
HAT TRICK	HUGHES WADE	3360 ORBIT DR	ANCHORAGE	AK	99517	Bristol Bay
HEIDI OF NORWAY	ISAKSEN GARY	7419 25TH ST NE	EVERETT	WA	98205	Bristol Bay
HELEN CHRISTINE	JOHN MARK	3833 SCENIC VIEW DR	ANCHORAGE	AK	99504	Bristol Bay
HERBERT CECIL	HERBERT CECIL INC	6196 N FORK RD	DEMING	WA	98244	Bristol Bay
HERNANDO 1	ACHESON ALLAN	2613 PINE ST	EVERETT	WA	98201	Bristol Bay
HERRING HOG	PAUL HERMAN	BOX 166	TOGIAK	AK	99678	Bristol Bay
HI STANDARD	QUINN JEFFREY	225 N 160TH ST	SEATTLE	WA	98133	Bristol Bay
HI TECH	MARTUSHEV ALEXAY	BOX 1765	HOMER	AK	99603	Bristol Bay
HIDE AWAY	WINTERHALTER KURT	5219 220TH NW	STANWOOD	WA	98292	Bristol Bay
HIGH ROLLER II	DEAVER DENNIS	84 LAS QUEBRADAS LN	ALAMO	CA	94507	Bristol Bay
HIGHWAYMAN	LITTLETON ROCKY	BOX 1373	PETERSBURG	AK	99833	Bristol Bay
HOBO	KESTER SAMMIE	BOX 4068	BELLINGHAM	WA	98227	Bristol Bay
HOLLOWAY	GRIFFIN RONALD	BOX 1953	KINGSTON	WA	98346	Bristol Bay
HOMEWARD	ANGASAN TREFON	8501 BLACKBERRY ST	ANCHORAGE	AK	99502	Bristol Bay
HOOD CANAL	IVERSEN ANDREW	23279 ALDO RD NW	POULSBO	WA	98370	Bristol Bay
HORIZON	BASARGIN GEORGE	BOX 1580	HOMER	AK	99603	Bristol Bay
HOSANNA	RESETARITS DOUGLAS	BOX 3063	HOMER	AK	99603	Bristol Bay

Vessel	Owner	Address	City	State	Zip	Area
HUNTER C	MAVAR JOHN	BOX 1468	ANACORTES	WA	98221	Bristol Bay
HYDRO	KOHUK STEPAN	BOX 253	TOGIAK	AK	99678	Bristol Bay
HYLDA MARIE	TRETIKOFF JOHN	BOX 11	NEWHALEN	AK	99606	Bristol Bay
I-C STRAIT	MCHALE BRYAN	6413 SANDRIDGE RD	LONG BEACH	WA	98631	Bristol Bay
ICARUS	OLMOS JULIO	21200 40TH PL SE	SAMMAMISH	WA	98075	Bristol Bay
ICE MAN	GREENFIELD KENNETH	BOX 237	CHINOOK	WA	98614	Bristol Bay
ICY BAY	KOHLHASE JASON	10753 HORIZON DR	JUNEAU	AK	99801	Bristol Bay
IDA A	ALEXIE ROY	BOX 401	BETHEL	AK	99559	Bristol Bay
IFICIENCY	KALUGIN DAVID	BOX 542	HOMER	AK	99603	Bristol Bay
ILLUSION	JOHNSON DONALD	762 SHELTER BAY DR	LACONNER	WA	98257	Bristol Bay
ILLUSION	SMEATON JOHN	BOX 895	DILLINGHAM	AK	99576	Bristol Bay
INA K	ANAVER JIMMY	BOX 108	QUINHAGAK	AK	99655	Bristol Bay
INAKAK MIKE II	CARL CYRIL	BOX 37007	TOKSOOK BAY	AK	99637	Bristol Bay
IN'EM	TIRRELL TROY	BOX 600	CORDOVA	AK	99574	Bristol Bay
INFINN	HILL PETE	BOX 269	NAKNEK	AK	99633	Bristol Bay
INGER B	PEDERSEN ROALD	873 ROCKY POINT DR	CAMANO ISLAND	WA	98282	Bristol Bay
INGOLF	SANDVIK RANDALL	901 SHAW RD E	PUYALLUP	WA	98372	Bristol Bay
INNOVATOR	FLEMING JOHN	11640 ELLEN AVE	ANCHORAGE	AK	99515	Bristol Bay
INTERNET	BALLUTA ROY	BOX 051	NONDALTON	AK	99640	Bristol Bay
INTREPID	HANEY STEVEN	7691 N NAN LN	PALMER	AK	99645	Bristol Bay
IRENE A	MARTUSHEV NICKOLAI	40929 HUNTLEY RD SE	STAYTON	OR	97383	Bristol Bay
IRON BELLY	BAKK DARREL	BOX 142	EGEGIK	AK	99579	Bristol Bay
IRON MAIDEN	CHELEDINAS BRIAN	BOX 10524	YAKIMA	WA	98909	Bristol Bay
IRONIC	MANN BRUCE	816 S 216TH ST #424	SEATTLE	WA	98198	Bristol Bay
ISADORE	FROST LAURA	BOX 229	TOGIAK	AK	99678	Bristol Bay
ISBJORN	BERLIN DAVID	7910 LADASA PL	ANCHORAGE	AK	99507	Bristol Bay
ISSAMA BOAT	SHADE STEVEN	BOX 872	DILLINGHAM	AK	99576	Bristol Bay

Vessel	Owner	Address	City	State	Zip	Area
ITALIAN LEPRACH	AIELLO RICHARD	500 SPENCER ST	MONTEREY	CA	93940	Bristol Bay
ITALIAN STALLION	KUNZ LUCAS	418 SR #105	RAYMOND	WA	98577	Bristol Bay
IVY DREAM	POPA CHRISTOPHER	2268 AQUA HILL RD	FALLBROOK	CA	92028	Bristol Bay
JACK AUSTIN	DOERTY KEVIN	BOX 1458	KALAMA	WA	98625	Bristol Bay
JACK OF HEARTS	TWO OCEANS CORP.	1704 HILLSIDE RD	STEVENSON	MD	21153	Bristol Bay
JACLYNN MICHELE	ALAKAYAK HENRY	BOX 25	MANOKOTAK	AK	99628	Bristol Bay
JAGULAR	ABELLA DAREN	3422 38TH AVE SW	SEATTLE	WA	98126	Bristol Bay
JAIME LEIGH	GEAGEL RUSSELL	BOX 4	SELDOVIA	AK	99663	Bristol Bay
JAN-D	DAVIS BARRY	200 W 34TH AVE #556	ANCHORAGE	AK	99503	Bristol Bay
JANET M	SMITH DELBERT	316 SE PIONEER WAY #560	OAK HARBOR	WA	98277	Bristol Bay
JANICE E	MOORE HARRY	BOX 10	PALMER	AK	99645	Bristol Bay
JANIS ANN	WILLARD RAYMOND	BOX 870302	WASILLA	AK	99687	Bristol Bay
JEAN ANN	NELSEN THOMAS	8355 NW WILDCAT LAKE RD	BREMERTON	WA	98312	Bristol Bay
JENDER	CROOKSHANKS DARREN	6130 WILLOW GROVE RD	LONGVIEW	WA	98632	Bristol Bay
JENNI LEE	CHUCKWUK CHRISTIAN	BOX 22	ALEKNAGIK	AK	99555	Bristol Bay
JENNIFER C	ODONNOGHUE JOSEPH	BOX 1776	KODIAK	AK	99615	Bristol Bay
JENNY JOE	BRIDGES MICHAEL	3230 JUNIPER DR	MOAB	UT	84532	Bristol Bay
JEREMIAH 333	GOSUK ALFRED	BOX 261	TOGIAK	AK	99678	Bristol Bay
JERONIMO	DERANJA BOZHO	1214 WESTERN AVE	GLENDALE	CA	91201	Bristol Bay
JERRY SUE II	THIELE CARL	#6 RIVER ST	ALEXANDER CREEK	AK	99695	Bristol Bay
JESS	PIATT ROBERT	4100 PALMDALE DR	WASILLA	AK	99654	Bristol Bay
JESSIE LUCILE	BURTNER MARCUS	1049 E ALTA VISTA ST	TUCSON	AZ	85719	Bristol Bay
JEWELINE M	ALAKAYAK LOUIE	BOX 27	MANOKOTAK	AK	99628	Bristol Bay
JIMMY JEFF	SWAB LUKE	901 GRAY RD	MERRITT	MI	49667	Bristol Bay
JIMMY JEFF II	SONGSTAD JEFFERY	4804 DARLINGTON LN	EVERETT	WA	98204	Bristol Bay
JIMMY JOE	JIMMY DAVID	BOX 6	CHEFORNAK	AK	99561	Bristol Bay
JJ	ALIOTTI GUISEPPE	5041 SUNSET VISTA DR	SEASIDE	CA	93955	Bristol Bay

Vessel	Owner	Address	City	State	Zip	Area
JO ANN	LEAGE GALE	4955 EL VERANO	ATASCADERO	CA	93422	Bristol Bay
JOANN TOO	GENTLES LARRY	3526 115TH ST SE	EVERETT	WA	98208	Bristol Bay
JO-BE	PHILPOTT KENNETH	2526 LAKERIDGE DR	FERNDALE	WA	98248	Bristol Bay
JOE LEIGH	BOROVINA JON	834 GRAND AVE	EVERETT	WA	98201	Bristol Bay
JOEY BOY II	GAMECHO JOSEPH	1121 ROSITARD	DEL REY OAKS	CA	93940	Bristol Bay
JOHANNA	FLORA MIKE	34710 MOONRISE ST	HOMER	AK	99603	Bristol Bay
JOHN C	CATALANO JOHN	799 SPENCER ST #B	MONTEREY	CA	93940	Bristol Bay
JOHNNY BOY III	GUERRA PETER	2 CARIBOU CT	MONTEREY	CA	93940	Bristol Bay
JOSEY WALES	VOLESKY BERNIE	22600 WINTERGREEN ST NW	BETHEL	MN	55005	Bristol Bay
JOSIE L	LEWIS WALTER	BOX 2	CHEFORNAK	AK	99561	Bristol Bay
JOY LEE	FROST LAURA	BOX 229	TOGIAK	AK	99678	Bristol Bay
JPC	CARLSON JENS	2739 SEAVIEW DR	PORT HEIDEN	AK	99549	Bristol Bay
JUAN XV	GOODRICH SHANE	3705 ARCTIC BLVD #1246	ANCHORAGE	AK	99503	Bristol Bay
JULIA LEE	INGRAM WALTER	407 13TH ST #300	BELLINGHAM	WA	98225	Bristol Bay
JULIE KAY	SIMPSON DAVID	3900 GREENLAND DR	ANCHORAGE	AK	99517	Bristol Bay
JUNEBUG	DUNSMORE KEN	6011 A BEVERLY LN	EVERETT	WA	98203	Bristol Bay
JUST-IN-TIME	ARNOLD JUSTIN	BOX 577	HOMER	AK	99603	Bristol Bay
K 16	LONG JIM	BOX 172	CHINOOK	WA	98614	Bristol Bay
K 17	MANN RANDOLPH	2211 ELDRIDGE AVE	BELLINGHAM	WA	98225	Bristol Bay
K 2	MUNRO MARK	BOX 1971	HOMER	AK	99603	Bristol Bay
K 3	WALDRON VINTON	3511 SW BALDA ST	OAK HARBOR	WA	98277	Bristol Bay
K 7	VUKAS MAXWELL	32209 7TH AVE SW	FEDERAL WAY	WA	98023	Bristol Bay
K 8	K 8 CORPORATION	22111 NE 217TH AVE	BATTLEGROUND	WA	98604	Bristol Bay
K 9	LAINE STEVEN	738 ELM ST	RAYMOND	WA	98577	Bristol Bay
K-2	MAVAR BRIAN	604 SAINT MARYS DR	ANACORTES	WA	98221	Bristol Bay
KA SITNA BAY	PAINE BRENT	4000 TAZLINA AVE	ANCHORAGE	AK	99517	Bristol Bay
KAMANU	GJERTSEN GEORGE	5727 14TH ST SE	EVERETT	WA	98208	Bristol Bay

Vessel	Owner	Address	City	State	Zip	Area
KANISTA	ROGOTZKE DAVID	3094 WHITESIDE RD	DULUTH	MN	55804	Bristol Bay
KARA K	GDK FISHING INC	23 280TH ST NE	ARLINGTON	WA	98223	Bristol Bay
KARISMA	MARTIN WARREN	5415 BELLWEST DR	BELLINGHAM	WA	98226	Bristol Bay
KARLY	CORMACK INC	2242157TH AVE SE	BOTHEL	WA	98021	Bristol Bay
KARMA	GIRVAN JOHN	2895 N HOBBS CREEK DR	LAYTON	UT	84404	Bristol Bay
KA-SE-RA	WYMAN GEOFFREY	349 RICHARD RD	OAK HARBOR	WA	98277	Bristol Bay
KASOTA	CROSBIE JOHN	BOX 1987	HOMER	AK	99603	Bristol Bay
KATANYA	GAUTHIER PHILLIP	21 AUBURN	ASTORIA	OR	97103	Bristol Bay
KATHERINE A	ANDREW RICHARD	BOX 105	ALEKNAGIK	AK	99555	Bristol Bay
KATHERINE B	PIERCEY GUY	720 CEDAR ST	EDMONDS	WA	98020	Bristol Bay
KATHY O	DEVEAU FREDERICK	BOX 12	DILLINGHAM	AK	99576	Bristol Bay
KATIE BLUE	ROGOTZKE TOM	27090 320TH ST	SLEEPY EYE	MN	56085	Bristol Bay
KATIE KRISTI	SHARP DAVID	1212 RAYMOND ST	BELLINGHAM	WA	98229	Bristol Bay
KATIE LADY	ANDERSON KAVIK	113 BANCROFT	KODIAK	AK	99615	Bristol Bay
KATYA DAWN	MARINKOVICH FRED	8721 137TH ST NW	GIG HARBOR	WA	98329	Bristol Bay
KAULI BOAT	COOPCHIAK TEDDY	BOX 84	TOGIAK	AK	99678	Bristol Bay
KAY GIRL	ARMSTRONG DANIEL	BOX 110468	ANCHORAGE	AK	99511	Bristol Bay
KAZBEK	MARTUSHEV VLADIMIR	BOX 5148	ANCHOR POINT	AK	99556	Bristol Bay
KB	HAGER KIM	BOX 1552	CORDOVA	AK	99574	Bristol Bay
KELLEY J	JANSEN PACIFIC LLC	10915 59TH AVE W	MUKILTEO	WA	98275	Bristol Bay
KELLI SUE	ROBERTSON RALPH	307 W NIAGARA AVE	ASTORIA	OR	97103	Bristol Bay
KELLY MARIE	AYOJIAK MOSES	BOX 104	TOGIAK	AK	99678	Bristol Bay
KENNY B	HENRY JOSEPH	BOX 37006	TOKSOOK BAY	AK	99637	Bristol Bay
KENNY C	MUCHA JERRY	2310 LINCOLN AVE	ANCHORAGE	AK	99517	Bristol Bay
KEREN LYNN	FV KEREN LYNN	BOX 2358	CORDOVA	AK	99574	Bristol Bay
KETOK	WASSILY HARRY	BOX 17	CLARKS POINT	AK	99569	Bristol Bay
KEYSTONE	MCMAHAN BRYAN	BOX 209	GAKONA	AK	99586	Bristol Bay

153

Vessel	Owner	Address	City	State	Zip	Area
KIMMY	ANGASAN MARTIN	BOX 70163	SOUTH NAKNEK	AK	99670	Bristol Bay
KINDRED SPIRIT	SPIELMAN KARL	2609 NW MARKET ST	SEATTLE	WA	98107	Bristol Bay
KING KRESIMIR	HULJEV JOHN	2824 GAFFEY ST	SAN PEDRO	CA	90731	Bristol Bay
KING LOUIE	POPA VICTOR	2268 AQUA HILL RD	FALLBROOK	CA	92028	Bristol Bay
KINGFISHER	KING LESLIE	83072 LOWER DRY CK RD	MILTON FREEWATER	OR	97862	Bristol Bay
KIRSIKKA	LEWIS JOSHUA	BOX 456	KODIAK	AK	99615	Bristol Bay
KIRSTEN G	MORTON RICHARD	BOX 1418	MUKILTEO	WA	98275	Bristol Bay
KISSA	ALAKAYAK MICHAEL	BOX 56	MANOKOTAK	AK	99628	Bristol Bay
KNEE DEEP	BARBER EDWARD	BOX 925	GIRDWOOD	AK	99587	Bristol Bay
KNUCKLES	WALL RANDALL	92416 SVENSEN MKT RD	ASTORIA	OR	97103	Bristol Bay
KNUCKLES II	HACHIYA DAMON	2479 LAGRANADA DR	THOUSAND OAKS	CA	91362	Bristol Bay
KOKOPELLI	KOKOPELLI LLC	84 SUDDEN VALLEY	BELLINGHAM	WA	98229	Bristol Bay
KOLOB	ANDERSON NORMAN	BOX 864	DILLINGHAM	AK	99576	Bristol Bay
KOMIZA	VARDY DAVID	15326 15TH AVE W	LYNNWOOD	WA	98087	Bristol Bay
KRIAD II	FALLEUR MIKE	1401 OSTER RD	GEARHART	OR	97138	Bristol Bay
KRISINDY	MEDJO TERRY	4426 DRAKE LN	GRAND ISLAND	NE	68801	Bristol Bay
KRISTEN BREE	HANSEN FREDERICK	BOX 153	DILLINGHAM	AK	99576	Bristol Bay
KRISTIN LYNN	TRIEWEILER ADAM	BOX 2905	HOMER	AK	99603	Bristol Bay
KRISTINA	NYHAMMER SVEIN	18504 RIDGEFIELD RD NW	SHORELINE	WA	98177	Bristol Bay
KRISTY	BENOIT GIFFORD	8770 JEWAL TERRACE	ANCHORAGE	AK	99511	Bristol Bay
KUDOS	NASH JAMES	236 E SHUMWAY	CAMANO ISLAND	WA	98282	Bristol Bay
KUSKO GAYLE	FRANKS MICHAEL	3565 SAILBOARD CIR	ANCHORAGE	AK	99516	Bristol Bay
KVAMME III	NICK LLOYD	BOX 252	TOGIAK	AK	99678	Bristol Bay
LADALE	BAKK DALE	BOX 6884	NIKISKI	AK	99635	Bristol Bay
LADY AMERICA	ANDERSON TY	BOX 310	KODIAK	AK	99615	Bristol Bay
LADY C	SHARABARIN VASILY	6363 S ZIMMERMAN RD	AURORA	OR	97002	Bristol Bay
LADY CAROL	LIND ORVILLE	BOX 379	KING SALMON	AK	99613	Bristol Bay

Appendix 5
Gill Netters, Salmon

Vessel	Owner	Address	City	State	Zip	Area
LADY DEA	WALDRON FRANKLIN	BOX 39093	NINILCHIK	AK	99639	Bristol Bay
LADY DEBORAH	OBLAD KELLY	267 OXBOW RD	RAYMOND	WA	98577	Bristol Bay
LADY HAWK	STYCZYNSKI ANGELA	4802 RURAL AVE	BELLINGHAM	WA	98226	Bristol Bay
LADY JASMINE	KRITZ MOSES	BOX 83	TOGIAK	AK	99678	Bristol Bay
LADY JAZZALYNN	ROSS CONNER	BOX 804	KODIAK	AK	99615	Bristol Bay
LADY JO RAE	WASSILLIE THOMAS	BOX 53	NEWHALEN	AK	99606	Bristol Bay
LADY JUNE	WOINOWSKY AURTHER	301 PTARMIGAN RD	UGASHIK	AK	99613	Bristol Bay
LADY KATE	BJAZEVICH PETER	1700 E LOPEZ CT	BELLINGHAM	WA	98229	Bristol Bay
LADY KATHERINE	CAMPO ANTHONY	525 MADISON #D	MONTEREY	CA	93940	Bristol Bay
LADY KONA	DEMOSKI ERNEST	200 W FALLEN LEAF CIR	WASILLA	AK	99654	Bristol Bay
LADY LAURA	CHRISTENSEN MACARLO	BOX 49014	PORT HEIDEN	AK	99549	Bristol Bay
LADY LYNDA	ANGASAN RALPH	BOX 633	KING SALMON	AK	99613	Bristol Bay
LADY O	PHILLIPS WILLIAM	15406 21ST AVE SW	SEATTLE	WA	98166	Bristol Bay
LADY ROSE	MACH LADISLAV	828 NW 125TH	SEATTLE	WA	98177	Bristol Bay
LANIKAI	DOWNS NICK	1100 5TH AVE N #1	SEATTLE	WA	98109	Bristol Bay
LAST CHANCE	NORA H CORPORATION	BOX 25	CHINOOK	WA	98614	Bristol Bay
LAUREN K	BURGRAFF MARION	BOX 380	KING SALMON	AK	99613	Bristol Bay
LAURI LYN	AIELLO SALVATORE	5397 BREEZEWOOD DR	PARADISE	CA	95969	Bristol Bay
LEADING EDGE	LOTHROP BRUCE	10230 SW 161ST ST	VASHON	WA	98070	Bristol Bay
LEGEND	PHILBRICK, KRISTA & RYAN	793 E APRIL AVE	GRAPEVIEW	WA	98546	Bristol Bay
LEILA M	BAUMGART JIM	210 BAYSIDE PL	BELLINGHAM	WA	98225	Bristol Bay
LENA LUCY	AITI SAMUEL	BOX 42	KWIGILLINGOK	AK	99622	Bristol Bay
LENA MAE III	AYOJIAK GABRIEL	BOX 61	MANOKOTAK	AK	99628	Bristol Bay
LENNY	ARNARIAK IVAN	2221 MULDOON 908	ANCHORAGE	AK	99504	Bristol Bay
LENNY BOY	GIANNO LEONARD	380 VIA PALO LINDA	FAIRFIELD	CA	94534	Bristol Bay
LESON	LINN SCOTT	1004 COMMERCIAL AVE	ANACORTES	WA	98221	Bristol Bay
LIBERTY	MIKKELSEN ROGER	BOX 271	DILLINGHAM	AK	99576	Bristol Bay

Vessel	Owner	Address	City	State	Zip	Area
LIGHTFOOT	GUIGGEY RYAN	3021 N SCHEVENE RD	FLAGSTAFF	AZ	86004	Bristol Bay
LIGHTHOUSE	PRYZMONT PHILLIP	BOX 712	NOME	AK	99762	Bristol Bay
LIL BUDDY	SCHILLE MICHAEL	6244 S WINDFALL	CLINTON	WA	98236	Bristol Bay
LIL NICK	JOHNSON LUDWIG	501 N KIMBERLY	WASILLA	AK	99654	Bristol Bay
LIL' PETE	CHRISTOPHER PETER	BOX 85	NEW STUYAHOK	AK	99636	Bristol Bay
LILA L	RUSSELL SHANE	3105 LAURELWOOD AVE	BELLINGHAM	WA	98225	Bristol Bay
LINDA K	LELAND TROY	2101 WEST SHORE DR	LUMMI ISLAND	WA	98262	Bristol Bay
LINDA K II	DAHL STANLEY	305 GROWLERS GULCH	CASTLE ROCK	WA	98611	Bristol Bay
LINDA SUE	MOORES JOHN	3840 ROBIN ST	ANCHORAGE	AK	99504	Bristol Bay
LINN LOUISE	DEMANTLE HARVEY	BOX 156	AKIAK	AK	99552	Bristol Bay
LITTLE CASINO	CORSON BRUCE	205 E DIMOND BLVD #395	ANCHORAGE	AK	99515	Bristol Bay
LITTLE COMFORT	HIRATSUKA RICHARD	BOX 312	DILLINGHAM	AK	99576	Bristol Bay
LITTLE ELLEN	GOSUK SAM	BOX 177	TOGIAK	AK	99678	Bristol Bay
LITTLE J	GULL DANIEL	BOX 395	FRENCHTOWN	MT	59834	Bristol Bay
LITTLE ROSEMARY	SHADE DOUGLAS	BOX 156	DILLINGHAM	AK	99576	Bristol Bay
LITTLE DOMENICI II	ASARO SALVATORE	630 OAK ST	MONTEREY	CA	93940	Bristol Bay
LOBO DEL MAR	LACHELT GENE	546 EMBASSY CIR	HENDERSON	NV	89015	Bristol Bay
LOKI	MUNRO MARK	BOX 1971	HOMER	AK	99603	Bristol Bay
LO-LO	WASSILLIE ROGER	BOX 287	TOGIAK	AK	99678	Bristol Bay
LOOKING GOOD	ALEXIE JOE	BOX 86	TOGIAK	AK	99678	Bristol Bay
LOOKOUT	BELMONT JORDAN	1206 S 10TH ST	MOUNT VERNON	WA	98273	Bristol Bay
LOON POINT	BERG JAMES	BOX 93	OAKVILLE	WA	98568	Bristol Bay
LORI DEE	BAVILLA THOMAS	BOX 44	ALEKNAGIK	AK	99555	Bristol Bay
LORI-D	MARKUSEN JEFF	8061 NISKA RD	BLAINE	WA	98230	Bristol Bay
LUCILLE D	LARSON ALBERT	BOX 702	DILLINGHAM	AK	99576	Bristol Bay
LUCKY BEAR	ANDREW PETER	BOX 1074	DILLINGHAM	AK	99576	Bristol Bay
LUCKY C	COFFEEN NAT	105 OHIMA DR	WALLA WALLA	WA	99362	Bristol Bay

Vessel	Owner	Address	City	State	Zip	Area
LUCKY LOGGER	SULLIVAN ROD	BOX 280	OAK HARBOR	WA	98277	Bristol Bay
LUCKY STRIKE	OCZKEWICZ EDWARD	BOX 186	NAKNEK	AK	99633	Bristol Bay
LULU	HANSEN SCOTT	1944 HWY 7	OROVILLE	WA	98844	Bristol Bay
LUND	LOGUSAK EVAN	BOX 216	TOGIAK	AK	99678	Bristol Bay
LUND BOAT	ANDREWS JOSEPH	BOX 103	TOGIAK	AK	99678	Bristol Bay
LYDIA RAELEEN	GROAT, CHARLES & KATHERINE	BOX 70047	SOUTH NAKNEK	AK	99670	Bristol Bay
LYNN C	CARLSON JENS	2739 SEAVIEW DR	PORT HEIDEN	AK	99549	Bristol Bay
LYNNE MARIE	UPTON HERBERT	44482 GENE AVE	KENAI	AK	99611	Bristol Bay
M & M	BAVILLA MARY	BOX 111	TOGIAK	AK	99678	Bristol Bay
MAC ATTACK	MCDONALD ROSS	57889 LEE VALLEY RD	COQUILLE	OR	97423	Bristol Bay
MADDIE C	RIDLEY CHARLES	2951 74TH AVE SE	MERCER ISLAND	WA	98040	Bristol Bay
MAE ANA	BROWN MELVIN	BOX 111566	ANCHORAGE	AK	99511	Bristol Bay
MAGGIE	WILDER LYLE	3323 DRY CREEK	PORT ALSWORTH	AK	99653	Bristol Bay
MAGGIE LYNN	DG INCORPORATED	BOX 24585	FEDERAL WAY	WA	99809	Bristol Bay
MAGIC	JACKSON JOHN	4817 PEAR POINT RD	FRIDAY HARBOR	WA	98250	Bristol Bay
MAGNUM	T & T MARINE INC	3754 S BAY DR	SEDRO WOOLLEY	WA	98284	Bristol Bay
MAIMED	BALCH PETER	BOX 80490	FAIRBANKS	AK	99708	Bristol Bay
MAJESTIC	KAHOOTEK	1005 RICHARDSON RD	LOPEZ ISLAND	WA	98261	Bristol Bay
MAJESTIC II	BOSKOFFSKY PAUL	BOX 408	NAKNEK	AK	99633	Bristol Bay
MALACHITE	MARTUSHEV IVAN	BOX 1939	HOMER	AK	99603	Bristol Bay
MANOWAR	DENNIS DANIEL	1501 MONTE MAR RD	VISTA	CA	92084	Bristol Bay
MARANATHA	KUZMIN VASILY	16727 LEARY RD	WOODBURN	OR	97071	Bristol Bay
MARGARET M	VINCENT TIMOTHY	16404 38TH AVE NW	STANWOOD	WA	98292	Bristol Bay
MARGIE MARIE II	ISHNOOK NATALIA	BOX 5029	KOLIGANEK	AK	99576	Bristol Bay
MARIA FRANCIS	MITBY ANDREW	2768 ST RT 105	GRAYLAND	WA	98547	Bristol Bay
MARIA GRAZIA II	COSTA VINCENZO	695 ELM AVE	SEASIDE	CA	93955	Bristol Bay

Vessel	Owner	Address	City	State	Zip	Area
MARIA J	JOHNSEN HERB	175 S HARRINGTON LAGOON RD	COUPEVILLE	WA	98239	Bristol Bay
MARIA S A	FERRARA MATTEO	7 1/2 RIVERVIEW RD	GLOUCESTER	MA	1930	Bristol Bay
MARIA THERESA	CURCURU SALINA	6 APPLE ST	GLOUCESTER	MA	1930	Bristol Bay
MARIAH	COLLINS DANIEL	BOX 1504	KETCHUM	ID	83340	Bristol Bay
MARIAH	GLOTFELTY JOHN	14931 SNOWSHOE LN	ANCHORAGE	AK	99516	Bristol Bay
MARIE	GRUBBS JASON	BOX 2267	KAPAA	HI	96746	Bristol Bay
MARIE JENSEN	LIE PALMER	21727 96TH AVE W	EDMONDS	WA	98020	Bristol Bay
MARIE K	KOLICH VINKO	818 S PATTON AVE #1	SAN PEDRO	CA	90731	Bristol Bay
MARJA-D	DOMINIS ANTHONY	1760 CHANDELEUR DR	SAN PEDRO	CA	90732	Bristol Bay
MARILYN MARIE	WALCOTT MICKIA	BOX 134	NEW STUYAHOK	AK	99636	Bristol Bay
MARI-LYNN	HAKALA MATTHEW	104 E PIONEER AVE	HOMER	AK	99603	Bristol Bay
MARINA JO	GUMLICKPUK IVAN	BOX 5037	KOLIGANEK	AK	99576	Bristol Bay
MARISSA	PALMGREN MICHAEL	2117 NORTH SHORE RD	BELLINGHAM	WA	98226	Bristol Bay
MARLEI	OLSON ROBERT	2465 GREEN ACRES LN	OAK HARBOR	WA	98277	Bristol Bay
MARLENE J	ZIMMER DOMINIC	12391 S ABBOTT-DOWNING WAY	NAMPA	ID	83686	Bristol Bay
MARMOT	JOHNSON CALEB	137 MOLEHULEHU LOOP	KAHULUI	HI	96732	Bristol Bay
MARQUTTAM	KASAK LEO	BOX 301	TOGIAK	AK	99678	Bristol Bay
MARY ANN	DARONE NED	24216 VIA SANTA CLARA	MISSION VIEJO	CA	92692	Bristol Bay
MARY JO II	MAYTON ROBERT	1417 HUNTLEY ST	ABERDEEN	WA	98520	Bristol Bay
MARY JOANN	POLISERI VINCENT	748 TAMARACK DR	SAN RAFAEL	CA	94903	Bristol Bay
MARY K	KALLENBERG WALTER	3705 ARCTIC BLVD #127	ANCHORAGE	AK	99503	Bristol Bay
MARY K	KONUKPEOK ALAKAY	BOX 27	TOGIAK	AK	99678	Bristol Bay
MARY M	MANUGUERRA VENTURA	4 ANTELOPE LN	MONTEREY	CA	93940	Bristol Bay
MARY MARGARET	PEARSON JON	38 HYLAND STRINGER RD	RAYMOND	WA	98577	Bristol Bay
MARYNA J	ROBERTSON RANDALL	BOX 62	NAKNEK	AK	99633	Bristol Bay
MASTER PHILIP	LAFATA MATTEO	3505 LINDSAY AVE	BELLINGHAM	WA	98229	Bristol Bay
MATCH POINT	LUDWIG JOEL	4018 226TH PL NE	ARLINGTON	WA	98223	Bristol Bay

Vessel	Owner	Address	City	State	Zip	Area
MATT AND JOE	RUSSO SALVATORE	4614 WINONA AVE	SAN DIEGO	CA	92115	Bristol Bay
MAVERICK	LARSEN RANDY	2493 MOUNTAIN VIEW RD	FERNDALE	WA	98248	Bristol Bay
MAXIMUS	ALIOTTI THOMAS	BOX 6093	BELLINGHAM	WA	98225	Bristol Bay
MAXINE W	WISE DREW	10805 23RD DR SE	EVERETT	WA	98208	Bristol Bay
MAYA ANN	KANULIE J.P	12420 LANDMARK ST	ANCHORAGE	AK	99515	Bristol Bay
MECCA	ARTUNER AHMET	1855 MARINE DR	BELLINGHAM	WA	98226	Bristol Bay
MEG J	MEG J LLC	BOX 1839	WAITSFIELD	VT	5673	Bristol Bay
MEGAN K	KUCHER MICHAEL	BOX 1780	CARMEL VALLEY	CA	93924	Bristol Bay
MEGAN M	J & M FISHERIES INC	1216 NW BLAKELY CT	SEATTLE	WA	98177	Bristol Bay
MELINDA LEE	JONES ANTHONY	BOX 402	KODIAK	AK	99615	Bristol Bay
MELINDA RAE	GARDINER THOMAS	BOX 1338	DILLINGHAM	AK	99576	Bristol Bay
MELISSA J	MYERS JAMES	BOX 197	NAKNEK	AK	99633	Bristol Bay
MELISSA M	GOSNELL ROBERT	1194 AL SERENO	LOS OSOS	CA	93403	Bristol Bay
MELODY LYNN	NODEN GLORIA	BOX 66	ALEKNAGIK	AK	99555	Bristol Bay
MENISCUS	STRAUB KRIS	BOX 56650	NORTH POLE	AK	99705	Bristol Bay
MERCHANT	FORSBERG DENNIS	1417 SE BLAIR	WASHOUGAL	WA	98671	Bristol Bay
MEREDITH CHARLENE	WATSON MARCUS	BOX 150	NAKNEK	AK	99633	Bristol Bay
MERIT	APOKEDAK CHRISTOPHER	BOX 34	LEVELOCK	AK	99625	Bristol Bay
MERLE J	JACKSON JOHN	4817 PEAR POINT RD	FRIDAY HARBOR	WA	98250	Bristol Bay
MICHAEL A	ANDREW TREFIM	BOX 12	ILIAMNA	AK	99606	Bristol Bay
MICHAEL VII	LINDSTROM DAVID	689 LEXINGTON	ASTORIA	OR	97103	Bristol Bay
MICHELLE DAWN	ABYO MIKE	BOX 445	PILOT POINT	AK	99649	Bristol Bay
MICHELLE M	MARBLE LEE	42 TARTE RD	FRIDAY HARBOR	WA	98250	Bristol Bay
MIGHTY JOE	EVICH ADAM	61 COTTAGE ST	FAIRHAVEN	MA	2719	Bristol Bay
MIGHTY LOETTA	JOHNSON GERALD	41244 SAINT MARYS LK RD	SAINT IGNATIUS	MT	59865	Bristol Bay

Vessel	Owner	Address	City	State	Zip	Area
MIGRATOR	BROCKHOFF, R. & A.	BOX 894	WESTPORT	WA	98595	Bristol Bay
MILDRED R	EVON ALVIN	BOX 31	MANOKOTAK	AK	99628	Bristol Bay
MIRAGE	DANESE DAVID	22241 MAYFIELD RD	GULF PORT	MS	39503	Bristol Bay
MISS	CARRIGLIO PASQUALE	775 ELM AVE	SESAIOLE	CA	93955	Bristol Bay
MISS BRIELLE	BORVE HANS	2138 THORNTON RD	FERNDALE	WA	98248	Bristol Bay
MISS CAROLYN	BROSTROM ED	959 QUEEN ST	BELLINGHAM	WA	98225	Bristol Bay
MISS CHELSEY	BIG CREEK FISHERIES LLC	3900 RAILWAY AVE	EVERETT	WA	98201	Bristol Bay
MISS CHOLI	WILCOX MARYJANE	BOX 147	TOGIAK	AK	99678	Bristol Bay
MISS CINDY	STECKER THOMAS	1321 24TH AVE	LONGVIEW	WA	98632	Bristol Bay
MISS COLLEEN	MAVAR NICK	BOX 70004	SOUTH NAKNEK	AK	99670	Bristol Bay
MISS DORY	SMITH ROY	BOX 20481	JUNEAU	AK	99802	Bristol Bay
MISS EMMA	MORGAN DOUGLAS	16339 HEADLANDS CIR	ANCHORAGE	AK	99516	Bristol Bay
MISS EVELYN	CLARK MICHAEL	28 HOWARD RD	CATHLAMET	WA	98612	Bristol Bay
MISS FRANCESCA	WELLER PATRICK	1208 234 PLACE	OCEAN PARK	WA	98640	Bristol Bay
MISS GAIL	HAMMER ARVE	3616 166 PL S W	LYNNWOOD	WA	98037	Bristol Bay
MISS GLADYS	HILL WILLIAM	BOX 483	NAKNEK	AK	99633	Bristol Bay
MISS JEAN	NOSTE KARL	112 BRITTANY ST	MOUNT VERNON	WA	98274	Bristol Bay
MISS JENNY	SMITH SAMUEL	BOX 54	MEKORYUK	AK	99630	Bristol Bay
MISS JULIE	COLE LESTER	BOX 194	CUSICK	WA	99119	Bristol Bay
MISS JULIE	SHERMAN KENT	BOX 4062	PALMER	AK	99645	Bristol Bay
MISS KRISTIN	FORSBERG VERNON	28811 NW MAIN	RIDGEFIELD	WA	98642	Bristol Bay
MISS KRISTY	WASSILY HENRY	BOX 36	CLARKS POINT	AK	99569	Bristol Bay
MISS LAUREN	FOSSO STEVEN	4116 R AVE	ANACORTES	WA	98221	Bristol Bay
MISS LISA	WEESE LYLA	5702 S 2ND AVE	EVERETT	WA	98203	Bristol Bay
MISS MADDISON	DISCHER RICHARD	101 HAVEN LANE #3	SITKA	AK	99835	Bristol Bay
MISS MARIA	ALIOTTI PAUL	1071 TRAPPERS TRAIL	PEBBLE BEACH	CA	93953	Bristol Bay
MISS MIA	RICE DARREN	4417 H AVE	ANACORTES	WA	98221	Bristol Bay

Vessel	Owner	Address	City	State	Zip	Area
MISS MORGAN	CATTOLICO ERASIMO	875 VENTURA DR	PITTSBURG	CA	94565	Bristol Bay
MISS NESSIE	MURPHY RICHARD	BOX 732	DILLINGHAM	AK	99576	Bristol Bay
MISS NILA	SMITH RORY	310 NARRAGANSETT ST NE	PALM BAY	FL	32907	Bristol Bay
MISS SHELLEY	ODELL MIKE	19117 15TH AVE NW	SHORELINE	WA	98177	Bristol Bay
MISS SUSIE	KASAK NORMAN	BOX 228	TOGIAK	AK	99678	Bristol Bay
MISS TANYA ANN	LABAR IVO	1235 W 13TH ST	SAN PEDRO	CA	90731	Bristol Bay
MISS TRACY	BLUNKA STEPHAN	BOX 17	NEW STUYAHOK	AK	99636	Bristol Bay
MISSION 3:16	CRACCHIOLO GIUSEPPE	40056 GLEN IVY ST	MURRIETA	CA	92563	Bristol Bay
MISTER A	ATAKITLIG BRADLEY	BOX 55	TOGIAK	AK	99678	Bristol Bay
MISTY	SIFSOF ERNEST	BOX 1449	DILLINGHAM	AK	99576	Bristol Bay
MODERATION	ETHELBAH HARLEY	BOX 972	PETERSBURG	AK	99833	Bristol Bay
MOLLY D	SWAB LUKE	901 GRAY RD	MERRITT	MI	49667	Bristol Bay
MONNIE MON BOAT	BAVILLA DANIEL	BOX 28	MANOKOTAK	AK	99628	Bristol Bay
MONTANA	CRAMER VICTOR	7890 FLETCHER BAY RD NE	BAINBRIDGE ISLAND	WA	98110	Bristol Bay
MORNING STAR	LEE ARNE	6200 NE LINCOLN RD E	POULSBO	WA	98370	Bristol Bay
MORNING STAR	OLSEN MATTHEW	4513 WOLF RUN DR	MEDFORD	OR	97504	Bristol Bay
MR BAISTA	NANALOOK MAURICE	BOX 2763	BETHEL	AK	99559	Bristol Bay
MR MIKE	BACKMAN GARY	301 E BIRNIE SLOUGH RD	CATHLAMET	WA	98612	Bristol Bay
MR SEA	ROHR JOHN	BOX 2621	HOMER	AK	99603	Bristol Bay
MS FISHER II	JOLMA ROGER	BOX 343	CLATSKANIE	OR	97016	Bristol Bay
MS MARIANA	AIELLO JACK	1563 MENDOCINO DR	CONCORD	CA	94521	Bristol Bay
MUD HEN	FV EDGE INC	BOX 1623	WESTPORT	WA	98595	Bristol Bay
MUMBO JUMBO	LAPEYRI BRIAN	BOX 448	PETERSBURG	AK	99833	Bristol Bay
MY GIRL	ALVAREZ RANDOLPH	BOX 4012	IGIUGIG	AK	99613	Bristol Bay
MY GIRLS	ANDERSON SCOTT	BOX 49027	PORT HEIDEN	AK	99549	Bristol Bay
MYCHAL SUE	CARPENTER LANDON	4739 MERMONT PL	EVERETT	WA	98203	Bristol Bay
MYRNA MAE	HEILALA MARK	7715 45TH PL W	MUKILTEO	WA	98275	Bristol Bay

Vessel	Owner	Address	City	State	Zip	Area
MZ LIZ	SPADARO GIUSEPPE	50 VIA ENCINA	MONTEREY	CA	93940	Bristol Bay
N 11	FUENTES SPENCER	BOX 251	SILVANA	WA	98287	Bristol Bay
N 16	BENNETT GEORGE	103 16TH ST	HOQUIAM	WA	98550	Bristol Bay
N 17	WINTERS ROBERT	47 HARVARD AVE #2	BROOKLINE	MA	2446	Bristol Bay
N 2	KEMMER JAMES	BOX 6	CHINOOK	WA	98614	Bristol Bay
N 20	BLAKEY BENJAMIN	6118 12TH AVE S	SEATTLE	WA	98108	Bristol Bay
N 5	TARABOCHIA DANIEL	7613 ELM CT SE	OLYMPIA	WA	98503	Bristol Bay
N 7 V	DEVRIES BRYAN	4566 NOON RD	BELLINGHAM	WA	98226	Bristol Bay
N 1	BROCK EDWARD	22845 ROSE RD	MOUNT VERNON	WA	98274	Bristol Bay
NAATO AAKII	HUFFER TOM	11551 TARGEE LP	EAGLE RIVER	AK	99577	Bristol Bay
NAKNEK	PIATT MICHAEL	3471 SEAGULL DR	PALMER	AK	99645	Bristol Bay
NANCY	SINGLETON JOSEPH	BOX 92	EGEGIK	AK	99579	Bristol Bay
NANCY LEE	REEL CHAD	3001 E KIBBY DR	WASILLA	AK	99654	Bristol Bay
NANCY O	VANDERLIND LAUREN	353 COURTNEY ST	ASHLAND	OR	97520	Bristol Bay
NATIVE SON	BELL RICHARD	BOX 575	KODIAK	AK	99615	Bristol Bay
NAUGHTY LADY	DEIGH RICHARD	BOX 40	EGEGIK	AK	99579	Bristol Bay
NEAR FALL	HENSHAW THOMAS	108 LILLIAN DR	SITKA	AK	99835	Bristol Bay
NELI BLY	NELI BLY INC	BOX 165	POULTNEY	VT	5764	Bristol Bay
NELLIE ANN II	ABRAHAM JOBE	BOX 71	CHEFORNAK	AK	99561	Bristol Bay
NELLIE G	GUDMUNDSON DENNIS	5973 RUTSATZ RD	DEMING	WA	98244	Bristol Bay
NEPTUNE	LOREE JEFFREY	10539 JONES RD SW	OLYMPIA	WA	98512	Bristol Bay
NERKA	GATENS JAMES	BOX 310	NAKNEK	AK	99633	Bristol Bay
NET INCOME	JONES RANDY	12825 129TH ST NE	LAKE STEVENS	WA	98258	Bristol Bay
NET PROFIT	FINBRATEN RIKKE	23220 49TH AVE SE	BOTHELL	WA	98021	Bristol Bay
NET SUM	ROSS MICHAEL	210 E WACO PL	BROKEN ARROW OK		74011	Bristol Bay
NETTA	ZIMIN CARVEL	BOX 70003	SOUTH NAKNEK AK		99670	Bristol Bay
NETWORK	SMITH MARK	11200 JEROME ST	ANCHORAGE	AK	99516	Bristol Bay

Vessel	Owner	Address	City	State	Zip	Area
NEW ERA	MCNEIL LOUISE	N 41218 GROVE RD	DEER PARK	WA	99006	Bristol Bay
NEW LIFE	NORTHERN WILD REDS INC	BOX 38	COLERAIN	NC	27924	Bristol Bay
NEW WAVE	SCHONBERG PAUL	BOX 1167	STANWOOD	WA	98292	Bristol Bay
NIGHT TRAIN II	BONANNO ROBERT	4552 WILDCAT CIR	ANTIOCH	CA	94531	Bristol Bay
NN-1	HEAVENER THERON	BOX 212771	ANCHORAGE	AK	99521	Bristol Bay
NO LIMIT	STEVENS ERICK	5762 STORR RD	FERNDALE	WA	98248	Bristol Bay
NOAH	BIG CREEK FISHERIES LLC	3900 RAILWAY AVE	EVERETT	WA	98201	Bristol Bay
NOAH	NORTHLAND FISHERIES LLC	3900 RAILWAY AVE	EVERETT	WA	98201	Bristol Bay
NOAH III	WHYMN FREDERICK	BOX 14	TOGIAK	AK	99678	Bristol Bay
NOLA RAE	ANGASAN STEVEN	BOX 193	NAKNEK	AK	99633	Bristol Bay
NOMAD	MULHOLLAND BRENDAN	4978 HIGHLAND DR	BLAINE	WA	98230	Bristol Bay
NON-SOLA FISHOLA	GREENFIELD KENNETH	BOX 237	CHINOOK	WA	98614	Bristol Bay
NON-SOLA FISHOLA	HEICHEL TODD	4414 290TH ST NW	STANWOOD	WA	98292	Bristol Bay
NORA-H	TRAINOR ROSS	624 WEST EWING ST	SEATTLE	WA	98119	Bristol Bay
NORINE LYNN II	COOPCHIAK BENJAMIN	BOX 94	TOGIAK	AK	99678	Bristol Bay
NORTH RUNNER	ZHAROFF AMANDA	259 MOUNTAIN VIEW DR	HOMER	AK	99603	Bristol Bay
NORTH SEA	WIDING WILLIAM	1445 NW 56TH ST	SEATTLE	WA	98107	Bristol Bay
NORTH STAR	ALIOTTI THOMAS	BOX 6093	BELLINGHAM	WA	98225	Bristol Bay
NORTH STAR	REEL CHAD	3001 E KIBBY DR	WASILLA	AK	99654	Bristol Bay
NORTHERN FLYER	MANNING BARRY	BOX 9194	KETCHIKAN	AK	99901	Bristol Bay
NORTHERN ZEPHYR	MERSHON PHILIP	BOX 536	COLLEGE PLACE	WA	99324	Bristol Bay
NOT ME	PAVELLA TIMMY	BOX 38	NEW STUYAHOK	AK	99636	Bristol Bay
NUMBER ONE	FRANKLIN ARLINE	BOX 84	MANOKOTAK	AK	99628	Bristol Bay
NUNAKA	GOLIA BERTHA	BOX 663	DILLINGHAM	AK	99576	Bristol Bay
NUNAKA	GOLIA PETER	BOX 663	DILLINGHAM	AK	99576	Bristol Bay
ODIC	WALTERS LEIF	2751 PALMER-WASILLA HWY	WASILLA	AK	99654	Bristol Bay
ODIE	SOLBERG REIDAR	4248 SQUALICUM LAKE RD	BELLINGHAM	WA	98225	Bristol Bay

Vessel	Owner	Address	City	State	Zip	Area
ODIN	FROSTAD KNUT	1051 D JORUP ST	CAMANO ISLAND	WA	98282	Bristol Bay
OFFENSE	PRINCEN JOSEPH	36005 6TH AVE SW	FEDERAL WAY	WA	98023	Bristol Bay
OHANA	MITCHELL JOHN	41 STRAWBERRY PT RD	BELLINGHAM	WA	98229	Bristol Bay
OI SEA	DEIGH KEVIN	BOX 40	EGEGIK	AK	99579	Bristol Bay
OLE MAN	BLUNKA BLUNKA	BOX 115	NEW STUYAHOK	AK	99636	Bristol Bay
OLY	WOOD ANTHONY	BOX 602	KING SALMON	AK	99613	Bristol Bay
ONE-50-ONE	BERTSCHI JERRY	BOX 455	LYLE	WA	98635	Bristol Bay
OOGRUK	WIRKKALA EAGER INC	BOX 141	CHINOOK	WA	98614	Bristol Bay
OPPORTUNITY	VOSS CHRISTOPHER	1743 HWY 154	SANTA BARBARA	CA	93105	Bristol Bay
ORACLE	MENISH FRITZ	BOX 1711	PETERSBURG	AK	99833	Bristol Bay
ORCA	MITBY ERIC	BOX 551	TOKELAND	WA	98590	Bristol Bay
OSCAR II	GUNLIK ARTHUR	BOX 135	KIPNUK	AK	99614	Bristol Bay
OSPREY 1	PETTERSEN PER	21515 CYPRESS WAY	LYNNWOOD	WA	98036	Bristol Bay
OUTSIDER	MUSTOLA GREGORY	80190 ALSTON MAYGER RD	CLATSKANIE	OR	97016	Bristol Bay
PAIGE	HATCH DAVID	1049 B AVE	EDMONDS	WA	98020	Bristol Bay
PAIL RIDER	DANESE DAVID	22241 MAYFIELD RD	GULF PORT	MS	39503	Bristol Bay
PALEGIA	NIELSEN DONALD	BOX 70151	SOUTH NAKNEK	AK	99670	Bristol Bay
PALUMMA II	ALIOTTI GASPARE	3057 BOSTICK AVE	MARINA	CA	93933	Bristol Bay
PASSING WIND	DEIGH KEVIN	BOX 40	EGEGIK	AK	99579	Bristol Bay
PATHFINDER	LIE SIGNAR	8022 149TH ST SE	SNOHOMISH	WA	98296	Bristol Bay
PATRICIA MARY	GEORGE GEORGE	13650 23RD ST	DADE CITY	FL	33525	Bristol Bay
PAULA D	MITCHELL BENJAMIN	1301 CLEARBROOK #25	BELLINGHAM	WA	98229	Bristol Bay
PAULA MAE	STRAUB KRIS	BOX 56650	NORTH POLE	AK	99705	Bristol Bay
PAULA.M	WOOD CHARLES	BOX 128	KING SALMON	AK	99613	Bristol Bay
PAULINE GLORIA	TOM NICK	BOX 90034	NIGHTMUTE	AK	99690	Bristol Bay
PAULINE II	PAUL DAVID	BOX 016	KIPNUK	AK	99614	Bristol Bay

Vessel	Owner	Address	City	State	Zip	Area
PEARL	NYBLOD LESLIE	9030 96TH ST NE #A	ARLINGTON	WA	98270	Bristol Bay
PEGGY LEE III	SNYDER WILLIAM	BOX 45	TOGIAK	AK	99678	Bristol Bay
PENTECOST	MSO FISHERIES INC	BOX 1814	SEQUIM	WA	98382	Bristol Bay
PEREGRIN	ANDERSON TY	BOX 310	KODIAK	AK	99615	Bristol Bay
PERIL STRAIT	BAUMGART HENRY	1504 FAIRVIEW	BELLINGHAM	WA	98229	Bristol Bay
PERSEVERE	CASTO GLENN	16120 DUBUQUE RD	SNOHOMISH	WA	98290	Bristol Bay
PHOENIX	THORSON RAYMOND	BOX 1130	DILLINGHAM	AK	99576	Bristol Bay
PICKENS II	NELSON ROBERT	BOX 388	GRAND MARAIS	MN	55604	Bristol Bay
PICKIN & GRINNIN	BECKER MARK	1395 SANTA RITA CIR	SANTA BARBARA	CA	93109	Bristol Bay
PIG	HOFFMAN CRYSTAL	3418 UPLAND DR	ANCHORAGE	AK	99504	Bristol Bay
PINNACLE	MAUDSLIEN ERIK	373 SW 176TH PLACE	SEATTLE	WA	98166	Bristol Bay
PIONEER	PENNEWELL RICHARD	3224 89TH AVE E	EDGEWOOD	WA	98371	Bristol Bay
PIRANHA	DUNCAN NORMAN	1798 SE WALL ST	ASTORIA	OR	97103	Bristol Bay
PIXIE GIRL	KRAUN ELAINE	4752 354TH AVE SE	FALL CITY	WA	98024	Bristol Bay
POIKEN J	JOHNSON MARTIN	1807 SAWMILL CREEK	SITKA	AK	99835	Bristol Bay
POINT DEFIANCE	NOSTE ERIK	20825 BULSON RD	MOUNT VERNON	WA	98274	Bristol Bay
POKEY II	COURTNEY MARSHALL	4854 W GLENHAVEN DR	EVERETT	WA	98203	Bristol Bay
POLAR BEAR	HAMMER KARL	1654 NW 204TH ST	SHORELINE	WA	98177	Bristol Bay
POLAR-ICE	SVASAND KURT	15812 71ST AVE NE	KENMORE	WA	98028	Bristol Bay
POLARIS	ALIOTTI GIACOMO & CARMELA	310 QUEBRADA DELMAR RD	MARINA	CA	93933	Bristol Bay
POLARSTAR	BASARGIN MARKEL	BOX 991	HOMER	AK	99603	Bristol Bay
POLLY'D	DAVID DAVID	BOX 78	KWIGILLINGOK	AK	99622	Bristol Bay
POST POINT	DAUBER GEORGE	BOX 5661	BELLINGHAM	WA	98227	Bristol Bay
POTENTIAL	LAWSON ELIJAH	543 N 82ND ST	SEATTLE	WA	98103	Bristol Bay
POUND BY POUND	FRANKLIN CLAYTON	7942 RENIC DR	SEDRO WOOLLEY	WA	98284	Bristol Bay
POWER PLAY	ANDERSON DARRIN	3290 S LAKESHORE LP	PALMER	AK	99645	Bristol Bay
PREDATOR	MANDICH DAVID	31 BOURSAW AVE	HOQUIAM	WA	98550	Bristol Bay

Vessel	Owner	Address	City	State	Zip	Area
PRELUDE	KRAUN FRED	4752 354TH AVE SE	FALL CITY	WA	98024	Bristol Bay
PREMO `LAI	ELK RIVER TRUST	378 RACCOON RD	OAKLAND	OR	97462	Bristol Bay
PROFISHNT	MARTUSHEV ANDREY	BOX 3113	HOMER	AK	99603	Bristol Bay
PROVIDER	EDENS DAVID	BOX 3456	HOMER	AK	99603	Bristol Bay
PUG	BARKER DAVE	126 E FAIRVEIW AVE	HOMER	AK	99603	Bristol Bay
PUTTY TAT	OLSON RUDOLPH	BOX 547	DILLINGHAM	AK	99576	Bristol Bay
QUANDARY	LOWRANCE JOHN	122 N 84TH ST	SEATTLE	WA	98107	Bristol Bay
QUEEN BEE	WASSILLIE WILLIE	BOX 28	TOGIAK	AK	99678	Bristol Bay
QUICK SET II	PHAM MINH	706 S 104TH ST	SEATTLE	WA	98168	Bristol Bay
QUICKSILVER II	KIRK WILLIAM	2011 MAC ARTHUR ST	RANCHO PALOS VERDE	CA	90275	Bristol Bay
R D & J	KALMAKOFF SHAWN	BOX 444	PILOT POINT	AK	99649	Bristol Bay
RJ	KURIAN STEVE	87 SCHOOLHOUSE LN	BLOOMSBURG	PA	17815	Bristol Bay
RACHEL ANNE	JACKSON MICHAEL	615 12TH ST	BELLINGHAM	WA	98225	Bristol Bay
RACHELLE DENAE	FIELDS WALLACE	BOX 1691	KODIAK	AK	99615	Bristol Bay
RADELL DAWN	THOMPSON DENNIS	19509 67TH AVE SE	SNOHOMISH	WA	98298	Bristol Bay
RAINSNOW	ARNARIAK WASSILLIE	BOX 66	TOGIAK	AK	99678	Bristol Bay
RAMBLING ROSE	LAWHEAD DONALD	BOX 879684	WASILLA	AK	99687	Bristol Bay
RANSOM	GREEN GARY	7342 RAVENNA AVE NE	SEATTLE	WA	98115	Bristol Bay
RAYGIN-T	TARABOCHIA JOHN	BOX 219	WARRENTON	OR	97146	Bristol Bay
RE RIG	ASPELUND SHAWN	2540 BRANDY CIR	ANCHORAGE	AK	99516	Bristol Bay
RED ALERT	KVERNVIK KURT	BOX 1081	PETERSBURG	AK	99833	Bristol Bay
RED HOOK TOO	RED HOOK INC	11 BEACH LN	LAKEWOOD	WA	98498	Bristol Bay
RED SOCK	BRILL RONALD	8775 46TH PL W	MUKILTEO	WA	98275	Bristol Bay
REDWING	CHYTHLOOK LEON	BOX 2815	SOLDOTNA	AK	99669	Bristol Bay
REGINA B	CHAKUCHIN JOHN	695 PYROLA DR	FAIRBANKS	AK	99709	Bristol Bay
REINHOLD	CHRISTOPHER FISHERIES INC	620 W LAKE SAMISH	BELLINGHAM	WA	98229	Bristol Bay
RELENTLESS	CORRICK JEFFREY	222 DECATUR ST NW	OLYMPIA	WA	98502	Bristol Bay

Vessel	Owner	Address	City	State	Zip	Area
RENEGADE	BROWN MARY	BOX 70161	SOUTH NAKNEK	AK	99670	Bristol Bay
RENEGADE II	ANDERSEN DENNIS	2709 SKILLMAN LN	PETALUMA	CA	94952	Bristol Bay
RESTLESS	FONDSE RAYMOND	BOX 335	SILVANA	WA	98287	Bristol Bay
RETROACTIVE	BRAMAN SEAN	3381 GODFREY DR	WASILLA	AK	99654	Bristol Bay
RICHIE A	AIELLO RICHARD	500 SPENCER ST	MONTEREY	CA	93940	Bristol Bay
RICOCHET	FOX MICHAEL	3417 38TH AVE W	SEATTLE	WA	98199	Bristol Bay
RIDIN DIRTY	FREDRICK FISHERIES LLC	BOX 1711	PETERSBURG	AK	99833	Bristol Bay
RIO DE ORO	HUNSINGER WILLIAM	BOX 1237	ASTORIA	OR	97103	Bristol Bay
RIP NET	HUGHES LANCE	2780 RUBY DR	ANCHORAGE	AK	99502	Bristol Bay
RIP RUNNER	WILLIS NOLAN	444 FREDRICKS DR	ANCHORAGE	AK	99504	Bristol Bay
ROADSTER	EDLING JOHN	BOX 3487	BLAINE	WA	98321	Bristol Bay
ROBERT DEAN	ALAKAYAK NICOLAI	BOX 10	MANOKOTAK	AK	99628	Bristol Bay
ROBINE	RUDEK RANDY	15308 50TH PL W	EDMONDS	WA	98026	Bristol Bay
ROCKINROCK	NESS NORMAN	8526 WARREN DR	GIG HARBOR	WA	98335	Bristol Bay
ROSEBUD	CRICHTON JAMES	318 SUNDSTROM LN	FRIDAY HARBOR	WA	98250	Bristol Bay
ROSER	ZIELINSKI DAVE	2429 S 121ST PL	SEATTLE	WA	98168	Bristol Bay
ROUND TRIP	TARABOCHIA DANIEL	7613 ELM CT SE	OLYMPIA	WA	98503	Bristol Bay
ROZELLA JUNE	SODERLUND MICHAEL	BOX 2269	MAPLE FALLS	WA	98266	Bristol Bay
RS-76	GNYP ELBOURNE	6209 PORTAL WAY	FERNDALE	WA	98248	Bristol Bay
RS-83	SCHLAUCH MARK	1221 BOREALIS CT	FORKED RIVER	NJ	8731	Bristol Bay
RS-84	HAKALA MATTHEW	104 E PIONEER AVE	HOMER	AK	99603	Bristol Bay
RS-84	TWOMEY TIM	7535 HILLSIDE WAY	ANCHORAGE	AK	99516	Bristol Bay
RUNOUT	LYON YAKOBI	50084 MOUNTAIN GLACIER CT	HOMER	AK	99603	Bristol Bay
RUTH M	HARA KIRI FISHERIES LLC	619 BIRCH AVE	RICHLAND	WA	99352	Bristol Bay
RYNE B	KOHLHASE ERNEST	BOX 240524	DOUGLAS	AK	99824	Bristol Bay
S K	HARSILA DAVID	20103 23RD AVE NW	SHORELINE	WA	98177	Bristol Bay
SABINA	MCKEOWN JAMES	230 MEADOWSIDE DR	VERONA	WI	53593	Bristol Bay

Vessel	Owner	Address	City	State	Zip	Area
SADIE B	COURTNEY DENNIS	4854 W GLENHAVEN DR	EVERETT	WA	98203	Bristol Bay
SADIE S	SMITH CAROLYN	1600 PENNSYLVANIA AVE	ALEKNAGIK	AK	99555	Bristol Bay
SALAMATOF	HEICHEL MELINDA	11172 MICHAEL PL	BURLINGTON	WA	98233	Bristol Bay
SALLY B	QUASHNICK DAVID	92296 WILLOW RD	ASTORIA	OR	97103	Bristol Bay
SALLY JEAN II	MARBLE ERIC	11278 SAHALIE RD	LACONNER	WA	98257	Bristol Bay
SALMON LADY	BAY JACK	21 SW 148TH AVE	BEAVERTON	OR	97006	Bristol Bay
SANDRA MARIE	LOPEZ BARBARA	BOX 906	DILLINGHAM	AK	99576	Bristol Bay
SANTA ROSALIA	NIENHUIS PHILIP	3095 N HUNT RD	OAK HARBOR	WA	98277	Bristol Bay
SARAH BESS	PALMBY PHILIP	BOX 777	DEMING	WA	98244	Bristol Bay
SARAH JEAN	GEAGEL RUSSELL	BOX 4	SELDOVIA	AK	99663	Bristol Bay
SARAH LOU	VAN.ARSDEL JOSEPH	12022 FARMINGTON RD	FARMINGTON	WA	99128	Bristol Bay
SASHA VIDA	JOHNSON DANIEL	3820 GALACTICA	ANCHORAGE	AK	99517	Bristol Bay
SAVAGE	WAHL GUST	BOX 949	DILLINGHAM	AK	99576	Bristol Bay
SAVANNAH TEAL	WILSON RICHARD	BOX 237	NAKNEK	AK	99633	Bristol Bay
SAWBILL	MATTSON CRAIG	BOX 530	NASELLE	WA	98638	Bristol Bay
SAY WHEN	BAKER CHARLES	3595 SUNRISE WAY	LUMMI ISLAND	WA	98262	Bristol Bay
SCHARELL	KOETJE RICK	17587 TIFFANY WAY	MOUNT VERNON	WA	98274	Bristol Bay
SCOTFREE	BIGHAM JOSHUA	BOX 553	LOVELL	WY	82431	Bristol Bay
SEA ANN	OLSEN MARVIN	BOX 133	EGEGIK	AK	99579	Bristol Bay
SEA BREEZE	LOBO TRAVIS	BOX 142	NAKNEK	AK	99633	Bristol Bay
SEA DEUCE II	LONT PAUL	BOX 298	QUILCENE	WA	98376	Bristol Bay
SEA DOG	ROBERTS KENT	550 S 100TH W	AMERICAN FORK	UT	84003	Bristol Bay
SEA DRAGON	EUFEMIO KIM	BOX 907	KODIAK	AK	99615	Bristol Bay
SEA ELF	HEIMBUCH KARL	7055 WHITEHALL	ANCHORAGE	AK	99502	Bristol Bay
SEA FALCON	PIATT CHRIS	4765 N DOTY CIR	WASILLA	AK	99654	Bristol Bay
SEA FIRE	WHITTINGHAM TOM	1294 HARTZOG LP	NORTH POLE	AK	99705	Bristol Bay
SEA HAG	SCHWANTES LUKE	BOX 774000 PMB 153	STEAMBOAT SPRINGS	CO	80477	Bristol Bay

Vessel	Owner	Address	City	State	Zip	Area
SEA HUNTER	MARBLE CURT	11278 SAHALIE RD	LA CONNER	WA	98257	Bristol Bay
SEA HUNTER II	KNUTSON HOWARD	BOX 91456	ANCHORAGE	AK	99509	Bristol Bay
SEA JAY	JOHNSON CHRIS	2013 DENELL WAY	BOISE	ID	83709	Bristol Bay
SEA MAID	NANALOOK PETER	BOX 95	MANOKOTAK	AK	99628	Bristol Bay
SEA MASTER	OLSEN MARVIN	BOX 133	EGEGIK	AK	99579	Bristol Bay
SEA MESSENGER	SHAVINGS HENRY	3922 SCENIC VIEW DR	ANCHORAGE	AK	99504	Bristol Bay
SEA POWER	REUTOV ALIZAR	12385 PORTLAND RD	GERVAIS	OR	97026	Bristol Bay
SEA QUE	IANI RYAN	8454 SE 47TH ST	MERCER ISLAND	WA	98040	Bristol Bay
SEA RULER	REUTOV TRIFILYI	BOX 793	HOMER	AK	99603	Bristol Bay
SEA SPY	BASKOVIC ANTE	13 HILLCREST MANOR	ROLLING HILLS EST	CA	90274	Bristol Bay
SEA TOO	GARDNER JACOB	1245 RUSSELL DR	COUPEVILLE	WA	98239	Bristol Bay
SEA WORLD	BASARGIN GAVRIIL	BOX 197	HOMER	AK	99603	Bristol Bay
SEABIRD	ALEXIE POSEN	BOX 43	TOGIAK	AK	99678	Bristol Bay
SEADUCER	STANLEY BRIAN	BOX 694	CATHLAMET	WA	98612	Bristol Bay
SEAFIRST	FINNEGAN TIMOTHY	BOX 603	KING SALMON	AK	99613	Bristol Bay
SEAQUILL	NASH JAMES	236 E SHUMWAY	CAMANO ISLAND	WA	98282	Bristol Bay
SEAWOLF	HARVATH JOHN	2501 MAYLEN CIR	ANCHORAGE	AK	99516	Bristol Bay
SEAWORTHY	KALUGIN DIMITIAN	BOX 1624	HOMER	AK	99603	Bristol Bay
SEAWORTHY	NEWMAN SCOTT	BOX 1348	PETERSBURG	AK	99833	Bristol Bay
SECOND CHANCE	MCMILLAN FISHERIES INC	BOX 503	OCEAN PARK	WA	98640	Bristol Bay
SECOND WIND	MATHEWS WILLIAM	BOX 8583	KODIAK	AK	99615	Bristol Bay
SEEKER	NOSTE MARK	2167 W BEACH RD	OAK HARBOR	WA	98236	Bristol Bay
SELMA	LITTLE JOHN	807 S MOUNTAIN AVE	ASHLAND	OR	97520	Bristol Bay
SELMA ANN	POPE DARRYL	3106 EDWARDS ST	BELLINGHAM	WA	98226	Bristol Bay
SHADOW	MARTINSON DONALD	15105 59TH PL W	EDMONDS	WA	98026	Bristol Bay
SHAGPOKE	HURULA GORDON	1164 OCEAN VIEW DR	ANCHORAGE	AK	99515	Bristol Bay
SHAMELESS	ADAMS MARK	8630 CAMBRIDGE LP	BLAINE	WA	98230	Bristol Bay

Vessel	Owner	Address	City	State	Zip	Area
SHANNARA	URE THOMAS	1120 HUFFMAN RD #24	ANCHORAGE	AK	99515	Bristol Bay
SHAWN MARIE	NORTHCUTT BARRY	17530 DUNBAR RD	MOUNT VERNON	WA	98273	Bristol Bay
SHAWN S II	DOCK THOMAS	BOX 203	TOGIAK	AK	99678	Bristol Bay
SHAWNA RAE	ROTHAUS RANDY	18224 SUNSET WY	EDMONDS	WA	98026	Bristol Bay
SHEARWATER	CARNEY DANIEL	BOX 871210	WASILLA	AK	99687	Bristol Bay
SHEILA	RING ALBERT	BOX 74	NAKNEK	AK	99633	Bristol Bay
SHERIE	CHEVALIER CHARLES	BOX 444	FRIDAY HARBOR	WA	98250	Bristol Bay
SHERMANATOR	VITA FISHERIES	1445 NW 56TH ST	SEATTLE	WA	98107	Bristol Bay
SHERYL LORENE	WASSILLIE TERRY	BOX 14	ILIAMNA	AK	99606	Bristol Bay
SHILLELAGH	CASSIDY ANDY	520 LYLA LN	BELLINGHAM	WA	98225	Bristol Bay
SHITTLE BUFF OUT	WERMERS ZACH	122 WHEELER MTN WAY	GALLATIN GATEWAY	MT	59730	Bristol Bay
SHODAN	OVERBY, TODD & LORI	7910 56TH AVE CT NW	GIG HARBOR	WA	98335	Bristol Bay
SHOONKIE	KINGSLEY RUSSELL	BOX 447	PILOT POINT	AK	99649	Bristol Bay
SHRIKE	EDSON JON	19808 PARSONS CK RD	SEDRO WOOLLEY	WA	98284	Bristol Bay
SIERRAN	JOHNSON RONALD	12022 275TH AVE SE	MONROE	WA	98272	Bristol Bay
SILENT PARTNER	HASTINGS DANIEL	BOX 3324	SOLDOTNA	AK	99669	Bristol Bay
SILENT PARTNER	HASTINGS LLC	BOX 3324	SOLDOTNA	AK	99669	Bristol Bay
SILVER BAY	EDVARDSEN MARK	18622 126TH ST SE	SNOHOMISH	WA	98290	Bristol Bay
SILVER BOUNTY	ANDERSON GLENN	920 ALDER ST	EDMONDS	WA	98020	Bristol Bay
SILVER BULLET	BACKMAN GARY	301 E BIRNIE SLOUGH RD	CATHLAMET	WA	98612	Bristol Bay
SILVER BULLET	HATCH BRYCE	3143 WILLOW CT	TWIN FALLS	ID	83301	Bristol Bay
SILVER BULLET	KONUKPEOK NORTON	BOX 172	NEW STUYAHOK	AK	99636	Bristol Bay
SILVER GULL	GULL DANIEL	BOX 395	FRENCHTOWN	MT	59834	Bristol Bay
SILVER KING	KING WILDON	BOX 1164	PALMER	AK	99645	Bristol Bay
SILVER LAND	NELSON FRED	GEN DEL	KOLIGANEK	AK	99576	Bristol Bay
SILVER MIST	OGREN BRUCE	BOX 214	SOUTH BEND	WA	98586	Bristol Bay
SILVER SEA	HELLER BRETT	17712 NE 189TH ST	BRUSH PRAIRIE	WA	98606	Bristol Bay
SILVER SIDE	BLUE BREAK LLC	815 RAMONA AVE	SPRING VALLEY	CA	91977	Bristol Bay

Vessel	Owner	Address	City	State	Zip	Area
SILVER SPOON	CARR MICHAEL	BOX 804	PORT TOWNSEND	WA	98368	Bristol Bay
SILVER SPOON	SILVER SPOON LLC	4461 OLD GARDINER RD	PORT TOWNSEND	WA	98368	Bristol Bay
SILVER VIKING	EDVARDSEN EGIL	BOX 4377	SOUTH COLBY	WA	98384	Bristol Bay
SILVERBOW	BUERGER JOHN	BOX 210846	AUKE BAY	AK	99821	Bristol Bay
SINBAD	NOSTE PAUL	1849 VALLEY VIEW DR	MOUNT VERNON	WA	98273	Bristol Bay
SINNER	LUTZ KEITH	7812 HUETTER CT SW	OLYMPIA	WA	98512	Bristol Bay
SIS VERA	ANDREW WASSILLIE	BOX 92	NEW STUYAHOK	AK	99636	Bristol Bay
SLAM DUNK	BARR DAN	2408 NOB HILL AVE N	SEATTLE	WA	98109	Bristol Bay
SLEEP ROBBER	GARDNER WILLIAM	2611 NW 54TH	SEATTLE	WA	98107	Bristol Bay
SLEEP ROBBER	JENSEN JEFFEREY	BOX 770955	EAGLE RIVER	AK	99577	Bristol Bay
SLIM	BREKKAA STAALE	17403 5TH AVE W	BOTHELL	WA	98012	Bristol Bay
SLUICEBOX	SCHAAD KONRAD	53200 N MCNEIL PT	HOMER	AK	99603	Bristol Bay
SMITH POINT	JOHNSON THOMAS	90222 YOUNG RIVER RD	ASTORIA	OR	97103	Bristol Bay
SNOOKIE	PSTROSS TOMAS	BOX 2614	CORDOVA	AK	99574	Bristol Bay
SNOWFLAKE	HATCH GRANT	939 16TH ST	CLARKSTON	WA	99403	Bristol Bay
SOCKEYE	ALBERT BRYAN	2831 WILEY POST	ANCHORAGE	AK	99517	Bristol Bay
SOFIA	WELLS JAMES	40969 GRAND VIEW RD	ASTORIA	OR	97103	Bristol Bay
SOLUS TOO	SEA Q INC	6363 S ZIMMERMAN RD	AURORA	OR	97002	Bristol Bay
SONIC	BERG GUNNAR	201 NORMAN ST	KENAI	AK	99611	Bristol Bay
SONJA ANN	ARDUSER RANDY	BOX 110833	ANCHORAGE	AK	99511	Bristol Bay
SONOVA BEACH	JOHNSON JOHN	BOX 2678	PALMER	AK	99645	Bristol Bay
SOPHIE IRENE II	CARL LAWRENCE	BOX 171	KIPNUK	AK	99614	Bristol Bay
SOUL RIDER	MARTUSHEV MIHAEL	40929 HUNTLEY RD	STAYTON	OR	97383	Bristol Bay
SOUND AND FURY	LEBOVIC ROBERT	257 RIVERVIEW DR	ASHEVILLE	NC	28806	Bristol Bay
SPECIAL K	ALIOTTI JOSEPH	BOX 3325	MONTEREY	CA	93942	Bristol Bay
SPIRIT	MIKKELSEN TIMOTHY	1260 N RAINBOW PARK DR	WASILLA	AK	99654	Bristol Bay
SPRIG III	HAGGARD RENETTA	2951 S BANK CIR	WASILLA	AK	99654	Bristol Bay

Vessel	Owner	Address	City	State	Zip	Area
ST BRENDAN	MARDESICH ANTHONY	5101 GUEMES ISLAND RD	ANACORTES	WA	98221	Bristol Bay
ST CHARLIETT	DANIELS C. PATRICK	429 COVE RD	BELLINGHAM	WA	98229	Bristol Bay
ST ELMO	CHEVALIER MATTHEW	169 TERRACE DR	FRIDAY HARBOR	WA	98250	Bristol Bay
ST GABRIEL	PAUK WILLIAM	BOX 36	MANOKOTAK	AK	99628	Bristol Bay
ST GABRIEL	TIM DAVID	BOX 37003	TOKSOOK BAY	AK	99637	Bristol Bay
ST JOHN	MAY AARON	1897 L ST #8	KODIAK	AK	99615	Bristol Bay
ST JOSEPHINE	HARMAN THOMAS	16131 BLACK BEAR DR	ANCHORAGE	AK	99516	Bristol Bay
ST VINCENT	SORENSON CHAD	320 BANNER LN #3	SOLDOTNA	AK	99669	Bristol Bay
ST. ELIAS	STONE VINCE	2711 GRAND AVE	EVERETT	WA	98201	Bristol Bay
STACI MARY	AITI SAMUEL	BOX 42	KWIGILLINGOK	AK	99622	Bristol Bay
STAG BAY	BELLAMY RAYMOND	62084 SKY LINE DR	HOMER	AK	99603	Bristol Bay
STAR LIGHT	COOPCHIAK BOBBY	BOX 181	TOGIAK	AK	99678	Bristol Bay
STARDUST	RASMUSSEN ROY	12332 19TH AVE SE	EVERETT	WA	98204	Bristol Bay
STARSHIP	KNIGHT JOHN	BOX 1133	PETERSBURG	AK	99833	Bristol Bay
STEINBIT	LEWIS STEVEN	2606 W 30TH AVE #B	ANCHORAGE	AK	99517	Bristol Bay
STELLA MICHAEL	JIMMIE ALEXIE	BOX 37127	TOKSOOK BAY	AK	99637	Bristol Bay
STEPHANIE ANN	ARKANAKYAK RACHEL	BOX 85	TOGIAK	AK	99678	Bristol Bay
STEVIE K	GIBBONS WARREN	430 PARKRIDGE RD	BELLINGHAM	WA	98225	Bristol Bay
STILLWATER	BANGS MICHAEL	BOX 1733	PETERSBURG	AK	99833	Bristol Bay
STINA	OCEAN RUN SEAFOODS INC	7710 S 106TH	SEATTLE	WA	98178	Bristol Bay
STINGRAY	YOUNG RIVER FISHERIES INC	90222 YOUNGS RIVER RD	ASTORIA	OR	97103	Bristol Bay
STORM CREST	PHILLIPS ALBERT	80610 WAGON WHEEL LP	IRRIGON	OR	97844	Bristol Bay
STORMY	ZUANICH NICHOLAS	BOX 2249	MAPLE FALLS	WA	98226	Bristol Bay
STUBBY	ENGBRETSON BRIAN	81008 HWY 202	JEWELL	OR	97138	Bristol Bay
SUMO	MCDOWELL CHRIS	2207 RADCLIFFE RD	JUNEAU	AK	99801	Bristol Bay
SUN WING	MJM INVESTMENTS INC	11753 SUNRISE DR NE	BAINBRIDGE ISLAND	WA	98110	Bristol Bay
SUNDANCE	BRUNO STEVEN	BOX 1054	CARMEL VALLEY	CA	93924	Bristol Bay

Vessel	Owner	Address	City	State	Zip	Area
SUNDOWNER	BRITO DUSTIN	BOX 1461	DILLINGHAM	AK	99576	Bristol Bay
SUNLIGHT III	MARINKOVICH MATTHEW	BOX 2084	FRIDAY HARBOR	WA	98250	Bristol Bay
SUNLIGHT IV	KOTLAR LEONARDO	4136 MERIDIAN N	SEATTLE	WA	98103	Bristol Bay
SUPER SPORT	NASH WILLIAM	BOX 2352	FRIDAY HARBOR	WA	98250	Bristol Bay
SURGE BAY	BUYS MURRAY	11201 MEYERS LN	LIVE OAK VALLEY	CA	95953	Bristol Bay
SURRENDER	NIVER MARK	955 LOCHNESS CT	WASILLA	AK	99654	Bristol Bay
SUSAN MARIE	SEABERG ERIC	15632 VIRGINIA POINT RD	POULSBO	WA	98370	Bristol Bay
SUSIE	PIATT MATTHEW	4100 PALMDALE DR	WASILLA	AK	99654	Bristol Bay
SUSIE G	TALLEKPALEK GUSTIE	BOX 16	LEVELOCK	AK	99625	Bristol Bay
SUSQUEHANNA	JOHNSON NICK	BOX 5048	KOLIGANEK	AK	99576	Bristol Bay
SUTHERLAND	OGLE JOHN	3705 ARCTIC BLVD #902	ANCHORAGE	AK	99503	Bristol Bay
SUZANNE C	TINKER NICHOLAS	BOX 26	ALEKNAGIK	AK	99555	Bristol Bay
SZENTA	CAPRI, REX & THERESA	255 NW 17TH ST	NEWPORT	OR	97365	Bristol Bay
T & T	ARNESTAD JOHN	4907 RUCKER	EVERETT	WA	98203	Bristol Bay
TAKU	KREIDER GARY	4829 OUTRIGGER LP	BLAINE	WA	98230	Bristol Bay
TALLAC	PERATA BACCI	BOX 15	EGEGIK	AK	99579	Bristol Bay
TALLY	DAVIS MICHAEL	BOX 155	DILLINGHAM	AK	99576	Bristol Bay
TAMI LEE	HEICHEL JERRY	1417 SUNDAY LAKE RD	STANWOOD	WA	98292	Bristol Bay
TANQUERAY	TANQUERAY	92732 FERNHILL RD	ASTORIA	OR	97103	Bristol Bay
TANQUERAY	WREN JOHN	8515 148TH ST COURT E	PUYALLUP	WA	98375	Bristol Bay
TARA	FLENSBURG GEORGE	BOX 77	DILLINGHAM	AK	99576	Bristol Bay
TARA MARIE	TARABOCHIA BRIAN	538 MCCLURE AVE	ASTORIA	OR	97103	Bristol Bay
TASK FORCE	HANSEN DAVID	BOX 1043	BELLINGHAM	WA	98227	Bristol Bay
TEDDY TERESA	MOSES CHARLES	BOX 37125	TOKSOOK BAY	AK	99637	Bristol Bay
TEMPEST	HOY GUY	3563 BRECKENRIDGE RD	EVERSON	WA	98247	Bristol Bay
TEN	CARPENTER CHARLES	4739 MERMONT PL	EVERETT	WA	98203	Bristol Bay

Vessel	Owner	Address	City	State	Zip	Area
TETER-TOTTER	GORMAN JASON	1369 JACKSON DR	ANCHORAGE	AK	99518	Bristol Bay
TETONIAN	MESAK THOMAS	BOX 176	KIPNUK	AK	99614	Bristol Bay
THE DRIFTER	SEYMOUR SHILOH	996 HILLFAIR CT	HOMER	AK	99603	Bristol Bay
THE GREAT RUBY	GREAT RUBY LLC	N 8986 SPRINGBROOK RD RIPON		WI	54971	Bristol Bay
THE ULTIMATE	SIFSOF VICTOR	BOX 815	DILLINGHAM	AK	99576	Bristol Bay
THE VIXEN	REYNOLDS THOMAS	BOX 246	CORTEZ	FL	34215	Bristol Bay
THREE COUSINS	BARTLETT DENNIS	BOX 876819	WASILLA	AK	99687	Bristol Bay
THUNDER BAY	KUMMER JERRET	BOX 1522	WESTPORT	WA	98595	Bristol Bay
TIANNA SEA	LIND KONAN	BOX 49071	PORT HEIDEN	AK	99549	Bristol Bay
TIDE RIP	FISCHER HENRY	BOX 526	NAKNEK	AK	99633	Bristol Bay
TIERA - NICOLE	SCHROEDER HUGH	BOX 102	DILLINGHAM	AK	99576	Bristol Bay
TIGER II	MCKEE MARC	690 BRICKYARD BLVD	SEDRO WOOLLEY	WA	98284	Bristol Bay
TIGGER	WEST JASON	2 EAST RD	CATHLAMET	WA	98612	Bristol Bay
TIMBER COUNTRY	NYGAARD DAVID	201 W IRVING	ASTORIA	OR	97103	Bristol Bay
TINA	LACHELT GENE	546 EMBASSY CIR	HENDERSON	NV	89015	Bristol Bay
TONANO	HUDDLESTON ERIC	89504 DELLMOOR LP	WARRENTON	OR	97146	Bristol Bay
TONI MARIE	ONGARO MICHAEL	20645 10TH PL SW	NORMANDY PARK	WA	98166	Bristol Bay
TORA	JOHNSON ROGER	43 RACE LN	ABERDEEN	WA	98520	Bristol Bay
TOURIST	TOURIST	BOX 762	MOUNT ANGEL	OR	97362	Bristol Bay
TRACY B	BENSON TERRY	64 KILLAPIE BEACH RD	PORT LUDLOW	WA	98365	Bristol Bay
TRANSPORTER	BASARGIN BORIS	BOX 1709	HOMER	AK	99603	Bristol Bay
TRANSPORTER	HOFFMAN RONALD	3418 UPLAND	ANCHORAGE	AK	99504	Bristol Bay
TRAVIS G	GLOKO FRANK	BOX 52	MANOKOTAK	AK	99628	Bristol Bay
TRIPLE B	BOUKER JOHN	BOX 1135	DILLINGHAM	AK	99576	Bristol Bay
TRISHA MARIE	FRANK WILLIE	BOX 8021	TUNTUTULIAK	AK	99680	Bristol Bay
TRITON	HAMBURG DAVID	9010 202ND PL SW	EDMONDS	WA	98026	Bristol Bay
TRI-UMPH	VUKAS JOHN	32209 7TH AVE SW	FEDERAL WAY	WA	98023	Bristol Bay

Vessel	Owner	Address	City	State	Zip	Area
TRUE NORTH	UTT MICHAEL	BOX 22200	SEATTLE	WA	98122	Bristol Bay
TSELANE SHERIE	ANGASAN VAL	BOX 1389	DILLINGHAM	AK	99576	Bristol Bay
TULUK	WALKER LOGAN	BOX 13	CLARKS POINT	AK	99569	Bristol Bay
TURBULENCE	WYMAN JOHN	4822 S GRAHAM ST	SEATTLE	WA	98118	Bristol Bay
TURN PT	NASH CHARLES	460 HARRISON ST	FRIDAY HARBOR	WA	98250	Bristol Bay
TUSK	STENBERG LUTHER	2430 20TH CT NE	OLYMPIA	WA	98506	Bristol Bay
TWO BROTHERS	COSTA GIUSEPPE	22 VIA DEL REY	MONTEREY	CA	93940	Bristol Bay
TWYLA DAWN	ANDREW JOHN	BOX 57	MANOKOTAK	AK	99628	Bristol Bay
TYONE	PERRY ALAN	BOX 1447	SOLDOTNA	AK	99669	Bristol Bay
U-8	PHILLIPS JOHN	BOX 3650	HAILEY	ID	83333	Bristol Bay
UNBELIEVABLE	MERCURIO SAM	1007 HELLAM ST	MONTEREY	CA	93940	Bristol Bay
UNCLE EINAR	ROCKNESS NORMAN	8526 WARREN DR	GIG HARBOR	WA	98335	Bristol Bay
UNCLE FRITZ	MANCUSO RALPH	BOX 181	NAKNEK	AK	99633	Bristol Bay
UNITED	VELSKO ERIK	780 DAYBREEZE CT	HOMER	AK	99603	Bristol Bay
UTNAPISHNUM	MULLINS DANIEL	131 N HAWTHORNE RD	DULUTH	MN	55812	Bristol Bay
UTOPIA II	BENTON J.SCOTT	108 MT ETNA DR	CLAYTON	CA	94517	Bristol Bay
VALLESTAD	WILLIAMS RICKEY	BOX 1321	PETERSBURG	AK	99833	Bristol Bay
VALI	THORNTON JOE	BOX 81532	FAIRBANKS	AK	99708	Bristol Bay
VELUX	ROSS WILLIAM	BOX 153	EGEGIK	AK	99579	Bristol Bay
VENTURE	JOLMA BRUCE	460 NE ALDER ST	CLATSKANIE	OR	97016	Bristol Bay
VERNON PAUL	JOHN SIMEON	BOX 37051	TOKSOOK BAY	AK	99637	Bristol Bay
VICKI K	OUTLAW INC	BOX 312	CATHLAMET	WA	98612	Bristol Bay
VIKING	BERTELSEN STEVE	1801 NAGLER RD	SELAH	WA	98942	Bristol Bay
VIKING SPIRIT	PETERSON GREG	8302 FREDERICK PL	EDMONDS	WA	98026	Bristol Bay
VORTEX	STEVENS ERICK	5762 STORR RD	FERNDALE	WA	98248	Bristol Bay
WARP-1	MARTINSEN MARC	404 E MAIN	SHERIDAN	OR	97378	Bristol Bay
WARRIOR	BENTON DANIEL	2111 E 37TH	ANCHORAGE	AK	99508	Bristol Bay

Vessel	Owner	Address	City	State	Zip	Area
WASALISA	LEUTHE CRAIG	3921 BRYANT RIDGE PL	ANCHORAGE	AK	99504	Bristol Bay
WATERMEN	GUFFEY SEAN	11245 ST RT E	ROLLA	MO	65401	Bristol Bay
WENDYS WEATHER	WHITEMAN JOHN	BOX 31776	BELLINGHAM	WA	98228	Bristol Bay
WESTERN FLYER	GLEGOR NICK	91981 GEORGE HILL RD	ASTORIA	OR	97103	Bristol Bay
WHIPPING POST	MARIFERN BRUCE	BOX 917	PETERSBURG	AK	99833	Bristol Bay
WHISKEY CREEK	CHILDERS JOSEPH	BOX 210522	AUKE BAY	AK	99821	Bristol Bay
WHITE CAINE	HOUGHTON RANDALL	2576 E LILLY DR	COEUR D'ALENE	ID	83814	Bristol Bay
WILD BUFFALO	GNYP ELLIS	5456 NW RD	BELLINGHAM	WA	98226	Bristol Bay
WILD GOOSE II	KINK MITCHELL	700 14TH ST	BELLINGHAM	WA	98225	Bristol Bay
WILD WIZARD	MULLEN BRYAN	36508 SE 25TH ST	FALL CITY	WA	98024	Bristol Bay
WILLAWAW	MITCHELL STEVEN	BOX 471	CLINTON	WA	98236	Bristol Bay
WINDSONG	HOUSLEY LAWRENCE	612 MCFADDENS TR	EAGAN	MN	55123	Bristol Bay
WINTER BLUES	IVY DAVID	BOX 2219	HOMER	AK	99603	Bristol Bay
WIZARD	BEISHLINE DANIEL	BOX 211447	AUKE BAY	AK	99821	Bristol Bay
WRANGLER	WREN CHARLES	85589 HWY 339	MILTON FREEWATER	OR	97862	Bristol Bay
YUKON	MARTUSHEV FEOKTIST	BOX 1765	HOMER	AK	99603	Bristol Bay
YUPIK	OLSON HJALMAR	BOX 456	DILLINGHAM	AK	99576	Bristol Bay
ZEPHYR	SAARHEIM AMIE	36608 VALLEY VISTA LN	ASTORIA	OR	97103	Bristol Bay
ZOLA BUDD	WIEBE MATTHEW	369 MONTEZUMA ST #248	SANTA FE	NM	87501	Bristol Bay

Appendix 6
Purse Seiners, Salmon

Vessel	Owner	Address	City	State	Zip	Area
LOGANS ARK Bay	HUBERT KIM	17636 TEKLANIKA DR	EAGLE RIVER	AK	99577	Bristol
ABSOLUT	OLSEN INVESTMENT INC	215 NW 198TH ST	SHORELINE	WA	98177	Chignik
ADVENTURESS	GRUNERT CLEMENS	BOX 28	CHIGNIK LAGOON	AK	99565	Chignik
ALASKA ROSE	ANDERSON BILLY	BOX 12	CHIGNIK	AK	99564	Chignik
ALEUT SISTERS	LIND JOHNNY	BOX 4	CHIGNIK LAKE	AK	99548	Chignik
ALEUT SISTERS 2	LIND JOHNNY	BOX 4	CHIGNIK LAKE	AK	99548	Chignik
ALEUTIAN VENTURE	GRUNERT CLEMENS	BOX 28	CHIGNIK LAGOON	AK	99565	Chignik
ALEXANDRIA	BRANDAL ALEC	BOX 170	CHIGNIK LAGOON	AK	99565	Chignik
ALICE A	ANDERSON HAROLD	2101 TUDOR HILLS CT	ANCHORAGE	AK	99507	Chignik
ALRENICE	ANDERSON H.GARY	BOX 47	CHIGNIK LAGOON	AK	99565	Chignik
AMY RAE	SKONBERG MINNIE	BOX 5	CHIGNIK	AK	99564	Chignik
ANTOINETTE RENEE	GREGORIO TONY	BOX 24	CHIGNIK LAGOON	AK	99565	Chignik
BAY VIEW	SHANGIN STEPHEN	10308 THIMBLEBERRY DR	ANCHORAGE	AK	99515	Chignik
CAPT'N JAY	ALEXANDER JASON	18315 87TH AVE SE	SNOHOMISH	WA	98296	Chignik
CHRISTINA J	FV NOMAD INC	BOX 30	CHIGNIK LAGOON	AK	99565	Chignik
CHRISTINE K	KASHEVAROF WILLIAM	4810 W 88TH AVE	ANCHORAGE	AK	99502	Chignik
CRYSTAL SEA	SHANGIN EDGAR	5531 RABBIT CR RD	ANCHORAGE	AK	99516	Chignik
DESIDERATA	LIND MITCHELL	320 LAKEVIEW DR	CHIGNIK LAKE	AK	99548	Chignik
ELLA-MAE	ODOMIN NICK	8850 CORDELL CR #3	ANCHORAGE	AK	99502	Chignik
ENDURANCE	ANDERSON RODNEY	BOX 188	CHIGNIK LAGOON	AK	99565	Chignik
GEOJ	JOHNSON PAUL	102 SHIPYARD RD	DECATUR ISLAND	WA	98221	Chignik
HEIDI LINEA	OLSEN KNUD	215 NW 198TH ST	SHORELINE	WA	98177	Chignik
KADIAK	JONES MORRIS	100 SHIPYARD RD	DECATUR ISLAND	WA	98221	Chignik
KARMA	LOUNSBURY BRETT	BOX 8947	KODIAK	AK	99615	Chignik
KIMBERLY	CARLSON ERNEST	BOX 21	CHIGNIK	AK	99564	Chignik
KIMBERLY DAWN	BUMPUS DONALD	BOX 167	CHIGNIK LAGOON	AK	99565	Chignik

Vessel	Owner	Address	City	State	Zip	Area
KURT ELDON	GRUNERT FRANK	BOX 17	CHIGNIK LAGOON	AK	99565	Chignik
LADY EVELYN	KOSBRUK PATRICK	BOX 110	PERRYVILLE	AK	99648	Chignik
LAURA JUNE	STEPANOFF ANDREW	BOX 11	CHIGNIK LAGOON	AK	99565	Chignik
LAURA JUNE	STEPANOFF ANDREW	BOX 11	CHIGNIK LAGOON	AK	99565	Chignik
LISA MARIE	LIND ELLIOT	BOX 48001	CHIGNIK LAKE	AK	99548	Chignik
LITTLE DI	CARLSON DALE	BOX 3	CHIGNIK	AK	99564	Chignik
MACKENZIE	CARLSON EUGENE	43633 SE 147TH LN	NORTH BEND	WA	98045	Chignik
MEMRY ANNE	SIERRA GALE FISHERIES INC	BOX 41	CHIGNIK LAGOON	AK	99565	Chignik
MICHELLE LEE	ORLOFF GEORGE	BOX 747	SEWARD	AK	99664	Chignik
MIDNIGHT SUN	ERICKSON CLARENCE	BOX 61	CHIGNIK LAGOON	AK	99565	Chignik
MISS ANGELINA	SHANGIN EDGAR	5531 RABBIT CR RD	ANCHORAGE	AK	99516	Chignik
MISS CLEMENTINE	SHANGIN CLEMENT	BOX 96	PERRYVILLE	AK	99648	Chignik
MUTINY	MORGAN JERRY	PMB 137 205 E DIMOND	ANCHORAGE	AK	99515	Chignik
MYLIA LYNN	KOPUN AXEL	16435 NICOLI WAY	EAGLE RIVER	AK	99577	Chignik
NORTHWIND	YAGIE JERRY	BOX 143242	ANCHORAGE	AK	99514	Chignik
PATTI ANN	ANDERSON DEAN	BOX 41	CHIGNIK LAGOON	AK	99565	Chignik
POWER	OLSEN INVESTMENT INC	215 NW 198TH ST	SHORELINE	WA	98177	Chignik
RAYMAR	ANDERSON EUGENE	BOX 87	SEWARD	AK	99664	Chignik
ROBYN	TALLERICO FRANK	4071 SAN PABLO DAM RD #305	EL SABRANTE	CA	94803	Chignik
SEAN CURTIS	ALEXANDER JASON	18315 87TH AVE SE	SNOHOMISH	WA	98296	Chignik
STELLOR	SUYDAM LOWELL	BOX 266	SELDOVIA	AK	99663	Chignik
TAJAHA	CARLSON DALE	BOX 3	CHIGNIK	AK	99564	Chignik
TEENER	KASHEVAROF WILLIAM	4810 W 88TH AVE	ANCHORAGE	AK	99502	Chignik
THUNDERBOLT	MORGAN JERRY	PMB 137 205 E DIMOND	ANCHORAGE	AK	99515	Chignik
VENTURE	ANDERSON AARON	BOX 43	CHIGNIK LAGOON	AK	99565	Chignik
AARON C	CARLSON CARL	BOX 2678	KODIAK	AK	99615	Chignik
ALASKAN FRONTIER	ABOUEID ALFREDO	BOX 26	CHIGNIK LAGOON	AK	99565	Chignik

Vessel	Owner	Address	City	State	Zip	Area
ALPEN GLOW	MACALUSO MICHAEL	BOX 2901	HOMER	AK	99603	Chignik
ALYSA JUNE	ANDERSON AL	BOX 10	CHIGNIK LAGOON	AK	99565	Chignik
CAPT'N SAM	GRUNERT MICHAEL	BOX 187	CHIGNIK LAGOON	AK	99565	Chignik
CARMALEE	SKONBERG BERNARD	BOX 15	CHIGNIK BAY	AK	99564	Chignik
COMMITMENT	ROWLAND ROGER	BOX 393	UNALASKA	AK	99685	Chignik
CRIMSON BEAUTY	SUYDAM STEVEN	BOX 987	KODIAK	AK	99615	Chignik
DESERT STORM	KALMAKOFF ARCHIE	BOX 69	PERRYVILLE	AK	99648	Chignik
DESPERADO	CARLSON ERNEST	BOX 21	CHIGNIK	AK	99564	Chignik
DOROTHY-M	MCKILLY GABRIEL	BOX 24	CHIGNIK	AK	99564	Chignik
GYPSY LADY	ANDERSON DAVID	BOX 5	CHIGNIK LAGOON	AK	99565	Chignik
ILLUSION	HINDERER WALLACE	BOX 13	CHIGNIK	AK	99564	Chignik
ISLANDER	JONES MORRIS	100 SHIPYARD RD	DECATUR ISLAND	WA	98221	Chignik
KEOKIE	ANDERSON GEORGE	2101 TUDOR HILLS CT	ANCHORAGE	AK	99507	Chignik
KIMBERLY	KOPUN ALOYS	BOX 74	CHIGNIK	AK	99564	Chignik
MIDGET MAID	CARLSON ERNEST	BOX 21	CHIGNIK	AK	99564	Chignik
MIRANDA LEIGH	SHANGIN DENNIS	203 CREST DR	SOLDOTNA	AK	99669	Chignik
OCEAN SPRAY	KALMAKOFF HARVEY	BOX 133	PERRYVILLE	AK	99648	Chignik
RAECHEL LOUISE	HINDERER WALLACE	BOX 13	CHIGNIK	AK	99564	Chignik
ROSALIE	SKONBERG CALVIN	BOX 2572	KODIAK	AK	99615	Chignik
SHARON ANN	FV SHARON ANN	BOX 72	CHIGNIK LAGOON	AK	99565	Chignik
SHARON DAWN	SHANGIN ANDY	BOX 116	PERRYVILLE	AK	99648	Chignik
SHARON LEE	ERICKSON CLARENCE	12119 263RD AVE NE	MONROE	WA	98275	Chignik
SPECTRE	WILKIE TIM	BOX 1726	SEWARD	AK	99664	Chignik
ZACHERY J	JONES JOHN	BOX 149	CHIGNIK LAGOON	AK	99565	Chignik

179

Vessel	Owner	Address	City	State	Zip	Area
ANNIE E	EJ JONES MORGAN	BOX 1044	HOMER	AK	99603	Cook Inlet
AQALEIT'	BRUDIE PHILIP	BOX 111	HOMER	AK	99603	Cook Inlet
BOUNCER	ROTH MARK	BOX 2008	HOMER	AK	99603	Cook Inlet
CADDIE	BRUDIE PHILIP	BOX 111	HOMER	AK	99603	Cook Inlet
CAPE NINILCHIK	EJ JONES MORGAN	BOX 1044	HOMER	AK	99603	Cook Inlet
CAPE PEIRCE	NUKA POINT FISHERIES INC	BOX 130	HOMER	AK	99603	Cook Inlet
DIABLO	PERRY CHRISTOPHER	BOX 1808	HOMER	AK	99603	Cook Inlet
DINERO	SPRINGER MATTHEW	BOX 2882	HOMER	AK	99603	Cook Inlet
DOUGLAS RIVER	CARROLL ALBERT	55090 BENJAMIN AVE #1	HOMER	AK	99603	Cook Inlet
FISH ASSASSIN	WISE PARTNERS	1930 EAST END RD #A	HOMER	AK	99603	Cook Inlet
GNAT	NUKA POINT FISHERIES INC	BOX 130	HOMER	AK	99603	Cook Inlet
GROG	COTTEN SAM	BOX 6405	HALIBUT COVE	AK	99603	Cook Inlet
GROO	COTTEN SAM	BOX 6405	HALIBUT COVE	AK	99603	Cook Inlet
INLET KAT	NELSON ROBERT	BOX 205	KASILOF	AK	99610	Cook Inlet
ISLAND GIRL	COTTEN SAM	BOX 6405	HALIBUT COVE	AK	99603	Cook Inlet
IVY LYNN	WALKDEN CHARLES	BOX 2017	HOMER	AK	99603	Cook Inlet
J R	CABANA JEFFERY	BOX 26	HOMER	AK	99610	Cook Inlet
JAEGER	MCELROY PATRICK	BOX 456	KASILOF	AK	99603	Cook Inlet
KILLIN TIME	PERRY CHRISTOPHER	BOX 1808	HOMER	AK	99603	Cook Inlet
KIRSHNER	CABANA LEROY	BOX 49	HOMER	AK	99603	Cook Inlet
LITTLE STAR	ROTH MARK	BOX 2008	HOMER	AK	99603	Cook Inlet
MALLARD MAID	WINSLOW ERIC	203 S VIRGINA AVE	SANFORD	FL	32771	Cook Inlet
MARATHON	ADVANCE NORTH LLC	2220 NORTH STAR #7	ANCHORAGE	AK	99503	Cook Inlet
MELISSA B	BUCHANAN THOMAS	BOX 821	SEWARD	AK	99664	Cook Inlet
MYA	WALKDEN CHARLES	BOX 2017	HOMER	AK	99603	Cook Inlet
NAHANI	NELSON THOMAS	BOX 1392	HOMER	AK	99603	Cook Inlet
NORTH STAR	ROTH PAUL	1011 SYCAMORE CR DR	JONESBOROUGH	TN	37659	Cook Inlet

Vessel	Owner	Address	City	State	Zip	Area
RHINO	GOLDEN JEFFREY	8322 SILVER LAKE RD	MAPLE FALLS	WA	98266	Cook Inlet
SCAT	NELSON ROBERT	BOX 205	KASILOF	AK	99610	Cook Inlet
SCOOTER	BUCHANAN THOMAS	BOX 925	SEWARD	AK	99664	Cook Inlet
SEA MAID	COTTEN SAM	BOX 6405	HALIBUT COVE	AK	99603	Cook Inlet
SILVER BULLIT	CAMELOT LTD	3733 BEN WALTERS LN #2	HOMER	AK	99603	Cook Inlet
SPIT BALL	CARROLL ALBERT	55090 BENJAMIN AVE #1	HOMER	AK	99603	Cook Inlet
STAR LIGHT	ALASKA STAR FLEET LLC	BOX 2008	HOMER	AK	99603	Cook Inlet
STAR WIND	ROTH ROBERT	BOX 1314	ANCHOR POINT	AK	99556	Cook Inlet
STARDUST	ROTH MARK	BOX 2008	HOMER	AK	99603	Cook Inlet
STINGER	HALPIN KENNETH	BOX 1022	HOMER	AK	99603	Cook Inlet
SUNDOG	MOSS CHRISTOPHER	BOX 1115	HOMER	AK	99603	Cook Inlet
TORQUE	CABANA JEFFERY	BOX 26	HOMER	AK	99603	Cook Inlet
C'RAINE	MOSS ROBERT	BOX 3428	HOMER	AK	99603	Cook Inlet
DOLLY B	BUCHANAN THOMAS	BOX 925	SEWARD	AK	99664	Cook Inlet
DOROLEE	CABANA LARRY	BOX 3388	HOMER	AK	99603	Cook Inlet
HANTA YO	MCDONALD TIMOTHY	BOX 25	SEWARD	AK	99664	Cook Inlet
INTERCEPTOR	NORMAN WAYNE	BOX 5546	PORT GRAHAM	AK	99603	Cook Inlet
MARANATHA	WINSLOW ERIC	203 S VIRGINA AVE	SANFORD	FL	32771	Cook Inlet
SILVER STREAK	WISE PARTNERS	1930 EAST END RD #A	HOMER	AK	99603	Cook Inlet
MITZI BEE	BLOSSOM DOUGLAS	BOX 289	CLAM GULCH	AK	99568	Cook Inlet
ALASKA LADY	NELSON THOMAS	BOX 101	PORT LIONS	AK	99550	Kodiak
ALCHEMIST	MANN DAVID	392 SUDDEN VALLEY	BELLINGHAM	WA	98229	Kodiak
ALPINE GIRL	JOHNSON CHARLES	4912 EAGLE PL	HOMER	AK	99603	Kodiak
ANNA MARIA	BRUDIE PHILIP	BOX 111	HOMER	AK	99603	Kodiak
ARCTIC MIST	MAGNUSEN CHRIS	BOX 516	KODIAK	AK	99615	Kodiak
ASHTEN MARIE	SCHAUFF WILLIAM	BOX 8774	KODIAK	AK	99615	Kodiak
BEACH MASTER	LINDSEY ROBERT	3162 SPRUCE CAPE RD	KODIAK	AK	99615	Kodiak

Vessel	Owner	Address	City	State	Zip	Area
BEAR PAW II	SCHAUFF CRAIG	BOX 8400	KODIAK	AK	99615	Kodiak
BELLAVANCE 22	FIELDS WALLACE	BOX 1691	KODIAK	AK	99615	Kodiak
BEVERLEE J	HENSON JON	BOX 176	KODIAK	AK	99615	Kodiak
BIG LOU	RISLEY RODNEY	3649 OLD PACIFIC HWY S	KELSO	WA	98626	Kodiak
BLACK HOLE	BRUDIE PHILIP	BOX 111	HOMER	AK	99603	Kodiak
BRINK	ALWARD MATTHEW	60082 CLARICE WAY	HOMER	AK	99603	Kodiak
CANDIDA DAWN C	CHRISTIANSEN DAVID	BOX 102	OLD HARBOR	AK	99643	Kodiak
CAPE CLEARE	COSTELLO FRANCIS	BOX 547	KODIAK	AK	99615	Kodiak
CAPE KARLUK	KULLER MARTIN	BOX 312	CATHLAMET	WA	98612	Kodiak
CAPE LOOKOUT	OLSEN DANIEL	BOX 1743	KODIAK	AK	99615	Kodiak
CHALLENGE	KEPLINGER MITCHELL	BOX 1006	KODIAK	AK	99615	Kodiak
CHALLENGER	ALWARD MATTHEW	60082 CLARICE WAY	HOMER	AK	99603	Kodiak
CHARLYDA	WATERBURY DOUGLAS	3373 MELNITSA LN	KODIAK	AK	99615	Kodiak
CLEARE	COSTELLO FRANCIS	BOX 547	KODIAK	AK	99615	Kodiak
CLUELESS	JOHNSON CHARLES	4912 EAGLE PL	HOMER	AK	99603	Kodiak
CRIMSON TIDE	HARRIS CHARLES	BOX 262	CLAM GULCH	AK	99568	Kodiak
DAHLIA BEATRIX	BERNS TRAVIS	BOX 33	OLD HARBOR	AK	99643	Kodiak
DANCIA	MCFARLAND DANIEL	BOX 1002	KODIAK	AK	99615	Kodiak
DARIA ANN	HUEY DENNIS	BOX 494	KODIAK	AK	99615	Kodiak
DREAMER	DENSMORE DAVID	41306 HILLCREST LP RD	ASTORIA	OR	97103	Kodiak
EMERALD BEAUTY	BEAUTY CORPORATION	BOX 987	KODIAK	AK	99615	Kodiak
ERIKA	ERIKA INC	BOX 8717	KODIAK	AK	99615	Kodiak
FIONA	MCWETHY CHARLES	BOX 8552	KODIAK	AK	99615	Kodiak
FISH HOOK	ROTH STEVEN	BOX 3171	HOMER	AK	99603	Kodiak
FV EL CAPORAL	PEREZ, EDWARDO & ENRIQUE	BOX 208	KODIAK	AK	99615	Kodiak
GALIVAT	ALPIAK JAMES	BOX 873752	WASILLA	AK	99687	Kodiak
GALLANT GIRL	HORN STEVEN	1210 MISSION RD	KODIAK	AK	99615	Kodiak

Vessel	Owner	Address	City	State	Zip	Area
GLACIER BAY	JOHNSON DAVID	BOX 15252	FRITZ CREEK	AK	99603	Kodiak
GLENNETTE C	CHRISTIANSEN HAROLD	BOX 129	OLD HARBOR	AK	99643	Kodiak
GRAYLING	TROSVIG CHRISTIAN	11132 LAKE ORBIN CIR	KODIAK	AK	99615	Kodiak
HALCYON	BLONDIN RONALD	1412 BARANOF ST	KODIAK	AK	99615	Kodiak
HEIDI MAY	BIEHL WILLIAM	BOX 36	PORT LIONS	AK	99550	Kodiak
HELEN DELL	NELSON MICHAEL	BOX 87	PORT LIONS	AK	99550	Kodiak
INFINITE GLORY	STAFFORD THOMAS	BOX 3403	HOMER	AK	99603	Kodiak
INFINITE GRACE	INFINITE GLORY FISHERS LLC	BOX 3403	HOMER	AK	99603	Kodiak
INTERCEPTOR	KING ROBERT	BOX 504	KODIAK	AK	99615	Kodiak
INVINCIBLE	FOGLE CHARLES	1136 WOLKOFF LN	KODIAK	AK	99615	Kodiak
JAMBOREE	MUTCH SAMUEL	210 B SHELIKOF	KODIAK	AK	99615	Kodiak
JERICHO	ALPIAK JAMES	BOX 873752	WASILLA	AK	99687	Kodiak
JILL-ANNE-I	SUYDAM GARY	BOX 2807	KODIAK	AK	99615	Kodiak
JJ	HENSON JON	BOX 176	KODIAK	AK	99615	Kodiak
KAOS	JOHNSON CLINT	BOX 909	KODIAK	AK	99615	Kodiak
KATIE LANAE	ALMETER PATRICIA	BOX 1365	KODIAK	AK	99615	Kodiak
KEEP CLEARE	COSTELLO FRANCIS	BOX 547	KODIAK	AK	99615	Kodiak
KELLY GIRL	ROTH STEVEN	BOX 3171	HOMER	AK	99603	Kodiak
KIPPER	SCIRROCO INC	2911 PLYMOTH DR	BELLINGHAM	WA	98225	Kodiak
KITTIWAKE	MACINTOSH IAN	910 STELLER WAY	KODIAK	AK	99615	Kodiak
KULSHAN	MCDONNELL ROBERT	230 SHALLOW SHORE RD	BELLINGHAM	WA	98229	Kodiak
LADY ASHLEY	MONROE SHIRLEY	BOX 1202	KODIAK	AK	99615	Kodiak
LAGUNA STAR	GOSSETT TIMOTHY	BOX 1277	KODIAK	AK	99615	Kodiak
LOT OF RED	BOTZ NORMAN	9163 JAMES BLVD	JUNEAU	AK	99801	Kodiak
LUBA MARIE	BERESTOFF ANDY	3478 PUFFIN DR	KODIAK	AK	99615	Kodiak
LYN MARK	PATITTUCCI MICHAEL	BOX 1511	KODIAK	AK	99615	Kodiak
MAIJA LIISA	FASTABEND TIM	91922 HWY 202	ASTORIA	OR	97103	Kodiak

Vessel	Owner	Address	City	State	Zip	Area
MARCO PURSE SEINE SK	BLAIR ANDREW	BOX 108	FOX ISLAND	WA	98333	Kodiak
MARTIN B II	TARABOCHIA MARCIA	3199 PLEASANT BCH DR	BAINBRIDGE ISLAND	WA	98110	Kodiak
MELINA	PESTRIKOFF EDWARD	BOX 56	OLD HARBOR	AK	99643	Kodiak
MERGANSER	JONES ROY	BOX 150	LARSEN BAY	AK	99624	Kodiak
MILLENNIUM	GUGEL GEROLD	1911 DOLLY VARDEN CIR	ANCHORAGE	AK	99516	Kodiak
MISS ADVENTURE	BALDRIDGE JAMES	BOX 3665	KENAI	AK	99611	Kodiak
MISS DESTINEE	MISS DESTINEE	2200 E 56TH	ANCHORAGE	AK	99507	Kodiak
MISS HOLLY	CHRISTIANSEN FRED	7051 CHAD ST	ANCHORAGE	AK	99518	Kodiak
MISS LYN	BOTZ JON	BOX 577	KODIAK	AK	99615	Kodiak
MISS MALISS	LOUTREL DAVID	1430 CRESCENT DR	ANCHORAGE	AK	99508	Kodiak
MISS MICHELLE	BOTZ JON	BOX 577	KODIAK	AK	99615	Kodiak
MISS RACHEL	BURTON ROY	9609 SUNRISE RD	BLAINE	WA	98230	Kodiak
MISS RACHEL SKF	BURTON ROY	9609 SUNRISE RD	BLAINE	WA	98230	Kodiak
MISS ROXANNE	RISLEY RODNEY	3649 OLD PACIFIC HWY S	KELSO	WA	98626	Kodiak
MISS-ALICE	ROTH STEVEN	BOX 3171	HOMER	AK	99603	Kodiak
MOONDANCE	BOWHAY BOB	BOX 187	KODIAK	AK	99615	Kodiak
NACY LYNNE	EBERLE RICK	4426 EDGEMONT PL	MOUNT VERNON	WA	98273	Kodiak
NATALIE	HEGGE MATTHEW	4705 SOCKEYE CIR	KENAI	AK	99611	Kodiak
NEW DAWN	IVANOFF TERRY	BOX 8883	KODIAK	AK	99615	Kodiak
NORTHWESTERN	SITKINAK INC	BOX 8985	KODIAK	AK	99615	Kodiak
OBA#20	KELLER DOUG	39980 FERNWOOD DR	HOMER	AK	99603	Kodiak
OBSESSION	KOMADINA KEVIN	19875 WAGONER RD	KIRKLAND	AZ	86332	Kodiak
OCEANIC	SHOLL RANDALL	BOX 681	KODIAK	AK	99615	Kodiak
OLSEN	SKONBERG JAMES	BOX 70	OUZINKIE	AK	99644	Kodiak
ORCA	COLE JAMES	BOX 102	PORT LIONS	AK	99550	Kodiak
OUTFOX	TARABOCHIA MICHAEL	3863 LINDSAY HILL RD	QUILCENE	WA	98376	Kodiak
PACIFIC PACER	PYLE DAVID	17423 SCHALIT WY	LAKE OSWEGO	OR	97035	Kodiak

Vessel	Owner	Address	City	State	Zip	Area
PATRICIA KAY	VANMATRE STANLEY	3199 PENINSULA RD	KODIAK	AK	99615	Kodiak
PATTI-ANN II	GILBERT JOHN	BOX 271	KODIAK	AK	99615	Kodiak
PINTAIL	MALONEY SEAN	11020 UGAK DR	KODIAK	AK	99615	Kodiak
PISCES	AGUILAR JOSE	1315 28TH ST	ANACORTES	WA	98221	Kodiak
PLUNGE BOB RAINPANTS	GABRIEL GREGORY	BOX 3392	SOLDOTNA	AK	99669	Kodiak
POS	JOHNSON GREGORY	BOX 52	HOMER	AK	99603	Kodiak
PRESTIGE	LAYFIELD KENNETH	BOX 644	WINTHROP	WA	98862	Kodiak
PURSUIT	THOMPSON ERIC	16945 HALL PL	MOUNT VERNON	WA	98273	Kodiak
RESURRECTION	REUTOV SEVEREAN	BOX 1879	KODIAK	AK	99615	Kodiak
ROZGMA	PETERSON CHARLES	1850 THREE SISTERS WY	KODIAK	AK	99615	Kodiak
RUBBER RAFT	FELLOWS ROBERT	266 E BAYVIEW	HOMER	AK	99603	Kodiak
RUBBER RAFT	SUYDAM GARY	BOX 2807	KODIAK	AK	99615	Kodiak
SABRINA C	BLONDIN BRIAN	BOX 4478	KODIAK	AK	99615	Kodiak
SANDRA JEAN	KUCZEK RONALD	BOX 91657	ANCHORAGE	AK	99509	Kodiak
SANTA ROSA	CARLSON KURT	2399 HEMLOCK	MORRO BAY	CA	93442	Kodiak
SCANDIA	ANDERSON LUKE	7901 ZERMATT AVE	ANCHORAGE	AK	99507	Kodiak
SCIRROCO LITTLE	SCIRROCO INC	2911 PLYMOTH DR	BELLINGHAM	WA	98225	Kodiak
SEA STAR	LINDHOLM JOE	11355 WHISTLE LAKE RD	ANACORTES	WA	98221	Kodiak
SEA WALKER	DUNCAN STANLEY	BOX 3444	KODIAK	AK	99615	Kodiak
SHADOWFAX	ROSENKRANZ BARRY	290 OLD STAGE WY	YAKIMA	WA	98908	Kodiak
SHERYL ANN	DEANE GREGORY	15739 YOKEKO DR	ANACORTES	WA	98221	Kodiak
SHINING SEA	MCWETHY CHARLES	BOX 8552	KODIAK	AK	99615	Kodiak
SLIPPERY FOX	KEPLINGER MITCHELL	BOX 1006	KODIAK	AK	99615	Kodiak
STAR POWER	OLSEN THORVOLD	BOX 322	KODIAK	AK	99615	Kodiak
STEADFAST	JOHNSON GREGORY	BOX 52	HOMER	AK	99603	Kodiak
SYDNEY ANN	JONES KENNY	4126 GINNETT RD	ANACORTES	WA	98221	Kodiak
SYLVIA STAR	KAVANAUGH RONALD	1533 SAWMILL CIR	KODIAK	AK	99615	Kodiak

Vessel	Owner	Address	City	State	Zip	Area
TIFFANY	TOTEFF JAMES	BOX 418	KALAMA	WA	98625	Kodiak
UNGALIKTHLUK	KEPLINGER MITCHELL	BOX 1006	KODIAK	AK	99615	Kodiak
VALKYRIE	FELLOWS ROBERT	266 E BAYVIEW	HOMER	AK	99603	Kodiak
VANISHING BREED	NEVIN JOHN	BOX 2125	KODIAK	AK	99615	Kodiak
VENTURESS	VENTURESS INC	1776 MISSION RD	KODIAK	AK	99615	Kodiak
WANDERING STAR	ROTH ALEX	BOX 2008	HOMER	AK	99603	Kodiak
WILD CARD	WILD ISLAND INC	BOX 804	KODIAK	AK	99615	Kodiak
WILD TOO	WILD ISLAND INC	BOX 804	KODIAK	AK	99615	Kodiak
WINDIGO	BARKER ADAM	126 E FAIRVIEW AVE	HOMER	AK	99603	Kodiak
ALITAKAN	METZGER RICHARD	BOX 5043	AKHIOK	AK	99615	Kodiak
HAIL MARY	FIORENTINO WILLIAM	BOX 1246	KAUNAKAKAI	HI	96748	Kodiak
JAIME MARIE	SCHAUFF WILLIAM	BOX 8774	KODIAK	AK	99615	Kodiak
KALA	TORMALA THOMAS	BOX 8829	KODIAK	AK	99615	Kodiak
KAREN KAY	KAREN KAY INC	BOX 8150	KODIAK	AK	99615	Kodiak
MANX	REID DANA	BOX 8935	KODIAK	AK	99615	Kodiak
MISS PALOMAR	AGUILAR JOSE	1315 28TH ST	ANACORTES	WA	98221	Kodiak
NAKCHAMIK	MYRVOLD LYLE	BOX 870181	WASILLA	AK	99687	Kodiak
ABBY JO	ORGAN KEITH	BOX 58	KODIAK	AK	99615	Kodiak
ALEUTIAN BELLE	IVANOFF STEVEN	1327 MOUNTAIN VIEW DR	KODIAK	AK	99615	Kodiak
ALPHA CENTAURI	EUFEMIO JAMES	BOX 907	KODIAK	AK	99615	Kodiak
ALYSA ANNE	HORN DAVID	717 UPPER MILL BAY RD	KODIAK	AK	99615	Kodiak
AMBASSADOR	BOGGS JOHN	BOX 1199	KODIAK	AK	99615	Kodiak
AMY LA RAE	ORTH HENRY	3462 N PARADISE LN	WASILLA	AK	99654	Kodiak
ANAPILAR	ANAPILAR LLC	8028 SIERRA DR	EDMONDS	WA	98026	Kodiak
ANNA LISA	NELSON HARRY	BOX 87	PORT LIONS	AK	99550	Kodiak
ASHLEE CHRISTINE C	TUELLER NATHAN	BOX 913	GIRDWOOD	AK	99587	Kodiak
AWTAM	CHRISTIANSEN MILES	BOX 45	OLD HARBOR	AK	99643	Kodiak

Vessel	Owner	Address	City	State	Zip	Area
BIG DIPPER	SMEDLEY DONOVAN	BOX 8529	KODIAK	AK	99615	Kodiak
CAPE PROVIDENCE	SCHAUFF CRAIG	BOX 8400	KODIAK	AK	99615	Kodiak
CAPTAIN KIDD	MARTIN MICHAEL	BOX 889	KODIAK	AK	99615	Kodiak
CARLA RAE C	CHRISTIANSEN EMIL	8211 DEBARR RD	ANCHORAGE	AK	99504	Kodiak
CARLSEN POINT	CARLSEN DENNIS	3629 REZANOFF #41	KODIAK	AK	99615	Kodiak
CARMELINA	CREAMER WILLIE	BOX 2003	HOMER	AK	99603	Kodiak
DIANA	PEDERSEN ALEC	BOX 8577	KODIAK	AK	99615	Kodiak
EIDER	LUKIN LESTER	BOX 62	PORT LIONS	AK	99550	Kodiak
EVENING STAR	CLARK MICHAEL	BOX 2009	KODIAK	AK	99615	Kodiak
FAMILY PRIDE	FAMILY PRIDE INC	3609 SUNSET DR	KODIAK	AK	99615	Kodiak
FISHIN' MAGICIAN	K C FISHERIES	1849 MARMOT DR	KODIAK	AK	99615	Kodiak
FV FIVE BROTHERS	TARABOCHIA MICHAEL	3863 LINDSAY HILL RD	QUILCENE	WA	98376	Kodiak
HANK	NELAND JOHN	BOX 414	ANCHOR POINT	AK	99556	Kodiak
ICY MIST	FV ICY MIST LLC	BOX 344	KODIAK	AK	99615	Kodiak
JACQUELYN W	WISNER HUGH	BOX 2783	KODIAK	AK	99615	Kodiak
JILL ALLISON	GILES LESLIE	BOX 275	SELDOVIA	AK	99663	Kodiak
JOMEL	KELLER DOUG	39980 FERNWOOD DR	HOMER	AK	99603	Kodiak
KATHY ANN	JOHNSON THOMAS	BOX 2885	KODIAK	AK	99615	Kodiak
KESTREL	ANDERSON STOSH	BOX 310	KODIAK	AK	99615	Kodiak
KILOKAK	KALCIC VITOMIR	BOX 2085	KODIAK	AK	99615	Kodiak
KIMBERLY ANN	ROBERTSON BRUCE	614 HILLSIDE ST	KODIAK	AK	99615	Kodiak
LA MER	BOWSER ROBERT	BOX 420	BURLEY	WA	98322	Kodiak
LADY KATHRYN	TANDLER JASON	BOX 2859	KODIAK	AK	99615	Kodiak
LARA LEE	GILBERT DANIEL	BOX 2531	KODIAK	AK	99615	Kodiak
LEGASEA	BLONDIN RONALD	1412 BARANOF ST	KODIAK	AK	99615	Kodiak
LISA GAYLE	HANKINS FRED	113 BANCROFT	KODIAK	AK	99615	Kodiak
LORENA MARIE	SKONBERG JAMES	BOX 70	OUZINKIE	AK	99644	Kodiak
LYNX	REID DANA	BOX 8935	KODIAK	AK	99615	Kodiak

Vessel	Owner	Address	City	State	Zip	Area
MAGGY J	PANAMAROFF ALEXANDER	BOX 6	LARSEN BAY	AK	99624	Kodiak
MARTIN B	TARABOCHIA MARCIA	3199 PLEASANT BCH DR	BAINBRIDGE ISLAND	WA	98110	Kodiak
MELISSA RAE	BERNS JAMES	BOX 44	OLD HARBOR	AK	99643	Kodiak
MIKADO	MIKADO FISHERIES	BOX 647	KODIAK	AK	99615	Kodiak
MISS LORI	MISS LORI INC	BOX 2843	KODIAK	AK	99615	Kodiak
MISS MICHELLE	GABRIEL GREGORY	BOX 3392	SOLDOTNA	AK	99669	Kodiak
MONICA JENE	NELSON ARNOLD	BOX 85	PORT LIONS	AK	99550	Kodiak
NORMA KAY	LINDSEY ROBERT	3162 SPRUCE CAPE RD	KODIAK	AK	99615	Kodiak
NORTH WIND	SARGENT FRED	3177 WOODY WAY LP	KODIAK	AK	99615	Kodiak
OCEAN BAY	HEGGE MATTHEW	4705 SOCKEYE CIR	KENAI	AK	99611	Kodiak
OCEAN PEARL	EBERLE RICK	4426 EDGEMONT PL	MOUNT VERNON	WA	98273	Kodiak
PAMELA DAWN	LINDBERG JOHN	BOX KWP	KODIAK	AK	99615	Kodiak
POLAR STAR	POLAR STAR INC	BOX 2843	KODIAK	AK	99615	Kodiak
RAGING BEAUTY	LESTER LUKE	BOX 553	KODIAK	AK	99615	Kodiak
RAVEN	PETERSON HENRY	1219 MADSEN AVE	KODIAK	AK	99615	Kodiak
REBECCA RAE	KNAGIN ALEXEI	BOX 1334	CORDOVA	AK	99574	Kodiak
REBEL	DOOLEY LARRY	BOX 2175	KODIAK	AK	99615	Kodiak
RENAISSANCE	ALEXSON PETER	BOX 661	HOMER	AK	99603	Kodiak
SALMON BARRY	ROSENKRANZ BARRY	290 OLD STAGE WY	YAKIMA	WA	98908	Kodiak
SALMON BAY	GLADU MARK	BOX 2862	KODIAK	AK	99615	Kodiak
SEA BARB	SKANA ENTERPRISES INC	BOX 2852	KODIAK	AK	99615	Kodiak
SHAWNEE	PIERSZALOWSKI WILLIAM	2412 KERRY AVE	CAMBRIA	CA	93428	Kodiak
SILVERSWORD	BOTZ NORMAN	9163 JAMES BLVD	JUNEAU	AK	99801	Kodiak
SISIUTL	STAGER FREDERICK	BOX 8243	KODIAK	AK	99615	Kodiak
SUSAN MARIE	GILBERT JOHN	BOX 271	KODIAK	AK	99615	Kodiak
THALASSA	CALHOUN JAMES	BOX 3805	HOMER	AK	99603	Kodiak
THREE ANGELS	KRAMER CHARLES	BOX 183	PORT LIONS	AK	99550	Kodiak

Vessel	Owner	Address	City	State	Zip	Area
TOP GUN	MARKOSKI JERRY	2215 WILLIAMS ST	BELLINGHAM	WA	98225	Kodiak
VIKING STAR	OLSEN THORVOLD	BOX 322	KODIAK	AK	99615	Kodiak
AQUARIUS	NEVIN JOHN	BOX 2125	KODIAK	AK	99615	Kodiak
DOLPHIN	LECHNER LUTHER	BOX 8538	KODIAK	AK	99615	Kodiak
FAYETTEJO	LIN RONALD	BOX 2022	KODIAK	AK	99615	Kodiak
KAIWIK	JOHNSON CLINT	BOX 909	KODIAK	AK	99615	Kodiak
LADY J	KATELNIKOFF NICK	BOX 170	OUZINKIE	AK	99644	Kodiak
MATILDA BAY	MARSHALL GEORGE	11185 WOMANS BAY DR	KODIAK	AK	99615	Kodiak
MONKS HABIT	MONKIEWICZ EDWARD	1110 PURTOV ST	KODIAK	AK	99615	Kodiak
NEW SONG	STIHL DANIEL	BOX 3373	KODIAK	AK	99615	Kodiak
ORION	ALLAN PETER	BOX 2160	KODIAK	AK	99615	Kodiak
PATRICIA SUE	PETERSON CHARLES	1850 THREE SISTERS WY	KODIAK	AK	99615	Kodiak
RED BEARD	DEPLAZES DOUGLAS	BOX 2923	KODIAK	AK	99615	Kodiak
STEPHANIE LYNN	BLONDIN SARAH	BOX 4478	KODIAK	AK	99615	Kodiak
SULINA	HOLM OLIVER	BOX 8749	KODIAK	AK	99615	Kodiak
SUSAN KAY	RUSSELL STEVEN	3152 WOODY WY LOOP	KODIAK	AK	99615	Kodiak
ADVANCER	BERNTSEN LOUIS	1216 NW BLAKELY CT	SEATTLE	WA	98177	Peninsula/Aleutian Islands
AGHILEEN	MITCHELL JOHN	41 STRAWBERRY PT RD	BELLINGHAM	WA	98229	Peninsula/Aleutian Islands
AMANDA DAWN	SAMUELSON HERMAN	8 MAIN ST	KING COVE	AK	99612	Peninsula/Aleutian Islands
ANNIE THERESA	KOSO RAYMOND	BOX 103	KING COVE	AK	99612	Peninsula/Aleutian Islands
AW 1	HOBLET TOM	BOX 108	FALSE PASS	AK	99583	Peninsula/Aleutian Islands
BD 2	DUSHKIN WILLIAM	BOX 135	SAND POINT	AK	99661	Peninsula/Aleutian Islands
CAPE CHEERFULL	HASTINGS RICHARD	1308 DINES POINT RD	GREENBANK	WA	98253	Peninsula/Aleutian Islands
CAPE ST ELIAS	INVICTUS LLC	BOX 749	GIRDWOOD	AK	99587	Peninsula/Aleutian Islands
COMMANDER	OSTERBACK ALVIN	BOX 920123	DUTCH HARBOR	AK	99692	Peninsula/Aleutian Islands
CRUSADER	GARDNER GLEN	BOX 444	SAND POINT	AK	99661	Peninsula/Aleutian Islands

Vessel	Owner	Address	City	State	Zip	Area
DEFENDER	BERNTSEN LOUIS	1216 NW BLAKELY CT	SEATTLE	WA	98177	Peninsula/Aleutian Islands
DESIRAE DAWN	DUSHKIN RUDY	8820 VERNON ST	ANCHORAGE	AK	99515	Peninsula/Aleutian Islands
DYNASTY	GUNDERSEN PAUL	BOX 134	SAND POINT	AK	99661	Peninsula/Aleutian Islands
FOUR WINDS II	GOULD ROBERT	BOX 52	KING COVE	AK	99612	Peninsula/Aleutian Islands
HAMMER TIME	HOBLET TOM	BOX 108	FALSE PASS	AK	99583	Peninsula/Aleutian Islands
JILL-ANNE-I	SAMUELSON ERIC	BOX 66	KING COVE	AK	99612	Peninsula/Aleutian Islands
JUST IN CASE	WILSON COREY	BOX 267	KING COVE	AK	99612	Peninsula/Aleutian Islands
KAREN EVICH	EVICH JOHN	2051 NORTHSHORE RD	BELLINGHAM	WA	98226	Peninsula/Aleutian Islands
KISER	MITCHELL JOHN	41 STRAWBERRY PT RD	BELLINGHAM	WA	98229	Peninsula/Aleutian Islands
KONA ROSE	BENKMAN BRYAN	10533 14TH AVE NW	SEATTLE	WA	98177	Peninsula/Aleutian Islands
LADY JOANNE	LADY JOANNE INC	BOX 6114	EDMONDS	WA	98026	Peninsula/Aleutian Islands
LAUREN L KAPP	KAPP DARRELL	338 BAYSIDE RD	BELLINGHAM	WA	98225	Peninsula/Aleutian Islands
LIAHONA	WADSWORTH RAY	200 E MAIN ST	OAKLEY	ID	83346	Peninsula/Aleutian Islands
LIL MAN	KOSO RAYMOND	BOX 103	KING COVE	AK	99612	Peninsula/Aleutian Islands
LITTLE TRACE	MACK HENRY	BOX 224	KING COVE	AK	99612	Peninsula/Aleutian Islands
MISS BRENDA	HOLMBERG JOHN	422 2ND AVE N	EDMONDS	WA	98020	Peninsula/Aleutian Islands
NAMORADA	WIEBE WILLIAM	5201 GJOSUND DR	HOMER	AK	99603	Peninsula/Aleutian Islands
NICHOLAS MICHAE	KURTZ MICHAEL	BPC 32265	BELLINGHAM	WA	98228	Peninsula/Aleutian Islands
NORTHERN DAWN	SEAWEST INC	BOX 98	SAND POINT	AK	99661	Peninsula/Aleutian Islands
NORTHERN DREAM	GOULD ROBERT	BOX 307	KING COVE	AK	99612	Peninsula/Aleutian Islands
NORTHERN STAR	GOULD DEAN	BOX 124	KING COVE	AK	99612	Peninsula/Aleutian Islands
PY.2	YATCHMENEFF PETER	BOX 75	FALSE PASS	AK	99583	Peninsula/Aleutian Islands
PATRICIA ANN	MCCALLUM HUBERT	BOX 2	SAND POINT	AK	99661	Peninsula/Aleutian Islands
PRIME TIME	HOLMBERG FRED	6829 QUEENVIEW CIR	ANCHORAGE	AK	99504	Peninsula/Aleutian Islands
PY1	YATCHMENEFF PETER	BOX 75	FALSE PASS	AK	99583	Peninsula/Aleutian Islands
RAND R	MAGIC FISH COMPANY	59065 MEADOW LN	HOMER	AK	99603	Peninsula/Aleutian Islands
RICKY	KOSO RICHARD	BOX 111053	ANCHORAGE	AK	99511	Peninsula/Aleutian Islands

Vessel	Owner	Address	City	State	Zip	Area
TINKER DOO	KOSO RAYMOND	BOX 103	KING COVE	AK	99612	Peninsula/Aleutian Islands
VICKI RAE	NUTT RAYMOND	BOX 122	SAND POINT	AK	99661	Peninsula/Aleutian Islands
YACKIE O	OVERA FISHERIES LLC	14010 154TH AVE SE	RENTON	WA	98059	Peninsula/Aleutian Islands
ALEUT KID	HOBLET IVAN	BOX 62	FALSE PASS	AK	99583	Peninsula/Aleutian Islands
ALEUT LADY	HOBLET TOM	BOX 108	FALSE PASS	AK	99583	Peninsula/Aleutian Islands
ALEUT SON	SAMUELSON FRANK	BOX 214	KING COVE	AK	99612	Peninsula/Aleutian Islands
ALEUTIAN STAR	WILSON VERNON	BOX 308	KING COVE	AK	99612	Peninsula/Aleutian Islands
BOBBI DEE	DUSHKIN WILLIAM	BOX 135	SAND POINT	AK	99661	Peninsula/Aleutian Islands
BREAKER	BERNTSEN LOUIS	1216 NW BLAKELY CT	SEATTLE	WA	98177	Peninsula/Aleutian Islands
CAMERON	OVERA FISHERIES LLC	14010 154TH AVE SE	RENTON	WA	98059	Peninsula/Aleutian Islands
COURTNEY NORAL	LARSEN NORMAN	BOX 52	SAND POINT	AK	99661	Peninsula/Aleutian Islands
CUB POINT	FOSTER BRUCE	BOX 46	SAND POINT	AK	99661	Peninsula/Aleutian Islands
CYNOSURE	HAT LLC	BOX 17911	SEATTLE	WA	98127	Peninsula/Aleutian Islands
DECISION	MELSETH FRANK	BOX 66	SAND POINT	AK	99661	Peninsula/Aleutian Islands
EQUINOX	SCHONBERGSEN INC	BOX 1988	KAILUA KONA	HI	96745	Peninsula/Aleutian Islands
HEATHER MARGENE	FOSTER DWAIN	BOX 162	SAND POINT	AK	99661	Peninsula/Aleutian Islands
JEANELLE	CARLSON CARL	BOX 44	SAND POINT	AK	99661	Peninsula/Aleutian Islands
JULIA SUE	YATCHMENEFF PETER	BOX 75	FALSE PASS	AK	99583	Peninsula/Aleutian Islands
KAREY GALE	GUNDERSEN CHARLES	BOX 24	SAND POINT	AK	99661	Peninsula/Aleutian Islands
KC	HOLMBERG RUEL	BOX 64	SAND POINT	AK	99661	Peninsula/Aleutian Islands
LADY LEE DAWN	NEWMAN ALVIN	BOX 248	KING COVE	AK	99612	Peninsula/Aleutian Islands
MISS ROXANNE	KOSO RAYMOND	BOX 877309	WASILLA	AK	99687	Peninsula/Aleutian Islands
MONGOOSE	OSBORNE ARTHUR	BOX 240925	DOUGLAS	AK	99824	Peninsula/Aleutian Islands
MS INGRID	JACOBSEN DICK	BOX 307	SAND POINT	AK	99661	Peninsula/Aleutian Islands
MY GRANDKIDS	HOLMBERG RUEL	BOX 64	SAND POINT	AK	99661	Peninsula/Aleutian Islands
MY OAR	REUTOV FEODOR	BOX 390	KODIAK	AK	99615	Peninsula/Aleutian Islands
NANA JOANN	WILSON OSCAR	BOX 144	KING COVE	AK	99612	Peninsula/Aleutian Islands

Vessel	Owner	Address	City	State	Zip	Area
NORSE MAID	CARLSON CARL	BOX 44	SAND POINT	AK	99661	Peninsula/Aleutian Islands
OCEANIA	JACOBSEN ANDREW	BOX 125	UNALASKA	AK	99685	Peninsula/Aleutian Islands
PACIFIC MAID	OSTERBACK DAVID	BOX 144	SAND POINT	AK	99661	Peninsula/Aleutian Islands
PERSEVERANCE	PERSEVERANCE LLC	2221 HALIBUT POINT RD	SITKA	AK	99835	Peninsula/Aleutian Islands
POINT COUNTESS	OGATA RAYMOND	BOX 181	SAND POINT	AK	99661	Peninsula/Aleutian Islands
PRIMUS	DEGROEN JOHN	9810 SW 148TH ST	VASHON	WA	98070	Peninsula/Aleutian Islands
SEA KING	HOLMBERG PAUL	BOX 3233	PALMER	AK	99645	Peninsula/Aleutian Islands
SHAREENA	FOSTER JACK	BOX 254	SAND POINT	AK	99661	Peninsula/Aleutian Islands
SHAWNA RAE	GALOVIN ANNETTE	BOX 327	SAND POINT	AK	99661	Peninsula/Aleutian Islands
SHONNA JACOLE	MACK KENNETH	5301 TRENA ST	ANCHORAGE	AK	99507	Peninsula/Aleutian Islands
ST FRANCIS	GRONHOLDT PAUL	BOX 288	SAND POINT	AK	99661	Peninsula/Aleutian Islands
ST LORETTA	DUSHKIN ESIAH	BOX 215	KING COVE	AK	99612	Peninsula/Aleutian Islands
STANLEY K	LAUKITIS MICHAEL	59065 MEADOW LN	HOMER	AK	99603	Peninsula/Aleutian Islands
TALIA	MENISH WILLIAM	BOX 877	PETERSBURG	AK	99833	Peninsula/Aleutian Islands
TAMMY ILENE	CALUGAN INVESTMENTS LLC	3115 MADISON WAY	ANCHORAGE	AK	99508	Peninsula/Aleutian Islands
TAURUS	CASTLE CAPE FISHERIES LTD	BOX 971	HOMER	AK	99603	Peninsula/Aleutian Islands
TEMPTATION	LARSEN MELVIN	BOX 33	SAND POINT	AK	99661	Peninsula/Aleutian Islands
TERN	HOLMBERG RUEL	BOX 64	SAND POINT	AK	99661	Peninsula/Aleutian Islands
TURNING POINT	FOSTER JOHN	BOX 225	SAND POINT	AK	99661	Peninsula/Aleutian Islands
ZEALOT	MISTY FJORD SEAFOOD INC	2450 TONGASS AVE #225	KETCHIKAN	AK	99901	Peninsula/Aleutian Islands
HOOK POINT	FOSTER BRUCE	BOX 34	SAND POINT	AK	99661	Peninsula/Aleutian Islands
SEA SPRAY	GUNDERSEN GEORGE	BOX 51	SAND POINT	AK	99661	Peninsula/Aleutian Islands
101ST MAN	SPURKLAND MEGAN	BOX 732	HOMER	AK	99603	Prince William Sound
A PENNY MORE	BURTON JAMES	BOX 6	CORDOVA	AK	99574	Prince William Sound
ABBY LOUISE	BOURGEOIS INC	BOX 1945	CORDOVA	AK	99574	Prince William Sound
ACHILLIS	ALBER LOUIE	BOX 111	CORDOVA	AK	99574	Prince William Sound
AGAVE	JONES KENNETH	BOX 1044	HOMER	AK	99603	Prince William Sound

Vessel	Owner	Address	City	State	Zip	Area
ALASKA GIRL	CARROLL DOUGLAS	BOX 1071	CORDOVA	AK	99574	Prince William Sound
ALASKA LEGACY	STEPHENS RONEL	10840 KASILOF BLVD	ANCHORAGE	AK	99507	Prince William Sound
ALASKAN SPIRIT	DAY PATRICK	BOX 788	VALDEZ	AK	99686	Prince William Sound
ALL IN	GABRIEL ANTHONY	BOX 137	KENAI	AK	99611	Prince William Sound
ALYS O	HERSCHLEB JOHN	BOX 447	GIRDWOOD	AK	99587	Prince William Sound
AMBER DAWN	CARROLL WESTON	1170 QUEETS CIR	HOMER	AK	99603	Prince William Sound
ARMADILLO	BEAUDRY LOUIS	BOX 1485	GIRDWOOD	AK	99587	Prince William Sound
ATLANTIS	PETERSON CHRISTOPHER	BOX 3982	KETCHUM	ID	83340	Prince William Sound
AYAKULIK	KILBREATH TERRANCE	26428 S BUTTONWOOD DR	SUN LAKES	AZ	85248	Prince William Sound
BABBLING BROOKE	JOHNSON JAMES	BOX 263	CORDOVA	AK	99574	Prince William Sound
BABE J	JOHNSON ELI	1564 SW APPERSON ST	MCMINNVILLE	OR	97128	Prince William Sound
BANKRUPT COMM	MCKENZIE FISHERIES INC	BOX 2071	CORDOVA	AK	99574	Prince William Sound
BASARGIN	ALASKA MAR. RESOURCES LLC	BOX 1976	CORDOVA	AK	99574	Prince William Sound
BATTLE STAR	SMITH GREGORY	BOX 2744	VALDEZ	AK	99686	Prince William Sound
BIG BLUE	BEAUDRY LOUIS	BOX 2225	CORDOVA	AK	99574	Prince William Sound
BIPOLAR	MARINA SKY LLC	BOX 2071	CORDOVA	AK	99574	Prince William Sound
BLUE C'S	CHESHIER ELMER	BOX 2264	CORDOVA	AK	99574	Prince William Sound
BONNIE JEAN	HONKOLA ROBERT	BOX 124	CORDOVA	AK	99574	Prince William Sound
BOUNTY	SUTTON RAY	BOX 2469	VALDEZ	AK	99686	Prince William Sound
BULLDOG	BOURGEOIS INC	BOX 1945	CORDOVA	AK	99574	Prince William Sound
CAPE ELRINGTON	GILDNES STEVEN	20032 HILL VUE ST	BURLINGTON	WA	98233	Prince William Sound
CAPE TRINITY	SUTTON PAUL	2647 W PALAIS DR	COUR D'ALENE	ID	83815	Prince William Sound
CAPTAIN'S BABY	BUTLER DAVID	BOX 141	CORDOVA	AK	99574	Prince William Sound
CENTURION	SPURKLAND MEGAN	BOX 732	HOMER	AK	99603	Prince William Sound
CHEERFUL II	LOPEZ THOMAS	233 LULLWATER	WILMINGTON	NC	28403	Prince William Sound
CHELSEA D	LEE BRIAN	31250 W LEE DR	SUTTON	AK	99674	Prince William Sound
CHRISTINE SUE	CARLSON ERLING	BOX 2369	CORDOVA	AK	99574	Prince William Sound

Vessel	Owner	Address	City	State	Zip	Area
CONSPIRACY	LOPEZ THOMAS	233 LULLWATER	WILMINGTON	NC	28403	Prince William Sound
COPASETIC	WILKIE TIM	BOX 1726	SEWARD	AK	99664	Prince William Sound
COVENTINA	WILLIAMS ZACHARY	7141 LINDEN DR	ANCHORAGE	AK	99502	Prince William Sound
DAMMIT JIM	GABRIEL GREGORY	BOX 3392	SOLDOTNA	AK	99669	Prince William Sound
DEFIANCE	DEAL STUART	7314 11TH NW	SEATTLE	WA	98117	Prince William Sound
DESTINY	DOHNER DENNIS	4321 BOBLETT RD	BLAINE	WA	98230	Prince William Sound
DUSTY-REK	RENNER OHN	BOX 756	CORDOVA	AK	99574	Prince William Sound
EQUINOX	BURTON CARL	BOX 1404	CORDOVA	AK	99574	Prince William Sound
ESPERANZA	LOVE JOHN	BOX 141	GIRDWOOD	AK	99587	Prince William Sound
FAST BREAK	LEE BRIAN	31250 W LEE DR	SUTTON	AK	99674	Prince William Sound
FAST BREAK	NELSON EMIL	BOX 130	HOMER	AK	99603	Prince William Sound
FAST BREAK II	NUKA POINT FISHERIES INC	BOX 130	HOMER	AK	99603	Prince William Sound
FAT BOY	ALWARD MATTHEW	60082 CLARICE WAY	HOMER	AK	99603	Prince William Sound
FINESSE	ROSAUER CHRIS	BOX 78	GIRDWOOD	AK	99587	Prince William Sound
FV GODSPEED	CORAZZA RICHARD	BOX 1320	HOMER	AK	99603	Prince William Sound
FV PAGAN	LONG JASON	BOX 1761	CORDOVA	AK	99574	Prince William Sound
GATOR	CABANA TIM	BOX 201	GIRDWOOD	AK	99587	Prince William Sound
GOTCHA	STEPHENS MONTY	10764 CHESHIRE WY	PALO CEDRO	CA	96073	Prince William Sound
GRAYLING	LINVILLE JOSEPH	BOX 1753	SEWARD	AK	99664	Prince William Sound
GUIDANCE	MILL RICHARD	BOX 39861	NINILCHIK	AK	99639	Prince William Sound
HADASSAH	CARROLL JEANNE	BOX 551	HOMER	AK	99603	Prince William Sound
HUMPY DORY	CARROLL DOUGLAS	BOX 1071	CORDOVA	AK	99574	Prince William Sound
JETSON	CABANA JEFFERY	BOX 26	HOMER	AK	99603	Prince William Sound
JIMANI	MEINTS MICHAEL	BOX 2402	CORDOVA	AK	99574	Prince William Sound
JITNEY	CHESHIER ELMER	BOX 2264	CORDOVA	AK	99574	Prince William Sound
JITNEY	VILLALON GONZALO	BOX 2695	CORDOVA	AK	99574	Prince William Sound
JITNEY II	CARROLL DOUGLAS	BOX 1071	CORDOVA	AK	99574	Prince William Sound

Vessel	Owner	Address	City	State	Zip	Area
JONATHAN S	SMALLWOOD GERALD	BOX 453	CORDOVA	AK	99574	Prince William Sound
JONES	MCCALLUM MARTIN	4351 S DISCOVERY BAY RD	PORT TOWNSEND	WA	98368	Prince William Sound
KELLY NATHAN	ROSAUER CHRIS	BOX 78	GIRDWOOD	AK	99587	Prince William Sound
KNOT 4 PLAY	ANDERSON KALE	BOX 2918	HOMER	AK	99603	Prince William Sound
KODIAK SOCKEYE	HARDER PAUL	839 51ST STREET	PORT TOWNSEND	WA	98368	Prince William Sound
KUPREANOF	BARCLAY TIMOTHY	BOX 3015	VALDEZ	AK	99686	Prince William Sound
LADY GRACE	BLACK CHARLES	BOX 666	HOMER	AK	99603	Prince William Sound
LADY KAY	EDENS MARK	BOX 641	HOMER	AK	99603	Prince William Sound
LADY SANDRA	CRUMP WILLIAM E	BOX 3731	VALDEZ	AK	99686	Prince William Sound
LAUNI LYNN	CAMERON ROBERT	2120 41ST ST	ANACORTES	WA	98221	Prince William Sound
LEAH C	CULBERTSON BERNARD	BOX 2906	VALDEZ	AK	99686	Prince William Sound
LUCKY	MILLER THANE	BOX 2961	VALDEZ	AK	99686	Prince William Sound
MALAGA	JOHNSON GERALD	BOX 1887	WESTPORT	WA	98595	Prince William Sound
MARANDAH	SEASCAPE INC	BOX 1646	HOMER	AK	99603	Prince William Sound
MARAUDER	PURATICH ROBERT	BOX 1223	GIG HARBOR	WA	98335	Prince William Sound
MARY M	MARKUSEN ROB	8358 DELTA LINE RD	CUSTER	WA	98240	Prince William Sound
MICKEY H	HALPIN KENNETH	BOX 1022	HOMER	AK	99603	Prince William Sound
MINE THREE	SMITH KRISTEN	BOX 2260	VALDEZ	AK	99686	Prince William Sound
MISHA'S TOY	JOHNSON GERALD	BOX 1887	WESTPORT	WA	98595	Prince William Sound
MISS GRANDE	JENSEN DOUGLAS	BOX 92535	ANCHORAGE	AK	99509	Prince William Sound
MISS KAYLEY	BABIC JACK	BOX 1208	CORDOVA	AK	99574	Prince William Sound
MISS MELODY	HATCH ARNE	BOX 346	SEWARD	AK	99664	Prince William Sound
MISS MOLLY	BOSICK GREGG	BOX 34	KASILOF	AK	99610	Prince William Sound
MOOT POINT	MACALUSO MICHAEL	BOX 2901	HOMER	AK	99603	Prince William Sound
MORNING STAR	MEINTS MICHAEL	BOX 2402	CORDOVA	AK	99574	Prince William Sound
MYRA JEAN	GILSON DANE	BOX 845	VALDEZ	AK	99686	Prince William Sound
MYRIAHE	COLANO DONALD	BOX 341	CORDOVA	AK	99574	Prince William Sound

Vessel	Owner	Address	City	State	Zip	Area
NACHO	JENSEN DOUGLAS	BOX 92535	ANCHORAGE	AK	99509	Prince William Sound
NAKCHAMIK	WILKIE TIM	BOX 1726	SEWARD	AK	99664	Prince William Sound
NANOOK	WILLIAMS DUKE	BOX 872425	WASILLA	AK	99687	Prince William Sound
NUKA POINT	NELSON EMIL	BOX 130	HOMER	AK	99603	Prince William Sound
OCEAN POINTE	OCEAN POINTE INC	BOX 2071	CORDOVA	AK	99574	Prince William Sound
ORCATRON II	MEADOWS MARK	4894 WENDY LN	KELSEYVILLE	CA	95451	Prince William Sound
ORION	WIDMANN ROBERT	BOX 879	CORDOVA	AK	99574	Prince William Sound
PACIFIC DREAM	DOHNER RODNEY	4786 SAGEBRUSH LN	BLAINE	WA	98230	Prince William Sound
PAGAN	RIEDEL STEPHEN	12300 ROCKRIDGE DR	ANCHORAGE	AK	99516	Prince William Sound
PERSISTENCE	WIDMANN ROBERT	BOX 879	CORDOVA	AK	99574	Prince William Sound
PILLAR CAPE	BLAKE HUGHIE	BOX 1236	CORDOVA	AK	99574	Prince William Sound
PRINCESS CHRISTINE	HONKOLA RAYMOND	BOX 100	CORDOVA	AK	99574	Prince William Sound
QUEST	SPRINGER MATTHEW	BOX 2882	HOMER	AK	99603	Prince William Sound
R/V MONTAGUE	MONTAGUE MAR. RESEARCH LLC	BOX 297	GIRDWOOD	AK	99587	Prince William Sound
RAFFERTY	JENSEN RODERICK	BOX 1601	CORDOVA	AK	99574	Prince William Sound
RAINBIRD	CHIPMAN DAVID	BOX 484	CORDOVA	AK	99574	Prince William Sound
RAVEN'S CHILD	HOPKINS JOHN	BOX 343	CORDOVA	AK	99574	Prince William Sound
REDEMPTION	TUTT STEVE	BOX 1105	HOMER	AK	99603	Prince William Sound
RIGOROUS	NORNES PETER	21316 92ND PL W	EDMONDS	WA	98020	Prince William Sound
RITA	SCHACTLER BRUCE	BOX 2254	KODIAK	AK	99615	Prince William Sound
RITUAL	BURTON CARL	BOX 1404	CORDOVA	AK	99574	Prince William Sound
RUDE	WIESE ROBERT	BOX 864	CORDOVA	AK	99574	Prince William Sound
RUTH M	MEADOWS MARK	4894 WENDY LN	KELSEYVILLE	CA	95451	Prince William Sound
SANTIAGO	COLLINS RICHARD	BOX 1734	CORDOVA	AK	99574	Prince William Sound
SARAH NICOLE	BARCLAY TIMOTHY	1207 CHUGACH WAY	ANCHORAGE	AK	99503	Prince William Sound
SCIRROCO	CANDY WATER CREEK LLC	2303 PERKINS LN W	SEATTLE	WA	98199	Prince William Sound
SEA DOG	HALTNESS ERIK	BOX 1818	VALDEZ	AK	99686	Prince William Sound

Appendix 6
Purse Seiners, Salmon

Capt. Jonathan Allen

Vessel	Owner	Address	City	State	Zip	Area
SEA HUNT	FULLER MARCUS	BOX 3205	VALDEZ	AK	99686	Prince William Sound
SEA KAT	NELSON ROBERT	BOX 205	KASILOF	AK	99610	Prince William Sound
SEA MIST	SCHOLLENBERG RICHARD	BOX 264	ANCHOR POINT	AK	99556	Prince William Sound
SHADOW DAWN	RENNER JOHN	BOX 756	CORDOVA	AK	99574	Prince William Sound
SHEAR WATER	WILLIAMS SHAWN	BOX 672505	CHUGIAK	AK	99567	Prince William Sound
SHILOH	CARROLL KIP	3744 627TH PL S	FEDERAL WAY	WA	98003	Prince William Sound
SOUND QUEST	ALLEN LESLIE	BOX 984	VALDEZ	AK	99686	Prince William Sound
SOUND STAR II	JONES KENNETH	BOX 1044	HOMER	AK	99603	Prince William Sound
ST ANDREW	VILLALON GONZALO	BOX 2695	CORDOVA	AK	99574	Prince William Sound
ST ZITA	GLENOVICH ROBERT	480 S STATE ST #102	BELLINGHAM	WA	98225	Prince William Sound
STAR SHADOW	LINDHOLM EVERETT	2310 25TH ST	ANACORTES	WA	98221	Prince William Sound
STRIDER	BB FISHERIES LLC	BOX 518	CORDOVA	AK	99574	Prince William Sound
SUNBABY	CARROLL WESTON	1170 QUEETS CIR	HOMER	AK	99603	Prince William Sound
SUSAN STARR	MAYBERRY JAMES	17500 17TH AVE W	LYNNWOOD	WA	98037	Prince William Sound
TATYANA RENEE	SMITH GREGORY	BOX 2744	VALDEZ	AK	99686	Prince William Sound
TEMPEST	LUNDLI FISHERIES LLC	17746 15TH AVE NW	SHORELINE	WA	98177	Prince William Sound
TERYN	WILLIAMS SHAWN	BOX 672505	CHUGIAK	AK	99567	Prince William Sound
THE GITNEY PESIDEN	FULLER MARCUS	BOX 3205	VALDEZ	AK	99686	Prince William Sound
THUNDER BOLT	GLASEN MICHAEL	BOX 432	CORDOVA	AK	99574	Prince William Sound
TOR	CARLSON ERLING	BOX 1008	CORDOVA	AK	99574	Prince William Sound
TRIAL	NIPPELL CHARLES	BOX 1041	CORDOVA	AK	99574	Prince William Sound
TUBE TIME	LONG JASON	BOX 1761	CORDOVA	AK	99574	Prince William Sound
VERA-B	LIDRAL LANCE	6986 S HIGH POINT DR	CLINTON	WA	98236	Prince William Sound
VORTEX	BLAKE HUGHIE	BOX 1236	CORDOVA	AK	99574	Prince William Sound
WESCO NO3	LYTLE LAWRENCE	BOX 336	CORDOVA	AK	99574	Prince William Sound
WEST POINT	MAYBERRY JAMES	17500 17TH AVE W	LYNNWOOD	WA	98037	Prince William Sound
WESTERLY	PLAIT JOHN	BOX 1085	CORDOVA	AK	99574	Prince William Sound

197

Vessel	Owner	Address	City	State	Zip	Area
WRESTLER	DANIELS DAVID	BOX 1555	VALDEZ	AK	99686	Prince William Sound
YO-SEMIDI-SAM	MILL RICHARD	BOX 39861	NINILCHIK	AK	99639	Prince William Sound
TOUCHDOWN	BABIC RUSSELL	BOX 1833	CORDOVA	AK	99574	Prince William Sound
ALEXANDRA	ALEXANDRA INC	2940 MALLARD LN	ANCHORAGE	AK	99508	Prince William Sound
ANDY SEA	SCUDDER BRADFORD	266 S MOBLEY LN	BOISE	ID	83712	Prince William Sound
ANGEJENL	LITTLETON ROCKY	BOX 1373	PETERSBURG	AK	99833	Prince William Sound
ANGELETTE	THOMASSEN JAY	BOX 1451	PETERSBURG	AK	99833	Prince William Sound
ARIEL	CLEMENS, MARY & DAVID	3735 DORA AVE	ANCHORAGE	AK	99516	Prince William Sound
AURIGA	CAMELOT LTD	3733 BEN WALTERS LN #2	HOMER	AK	99603	Prince William Sound
BOULDER BAY	MCLEAN JOHN	BOX 2191	HOMER	AK	99603	Prince William Sound
CARMEN ROSE	SANDELIN FISHERIES INC	409 LONGRTIME LN	SEDRO WOOLLEY	WA	98284	Prince William Sound
CAT-BIL-LU	NAHANNI FISHERIES INC	1470 FLINTRIDGE AVE	EUGENE	OR	97401	Prince William Sound
CRESCENT MOON	NELSON THOMAS	BOX 1392	HOMER	AK	99603	Prince William Sound
CRICKET	BURTON CARL	BOX 81	CORDOVA	AK	99574	Prince William Sound
DEBORAH ANN	DEXTER RODERICK	3726 BROAD ST	BELLINGHAM	WA	98229	Prince William Sound
DESERIE LYNNE	PWS CONNECTION INC	BOX 534	VALDEZ	AK	99686	Prince William Sound
DEVOTION	KILOKAK INC	BOX 848	KODIAK	AK	99615	Prince William Sound
EXCELLER	EXCELLER FISHERIES INC	BOX 5993	BELLINGHAM	WA	98227	Prince William Sound
GORE POINT	CABANA TIM	BOX 201	GIRDWOOD	AK	99587	Prince William Sound
HISTORIAN	ROGERS KENNETH	1060 JEFFREY AVE	HOMER	AK	99603	Prince William Sound
HUNGRY RAVEN	HARRIS RAYMOND	BOX 1318	SEWARD	AK	99664	Prince William Sound
INDIANA	MCCALLUM MARTIN	4351 S DISCOVERY BAY RD	PORT TOWNSEND	WA	98368	Prince William Sound
INTREPID	ROSAUER CHRIS	BOX 78	GIRDWOOD	AK	99587	Prince William Sound
JOSEPH BOONEY	PIRTLE TOM	BOX 774	CORDOVA	AK	99574	Prince William Sound
JOURNEYMAN	KAPP ALAN	BOX 3312	VALDEZ	AK	99686	Prince William Sound
KENDAL	STEPHENS MONTY	10764 CHESHIRE WY	PALO CEDRO	CA	96073	Prince William Sound
KETA	BURTON JAMES	BOX 6	CORDOVA	AK	99574	Prince William Sound

Vessel	Owner	Address	City	State	Zip	Area
KILLIN TIME	ANDERSON KALE	BOX 2918	HOMER	AK	99603	Prince William Sound
KYLE DAVID	BUTLER DAVID	BOX 141	CORDOVA	AK	99574	Prince William Sound
LADY SAMANTHA	ESTES ROXY	BOX 1709	CORDOVA	AK	99574	Prince William Sound
LAUN C	CAMERON ROBERT	2120 41ST ST	ANACORTES	WA	98221	Prince William Sound
LIVELY JANE	ANDREWS JON	BOX 1034	SEWARD	AK	99664	Prince William Sound
MAKAI	FLYNN OLIVER	BOX 2106	HOMER	AK	99603	Prince William Sound
MALAMUTE KID	CORAZZA SONJA	BOX 1320	HOMER	AK	99603	Prince William Sound
MINE TOO	SMITH KRISTEN	BOX 2260	VALDEZ	AK	99686	Prince William Sound
MISS EMILY	KALLANDER JAMES	BOX 2272	CORDOVA	AK	99574	Prince William Sound
MISS OLIVIA	WHITTOCK TYSON	10601 ELLIS DR	ANCHORAGE	AK	99516	Prince William Sound
MISS ROXANNE	FEENSTRA STEVEN	8869 SEMIAHMOO DR	BLAINE	WA	98230	Prince William Sound
MORNING THUNDER	GLASEN MICHAEL	BOX 432	CORDOVA	AK	99574	Prince William Sound
NEPTUNE	CHINA B FISHERIES INC	BOX 1945	CORDOVA	AK	99574	Prince William Sound
ODYSSEY	BLAKE RONALD	BOX 1236	CORDOVA	AK	99574	Prince William Sound
PARKS 19	ALASKA MAR. RESOURCES LLC	BOX 1976	CORDOVA	AK	99574	Prince William Sound
PATRIOT	FRONTIER FISHERIES INC	BOX 20373	JUNEAU	AK	99801	Prince William Sound
RAI DAWN	SMAC FISHERIES LLC	BOX 2071	CORDOVA	AK	99574	Prince William Sound
REGALIA	BLAKE RONALD	BOX 1236	CORDOVA	AK	99574	Prince William Sound
REJOYCE	BEAUDRY LOUIS	BOX 1485	GIRDWOOD	AK	99587	Prince William Sound
REMEDY	TRUE NORTH ENTERPRISES LLC	BOX 1904	CORDOVA	AK	99574	Prince William Sound
RHEMA	JENSEN JAMES	BOX 365	CORDOVA	AK	99574	Prince William Sound
SEA HUNTER	FRARY JIM	BOX 1019	HOMER	AK	99603	Prince William Sound
SEA PRINCE	NELSON ROBERT	BOX 205	KASILOF	AK	99610	Prince William Sound
SILVER STORM	YAKUNIN SERGEY	BOX 5044	NIKOLAEVSK	AK	99556	Prince William Sound
SISU	CLEMENS, MARY & DAVID	3735 DORA AVE	ANCHORAGE	AK	99516	Prince William Sound
STEVEN-DANIEL	ALLEY STEVEN	BOX 921	VALDEZ	AK	99686	Prince William Sound
TENACIOUS	TEN FISH LLC	2220 NORTH STAR #7	ANCHORAGE	AK	99503	Prince William Sound

Vessel	Owner	Address	City	State	Zip	Area
TRIBUTE	WILKIE TIM	BOX 1726	SEWARD	AK	99664	Prince William Sound
ALASKAN PRIDE	YAKUNIN SERGEY	BOX 5044	NIKOLAEVSK	AK	99556	Prince William Sound
SHERIN D	DANIELS DAVID	BOX 1555	VALDEZ	AK	99686	Prince William Sound
ADIRONDACK	JACKLET ALAN	4521 325TH AVE NE	CARNATION	WA	98014	Southeast
ALASKAN	DONTOS LARRY	2334 FAIRWAY LN	OAK HARBOR	WA	98277	Southeast
ALERT	BRUNSMAN JAMES	BOX 105	DAYVILLE	OR	97825	Southeast
ALESHALEY	GRANBERG KEVIN	BOX 2002	PETERSBURG	AK	99833	Southeast
ALPHA OMEGA	EVENS ERIC	BOX 1412	PETERSBURG	AK	99833	Southeast
ANIKA	GILBERT BROS. FISHERIES INC	BOX 4103	KODIAK	AK	99615	Southeast
ANITA	MATSON PAUL	6201 15TH AVE NW PMB G700	SEATTLE	WA	98107	Southeast
ANTHONY G	GEORGE RICHARD	515 N FOREST	BELLINGHAM	WA	98225	Southeast
ARCTIC	MCGEE GARY	40 DRAYTON CT	BLAINE	WA	98230	Southeast
ARCTIC FOX	CROME DANIEL	BOX 1243	PETERSBURG	AK	99833	Southeast
ARIEL	WARTMAN BRIAN	2144 NW 204TH	SEATTLE	WA	98177	Southeast
ARLINE	PLANCICH GERALD	9925 SW WINDMILL ST	VASHON	WA	98070	Southeast
BARANOF QUEEN	JENSEN BRAD	813 52ND	PORT TOWNSEND	WA	98368	Southeast
BARBARA	THOMASSEN TROY	BOX 152	PETERSBURG	AK	99833	Southeast
BARBARA ANN	MARSDEN CLINTON	BOX 815	METLAKATLA	AK	99926	Southeast
BARBRA B	VEITEHANS GREGORY	302 GARDEN CLUB RD	NORDLAND	WA	98358	Southeast
BFD	BALOVICH FRANK	BOX 1396	SITKA	AK	99835	Southeast
BLUE PACIFIC	HOLMSTROM MICHAEL	17952 MCLEAN RD	MOUNT VERNON	WA	98273	Southeast
BLUNDER	HEAVY DUTY LLC	3401 W LAWTON ST	SEATTLE	WA	98199	Southeast
BOULDER BAY	NELSON ERIC	BOX 507	NEWPORT	OR	97365	Southeast
BURKE	BURKE ARNOLD	1541 MADISON AVE	BLAINE	WA	98230	Southeast
CALOGERA A	ALFIERI, JOHN, NICK, & ANTHONY	1266 MOANA DR	SAN DIEGO	CA	92107	Southeast
CANUCK	SILVER BAY SEAFOODS	4400 SAWMILL CREEK RD #B	SITKA	AK	99835	Southeast
CANUCK II	SILVER BAY SEAFOODS	4400 SAWMILL CREEK RD #B	SITKA	AK	99835	Southeast

Vessel	Owner	Address	City	State	Zip	Area
CHALLENGER	GOLDEN JEFFREY	8322 SILVER LAKE RD	MAPLE FALLS	WA	98266	Southeast
CHASINA	DOBSZINSKY KURT	2023 E SIMS WAY #353	PORT TOWNSEND	WA	98368	Southeast
CHIQUITA	ONEIL DENNIS	BOX 1083	PETERSBURG	AK	99833	Southeast
CHRISTIAN S	UTTLEY ROSS	2201 5TH ST	EVERETT	WA	98201	Southeast
CHRISTINA DAWN	ROSTAD PAUL	BOX 183	KAKE	AK	99830	Southeast
CHRISTOPHER DAVID	DEMMERT KARL	BOX 556	CRAIG	AK	99921	Southeast
CINNAMON GIRL	EVENS CHRIS	BOX 886	PETERSBURG	AK	99833	Southeast
CONFIDENCE	JOHNS LEROY	BOX 290	CRAIG	AK	99921	Southeast
COOPER II	HUKILAU LLC	3009 HALIBUT POINT RD	SITKA	AK	99835	Southeast
CORAL	ESQUIRO IZAAK	BOX 984	WARM SPRINGS	OR	97761	Southeast
CRUSADER	BROWN BEAR FISHERIES INC	1900 W NICKERSON #213	SEATTLE	WA	98119	Southeast
CRYSTAL BAY	NAGAMINE ROSS	1134 SALMON RD 2-B	KETCHIKAN	AK	99901	Southeast
DONNA-C-2	JENSEN JEREMY	BOX 1688	PETERSBURG	AK	99833	Southeast
DREAM ON	RECORDS RONALD	BOX 307	HYDABURG	AK	99922	Southeast
EAGLE III	JENSEN ERIC	17403 COLONY RD	BOW	WA	98232	Southeast
EIGHTEEN WHEELER	OTOOLE KEVIN	BOX 1875	CORDOVA	AK	99574	Southeast
ELAINE B	CHENEY SCOTT	948 SUDDEN VALLEY	BELLINGHAM	WA	98229	Southeast
ENDURANCE	LIDDICOAT FISHERIES INC	4115 BAKER AVE NW	SEATTLE	WA	98107	Southeast
F/V LEGEND	MUNKRES MICHAEL	12818 6TH AVE CT NW	GIG HARBOR	WA	98332	Southeast
FAREWELL	MARKUSEN JEFF	8061 NISKA RD	BLAINE	WA	98230	Southeast
FAVORITE	FINTAN FISHERIES LLC	2888 S 355 ST	FEDERAL WAY	WA	98003	Southeast
FREEDOM	LUNDQUIST LOREN	723 SHELTER BAY DR	LACONNER	WA	98257	Southeast
FREEDOM	MARIFERN BRUCE	BOX 917	PETERSBURG	AK	99833	Southeast
FV FOX ISLAND	ADAMS MARK	8630 CAMBRIDGE LP	BLAINE	WA	98230	Southeast
GEORGE L	JERKOVICH NANCY	3710 HARBORVIEW DR	GIG HARBOR	WA	98332	Southeast
GORBUSCHA	LEACH LAUCHLIN	2318 NE 105TH ST	SEATTLE	WA	98125	Southeast
HAIDA LADY	SKULTKA CHARLES	BOX 665	SITKA	AK	99835	Southeast

Vessel	Owner	Address	City	State	Zip	Area
HAIDA WARRIOR	FRANKLIN C.DAVID	3401 W LAWTON ST	SEATTLE	WA	98199	Southeast
HALCYON	FINTAN FISHERIES LLC	2888 S 355 ST	FEDERAL WAY	WA	98003	Southeast
HARBOR GEM	LOVROVICH TIM	7021 120TH ST CT NW	GIG HARBOR	WA	98332	Southeast
HEAVY DUTY	HEAVY DUTY LLC	3401 W LAWTON ST	SEATTLE	WA	98199	Southeast
HIN 1	LOVROVICH TOM	9705 JACOBSEN LN	GIG HARBOR	WA	98332	Southeast
HOME SHORE	KYLE JAMES	4102 LINNELL RD	DEMING	WA	98244	Southeast
INGRID HELENA	THORSTENSON ROBERT	410 CALHOUN AVE	JUNEAU	AK	99801	Southeast
INTREPID	MCCULLOUGH CHARLES	BOX 707	PETERSBURG	AK	99833	Southeast
ISLAND GIRL	KVERNVIK KURT	BOX 1081	PETERSBURG	AK	99833	Southeast
ISLAND QUEEN	MOLLER RICHARD	BOX 1081	GIG HARBOR	WA	98332	Southeast
IVER P NORE	WALTZ JAMES	1418 191ST DR SE	SNOHOMISH	WA	98290	Southeast
JADE ANN	KADAKE DELBERT	BOX 554	KAKE	AK	99830	Southeast
JEAN D	JEAN D INC	17002 12TH AVE SW	NORMANDY PARK	WA	98166	Southeast
JENNIFER TARA	JOHANSON RUDY	BOX 276	KLAWOCK	AK	99925	Southeast
JENSEN REAGAN	FISHER ARTHUR	13506 96TH AVE NW	GIG HARBOR	WA	98329	Southeast
JOHNNIE B	COLD STREAM LLC	540 WATER ST #302	KETCHIKAN	AK	99901	Southeast
JOSIE J	FV JOSIE J INC	2417 TONGASS AVE 111-141	KETCHIKAN	AK	99901	Southeast
JULIA KAE	S L DEMMERT FISHERIES INC	13619 MUKILTEO SPEEDWAY D5-343	LYNNWOOD	WA	98087	Southeast
JULIE ANN	MUNKRES MATTHEW	7321 96TH ST NW	GIG HARBOR	WA	98332	Southeast
KAREN JEAN	GIERARD BRIAN	BOX 7343	KETCHIKAN	AK	99901	Southeast
KATHY N	NEWMAN DONALD	415 NW 120TH	SEATTLE	WA	98177	Southeast
KATLIAN	SKINNA BYRON	BOX 308	KLAWOCK	AK	99925	Southeast
KEELY ROSE	SWANSON JOHN	BOX 1546	PETERSBURG	AK	99833	Southeast
KELSEY NICOLE	SALMON FALLS INC	BOX 5454	KETCHIKAN	AK	99901	Southeast
LADY BRENDA	DEMMERT LAWRENCE	16136 41ST AVE NE	LAKE FOREST PARK	WA	98155	Southeast
LAKE BAY	MARRESE ANDREW	13041 4TH AVE NW	SEATTLE	WA	98177	Southeast
LAURIANNE	GOSPODINOVIC DENNIS	5087 ZANDER DR	BELLINGHAM	WA	98226	Southeast

Appendix 6
Purse Seiners, Salmon

Vessel	Owner	Address	City	State	Zip	Area
LEADING LADY	ALBER LOUIE	BOX 111	CORDOVA	AK	99574	Southeast
LISA MARIE	CHANEY DOUGLAS	11719 MADERA DR SW	LAKEWOOD	WA	98499	Southeast
LISA SAN	SITKA SOUND SEAFOODS	329 KATLIAN ST	SITKA	AK	99835	Southeast
LITTLE JOE	LINDHOLM EVERETT	2310 25TH ST	ANACORTES	WA	98221	Southeast
LUCIA	BABICH NICK	13310 PURDY DR NW	GIG HARBOR	WA	98332	Southeast
MADRE DOLOROSA	EINARSON ED	9311 VALLEY VIEW RD	BLAINE	WA	98230	Southeast
MANDI J	ROONEY ROBERT	BOX 2179	WRANGELL	AK	99929	Southeast
MARAUDER	THOMASSEN STEVEN	BOX 424	WRANGELL	AK	99929	Southeast
MARENE	PETERSON STEVE	BOX 309	ELLENSBURG	WA	98926	Southeast
MARSHAL TITO	LORAX INC	812 W CONNECTICUT	BELLINGHAM	WA	98225	Southeast
MARTHA K	KITKA HARVEY	BOX 1144	SITKA	AK	99835	Southeast
MARY LOUISE B	MCILRAITH THOMAS	BOX 1198	ORTING	WA	98360	Southeast
MILLER JITNEY	ALBER LOUIE	BOX 111	CORDOVA	AK	99574	Southeast
MISS SHERRI	GREEN JAMES	BOX 1154	PETERSBURG	AK	99833	Southeast
MISS TAMMY	VERRALL LARRY	12364 RAINIER DR	BURLINGTON	WA	98233	Southeast
MISS TINA	GREEN JAMES	BOX 1154	PETERSBURG	AK	99833	Southeast
MISTY MOON	BEAUDIN DAVID	BOX 983	BELLINGHAM	WA	98227	Southeast
MOUNT PAVLOF	ROOD RICHARD	BOX 3466	LYNNWOOD	WA	98046	Southeast
MUZON	DEMMERT LONNIE	BOX 2683	STANWOOD	WA	98292	Southeast
MY SONS	DEMMERT LAWRENCE	16136 41ST AVE NE	LAKE FOREST PARK	WA	98155	Southeast
MYSTIC LADY	BABICH MICHAEL	13510 GOODNOUGH DR NW	GIG HARBOR	WA	98332	Southeast
NANCY ROSE	BRISCOE JIM	1714 WILSON AVE	BELLINGHAM	WA	98225	Southeast
NEW OREGON II	BLAIR ANDREW	BOX 108	FOX ISLAND	WA	98333	Southeast
NORSEL	NORSEL LLC	12704 471ST AVE SE	NORTH BEND	WA	98045	Southeast
OCEAN DREAM	BABICH ANDREW	8306 25TH AVE CT NW	GIG HARBOR	WA	98332	Southeast
OCEAN RIPPLE	SUMMER FISHING LTD	1201 THIRD AVE #2200	SEATTLE	WA	98101	Southeast
OCEAN SPIRIT	LUNDE JAN	14202 BEVERLY PARK RD	EDMONDS	WA	98026	SoutheastLinda,

Vessel	Owner	Address	City	State	Zip	Area
ORCA SONG	HUDSON CLIFFORD	BOX 480	METLAKATLA	AK	99926	Southeast
OUTLOOK	MILLER AARON	BOX 2144	PETERSBURG	AK	99833	Southeast
OWYHEE	MCALLISTER THOMAS	316 DISTIN AVE	JUNEAU	AK	99801	Southeast
PACIFIC FISHER	CARLE, JOHN & JAN	BOX 1	HYDABURG	AK	99922	Southeast
PACIFIC JADE	MARTINEZ MARTY	BOX 513	METLAKATLA	AK	99926	Southeast
PACIFIC NOMAD	PACIFIC NOMAD INC	BOX 2232	WRANGELL	AK	99929	Southeast
PACIFIC SKYE	CHANEY DOUGLAS	11719 MADERA DR SW	LAKEWOOD	WA	98499	Southeast
PAIGE MARIE	SORO INC	510 OLMSTEAD LN SW	OLYMPIA	WA	98512	Southeast
PAMELA DENISE	WELLINGTON VICTOR	BOX 69	METLAKATLA	AK	99926	Southeast
PAMELA RAE	THORSTENSON ROBERT	410 CALHOUN AVE	JUNEAU	AK	99801	Southeast
PAMELA RAE SKIF	THORSTENSON ROBERT	410 CALHOUN AVE	JUNEAU	AK	99801	Southeast
PARAGON	BABICH RANDALL	BOX 429	LAKEBAY	WA	98349	Southeast
PARTISAN	SVENSON MIKE	104 SHARON DR	SITKA	AK	99835	Southeast
PRIME PLUS	TROKA PAUL	8602 SOBEK LN	CONCRETE	WA	98237	Southeast
PROZAC	MARINA SKY LLC	BOX 2071	CORDOVA	AK	99574	Southeast
QUANDARY	PAWLAK THOMAS	2010 JACKMAN ST	PORT TOWNSEND	WA	98368	Southeast
REALITY	CURRY JOHN	9445 SUNRISE RD	BLAINE	WA	98230	Southeast
RELENTLESS	MCFADYEN JEFFREY	BOX 592	PETERSBURG	AK	99833	Southeast
RENAISSANCE	RENAISSANCE LLC	16212 BOTHELL EVERETT HWY #F340	MILL CREEK	WY	98212	Southeast
RETRIEVER	RETRIEVER ALASKA LLC	1100 W EWING ST	SEATTLE	WA	98105	Southeast
ROGUE	THURSTON DONALD	9224 LOHRER LN NE	OLYMPIA	WA	98516	Southeast
SAINT JANET	ISLAND RAVEN SEAFOODS	349 RAVEN HILL RD	LOPEZ	WA	98261	Southeast
SAMANTHA RAE	MARSDEN DANIEL	BOX 15	METLAKATLA	AK	99926	Southeast
SARA B	HAYNES DANNY	BOX 7036	KETCHIKAN	AK	99901	Southeast
SARAH B	FV EMILY NICOLE INC	5166 SHORELINE DR N	KETCHIKAN	AK	99901	Southeast
SAVANNAH JEAN	BJORNSON TERRY	10980 FALK RD NE	BAINBRIDGE ISLAND	WA	98110	Southeast
SCREAMIN EAGLE	JAMES LARRY	BOX 1222	CRAIG	AK	99921	Southeast

Vessel	Owner	Address	City	State	Zip	Area
SEA BREAKER	CHRISTENSEN STEVE	6302 VISTA DR	FERNDALE	WA	98248	Southeast
SEA FURY	LOVROVICH GREGG	5310 72ND AVE NW	GIG HARBOR	WA	98335	Southeast
SEA GEM	CORNWELL CHRIS	4220 CRYSTAL SPRINGS DR	BAINBRIDGE ISLAND	WA	98110	Southeast
SEA GYPSY	HIGGINS GENE	109 DIGBY RD	MOUNT VERNON	WA	98273	Southeast
SECURE	BAILEY KWIN	BOX 1369	PORT TOWNSEND	WA	98368	Southeast
SHREDDER	WYMAN PHILLIP	BOX 2507	SITKA	AK	99835	Southeast
SHREK	WYMAN PHILLIP	BOX 2507	SITKA	AK	99835	Southeast
SIDE BET	DODSON FORREST	607 ETOLIN ST	SITKA	AK	99835	Southeast
SNATCH IT	WHITETHORN LUKE	BOX 1716	PETERSBURG	AK	99833	Southeast
SOUND STAR	MANNING EDWARD	11170 RIDGERIM TRAIL SE	PORT ORCHARD	WA	98367	Southeast
SPARTAN	SMITH ALLEN	3974 SALT SPRINGS DR	FERNDALE	WA	98248	Southeast
ST JOHN	ESQUIRO GEORGE	BOX 1993	PORT TOWNSEND	WA	98368	Southeast
ST TERESA	BRISCOE ROBERT	BOX 10	FERNDALE	WA	98248	Southeast
SYLVI ELISE	THORSTENSON ROBERT	410 CALHOUN AVE	JUNEAU	AK	99801	Southeast
TEASHA	DOBRYDNIA RANDALL	69 W MATTLE RD #N	KETCHIKAN	AK	99901	Southeast
THE BIG UNIT	BLANKENSHIP BRIAN	104 CHIRIKOV DR	SITKA	AK	99835	Southeast
TIFFANY ROSE	CHANEY DOUGLAS	11719 MADERA DR SW	LAKEWOOD	WA	98499	Southeast
TLINGIT LADY	DEMMERT BRENDA	16136 41ST AVE NE	LAKE FOREST PARK	WA	98155	Southeast
TRAC	LINDHOLM EVERETT	2310 25TH ST	ANACORTES	WA	98221	Southeast
TRADITION	LOVROVICH TOM	9705 JACOBSEN LN	GIG HARBOR	WA	98332	Southeast
TREJO	JONES KENNETH	4092 GINNETT RD	ANACORTES	WA	98221	Southeast
VERNON	ANK ROBERT	19316 133RD PL SE	RENTON	WA	98058	Southeast
VIKING MAID	COCKRUM RUSSELL	5791 N TONGASS HWY	KETCHIKAN	AK	99901	Southeast
WESTERN ROAMER	MALICH JOHN	7809 OLYMPIC VIEW DR	GIG HARBOR	WA	98335	Southeast
WIND WALKER	BARRY DAVID	BOX 6276	SITKA	AK	99835	Southeast
WONDERLAND	KELLS INCORPORATED	2888 S 355TH ST	FEDERAL WAY	WA	98003	Southeast
XIP 28	OCEAN BEAUTY ALASKA LLC	BOX 70739	SEATTLE	WA	98127	Southeast

Vessel	Owner	Address	City	State	Zip	Area
XIP 37	FORBUSH MIKE	BOX EXI	JUNEAU	AK	99850	Southeast
XIP 61	MOLLER RICHARD	BOX 1081	GIG HARBOR	WA	98332	Southeast
XIP59	OCEAN BEAUTY ALASKA LLC	BOX 70739	SEATTLE	WA	98127	Southeast
YANKEE BOY	GLENOVICH JAMES	818 17TH ST	BELLINGHAM	WA	98225	Southeast
YANKEE MAID	TROKA PAUL	8602 SOBEK LN	CONCRETE	WA	98237	Southeast
ZOKIAC	MARRESE ANDREW	13041 4TH AVE NW	SEATTLE	WA	98177	Southeast
PACIFIC LADY	RECORDS RONALD	BOX 307	HYDABURG	AK	99922	Southeast
PF #9	MCCAY RODERICK	BOX 161	PETERSBURG	AK	99833	Southeast
PF#7	BLANKENSHIP BRIAN	4316 VALLHALLA DR	SITKA	AK	99835	Southeast
PF#7	MCCAY RODERICK	BOX 161	PETERSBURG	AK	99833	Southeast
AARALYN	VICK STEWART	BOX 1271	PETERSBURG	AK	99833	Southeast
ALASKA GEM	HAYWARD, R & KING, S	BOX 161	METLAKATLA	AK	99926	Southeast
ALASKAN LADY	ALASKAN LADY LLC	BOX 749	GIRDWOOD	AK	99587	Southeast
ALASKAN ROSE	JOHANSON JOHN	BOX 276	KLAWOCK	AK	99925	Southeast
ALEUTIAN DREAM	NILSEN ROBERT	BOX 838	PETERSBURG	AK	99833	Southeast
ALEUTIAN SUN	ASH CREEK LLC	BOX 2192	PETERSBURG	AK	99833	Southeast
ALSEK	PECKHAM JOHN	BOX 8394	KETCHIKAN	AK	99901	Southeast
ARCHANGEL	WYMAN PHILLIP	BOX 2507	SITKA	AK	99835	Southeast
ARLICE	PETTICREW CHARLES	BOX 971	WRANGELL	AK	99929	Southeast
ARTEMIS	UNDERHILL JOHN	103 KRESTOF DR	SITKA	AK	99835	Southeast
BANTER BAY	ONEIL DENNIS	BOX 1083	PETERSBURG	AK	99833	Southeast
BILLY & I	DEMMERT ARTHUR	BOX 180	KLAWOCK	AK	99925	Southeast
BONNIE	WAGNER WALTER	BOX 107	METLAKATLA	AK	99926	Southeast
CAPE CAUTION	PIECUCH CHARLES	4737 4TH AVE NE	SEATTLE	WA	98105	Southeast
CAPE RELIANT	CAPE RELIANT FISHERIES IN	BOX 61	PETERSBURG	AK	99833	Southeast
CAROLE D	BALOVICH FRANK	BOX 1396	SITKA	AK	99835	Southeast
CATHIA ROSE	DEMMERT ARCHIE	BOX 223	KLAWOCK	AK	99925	Southeast

Vessel	Owner	Address	City	State	Zip	Area
CHARLENE MARIE	LINDEMUTH LONNIE	BOX 2069	SNOHOMISH	WA	98291	Southeast
CHELSEA DAWN	YOUNG MARK	BOX 2016	SITKA	AK	99835	Southeast
CHIKAMIN	SAVLAND STANLEY	2413 KA-SEE-ANN DR	JUNEAU	AK	99801	Southeast
CHIRIKOF	DEMMERT DAVID	16116 68TH AVE W	EDMONDS	WA	98026	Southeast
CLOUD NINE	JOHNSON MOSES	2604 SAWMILL CREEK RD	SITKA	AK	99835	Southeast
COMMANDER	OTNESS ALAN	BOX 317	PETERSBURG	AK	99833	Southeast
CORA J	SLAVEN GARY	BOX 205	PETERSBURG	AK	99833	Southeast
CORVA MAY	ALMA J INC	16708 MARINE DR #1	STANWOOD	WA	88292	Southeast
DEFIANT	ROSVOLD ERIC	BOX 1144	PETERSBURG	AK	99833	Southeast
DONNA-ANN	VELER WILLIAM	BOX 387	HOONAH	AK	99829	Southeast
DONNA-JEAN	KADAKE HENRICH	BOX 188	KAKE	AK	99830	Southeast
DREAM MAID	LEEKLEY ROBERT	BOX 217	PETERSBURG	AK	99833	Southeast
ELVAGENE	ERTZBERGER ROCKY	404 BARR RD	GRAYS RIVER	WA	98621	Southeast
EMILY NICOLE	FV EMILY NICOLE INC	5166 SHORELINE DR N	KETCHIKAN	AK	99901	Southeast
EMPRESS	HAYNES BRADLEY	BOX 1152	WARD COVE	AK	99928	Southeast
ERIKA ANN	CHRISTENSEN CHARLES	BOX 824	PETERSBURG	AK	99833	Southeast
EXPATRIATE	SEAMOUNT INC	BOX 1364	PETERSBURG	AK	99833	Southeast
GALLANT MAID	BROADHEAD WILLIAM	BOX 221	WILSON	WY	83014	Southeast
GJOA	CHRISTENSEN DAVID	7302 164TH PL SW	EDMONDS	WA	98026	Southeast
GUARDIAN	VERSTEEG KORY	BOX 1752	PETERSBURG	AK	99833	Southeast
HAAKON	WHITETHORN LUKE	BOX 1716	PETERSBURG	AK	99833	Southeast
HALEY MARIE	PFUNDT ALEC	BOX 1342	PETERSBURG	AK	99833	Southeast
HARVESTER	JENSEN JEREMY	BOX 1688	PETERSBURG	AK	99833	Southeast
HOTSPUR	HOTSPUR INC	3401 W LAWTON ST	SEATTLE	WA	98199	Southeast
HUKILAU	OLSON CHARLES	3009 HALIBUT POINT RD	SITKA	AK	99835	Southeast
ICY QUEEN	FILE SCOTT	4515 TRAFALGAR	JUNEAU	AK	99801	Southeast
INTANGIBLE	ROSVOLD ERIC	BOX 1144	PETERSBURG	AK	99833	Southeast

Vessel	Owner	Address	City	State	Zip	Area
ISLAND PRIDE	HALTINER DEAN	BOX 443	PETERSBURG	AK	99833	Southeast
JACKIE	GUTHRIE GLENN	BOX 686	METLAKATLA	AK	99926	Southeast
JEAN C	CURRY CLYDE	BOX 572	PETERSBURG	AK	99833	Southeast
JEANINE KATHLEEN	INGMAN ROGER	BOX 1155	SITKA	AK	99835	Southeast
JERILYN	EDENSHAW SIDNEY	BOX 352	HYDABURG	AK	99922	Southeast
JOHNNY A	HINCHMAN PAULINE	808 EVANS DR	SEDRO WOOLLEY	WA	98284	Southeast
JOHNNY L	CASTLE JAMES	87 SHOUP ST	KETCHIKAN	AK	99901	Southeast
JOYCE MARIE	TARABOCHIA MARK	BOX 902	ASTORIA	OR	97103	Southeast
KALLISTE	SCHWANTES J.CARLOS	BOX 2335	SITKA	AK	99835	Southeast
KAREN RAE	MAJORS DANIEL	BOX 5358	KETCHIKAN	AK	99901	Southeast
KARINE BRIT	ROSVOLD ERIC	BOX 1144	PETERSBURG	AK	99833	Southeast
KATHI	EVENS ERIC	BOX 1412	PETERSBURG	AK	99833	Southeast
KELSIE JAYCE	HAYWARD BYRON	BOX 446	METLAKATLA	AK	99926	Southeast
KIMBER	KIMBER FISHERIES LLC	BOX 1162	PETERSBURG	AK	99833	Southeast
LADY JANE	MUSTAPPA FRANK	1517 HARRIS AVE	BELLINGHAM	WA	98225	Southeast
LADY LOUISE	JACKSON JEFFREY	BOX 297	KAKE	AK	99830	Southeast
LIBERTY	CARLE MATTHEW	BOX 32	HYDABURG	AK	99922	Southeast
LISA JEAN	BLANKENSHIP BRIAN	104 CHIRIKOV DR	SITKA	AK	99835	Southeast
LITTLE LADY	CASTLE DANIEL	4430 S TONGASS HWY	KETCHIKAN	AK	99901	Southeast
LITTLE LADY	SCHWANTES J.CARLOS	BOX 2335	SITKA	AK	99835	Southeast
LITTLE SIOUX	WARE DOUG	BOX 1291	PETERSBURG	AK	99833	Southeast
LOGAN T	SWANSON JOHN	BOX 1546	PETERSBURG	AK	99833	Southeast
LOVEY JOANN	NELSON NORVAL	1625 FRITZ COVE RD	JUNEAU	AK	99801	Southeast
LUCKY STAR	BABICH NICK	13310 PURDY DR NW	GIG HARBOR	WA	98332	Southeast
LUCY O	OLNEY-MILLER NICK	3006 BARKER ST	SITKA	AK	99835	Southeast
MARATHON	MATHISEN SIGURD	BOX 1460	PETERSBURG	AK	99833	Southeast
MARTINA	GROSS BEN	7362 W PARK HWY #696	WASILLA	AK	99654	Southeast

Vessel	Owner	Address	City	State	Zip	Area
MARY ANN	OLSON DARRYL	BOX 1304	PETERSBURG	AK	99833	Southeast
MARY JOANNE	MILLS PATRICK	BOX 301	HOONAH	AK	99829	Southeast
MEMENTO	HANSON BRET	2916 ST CLAIR ST	BELLINGHAM	WA	98226	Southeast
MERMAID	WHITE JACOB	BOX 361	HOONAH	AK	99829	Southeast
MIDDLETON	HANSEN KURT	5521 33RD AVE NE	SEATTLE	WA	98105	Southeast
MISS DANICA	MOROVIC DARKO	BOX 756	WESTPORT	WA	98595	Southeast
MISS SUSAN	STEVENS GARY	BOX 1572	WRANGELL	AK	99929	Southeast
NEW OREGON	BLAIR ANDREW	BOX 108	FOX ISLAND	WA	98333	Southeast
NORTH CAPE	HAYNES, GARY & ELIZABETH	625 SUNSET DR	KETCHIKAN	AK	99901	Southeast
OBSESSION	CAPE RELIANT FISHERIES IN	BOX 61	PETERSBURG	AK	99833	Southeast
OCEAN STORM	ALFIERI MICHAEL	2273 66TH AVE SE	MERCER ISLAND	WA	98040	Southeast
ODIN	SEVERSON MARK	BOX 1502	PETERSBURG	AK	99833	Southeast
OLYMPIC	PIECUCH JUSTIN	1923 NE LAURIE VIEW	POULSBO	WA	98370	Southeast
ORION	EVENS CRAIG	BOX 585	PETERSBURG	AK	99833	Southeast
OSPREY	KALK DONALD	3980 N DOUGLAS HWY	JUNEAU	AK	99801	Southeast
PACIFIC BELLE	ALEX WAYNE	BOX 20095	JUNEAU	AK	99802	Southeast
PACIFIC RAIDER	JERKOVICH NICK	3710 HARBORVIEW DR	GIG HARBOR	WA	98332	Southeast
PACIFIC SEA	WARFEL FRANK	BOX 1512	WRANGELL	AK	99929	Southeast
PACIFIC VENTURE	MANOS WILLIAM	BOX 1365	WARD COVE	AK	99928	Southeast
PATTY LYNN	VAUGHAN JAMES	BOX 770	CRAIG	AK	99921	Southeast
PILLAR BAY	BARRY JOHN	339 WORTMAN LP	SITKA	AK	99835	Southeast
PROVIDENCE	KANDOLL BRIAN	BOX 1363	PETERSBURG	AK	99833	Southeast
PUFFIN	WILLS CHARLES	BOX 7554	KETCHIKAN	AK	99901	Southeast
QUETZAL	GOOD STEVEN	BOX 85540	SEATTLE	WA	98145	Southeast
REIVER	MARTENS COLLIN	BOX 623	PETERSBURG	AK	99833	Southeast
RIO GRANDE	MURPHY FRANCIS	BOX 1158	WARD COVE	AK	99928	Southeast
ROSE LEE	EIDE MITCHEL	BOX 981	PETERSBURG	AK	99833	Southeast
ROSIE M	MCCAY RODERICK	BOX 161	PETERSBURG	AK	99833	Southeast

Vessel	Owner	Address	City	State	Zip	Area
SARA DAWN	KITTAMS ANDREW	BOX 1544	PETERSBURG	AK	99833	Southeast
SEA PRIDE	BOROVINA MICHAEL	3616 COLBY #731	EVERETT	WA	98201	Southeast
SEA VIEW	KACH-MOR INC	5301 BLUEBERRY LN	JUNEAU	AK	99801	Southeast
SEANNA	CLARKE DAVID	1225 E SUNSET DR #727	BELLINGHAM	WA	98225	Southeast
SELMA	BLANDOV BRIAN	BOX 436	METLAKATLA	AK	99926	Southeast
SIERRA GALE	PEELER ALFRED	BOX 761	PETERSBURG	AK	99833	Southeast
SIERRA MAR	SEABECK KEVIN	8555 30TH NW	SEATTLE	WA	98117	Southeast
SIGNE LYNN	HALTINER ROBERT	BOX 808	PETERSBURG	AK	99833	Southeast
SILVER WAVE	CARLE MATTHEW	BOX 32	HYDABURG	AK	99922	Southeast
SIREN	FILE MICHAEL	BOX 1666	PETERSBURG	AK	99833	Southeast
SPICY LADY	MARTENS COLLIN	BOX 623	PETERSBURG	AK	99833	Southeast
SPRITE	PETERMAN TIMOTHY	BOX 2336	WRANGELL	AK	99929	Southeast
ST PETER	ST PETER COMPANY	BOX 1572	ANACORTES	WA	98221	Southeast
STORMBRINGER	BLANKENSHIP BRIAN	4316 VALLHALLA DR	SITKA	AK	99835	Southeast
SYMPHONY	MATHISEN WAYNE	BOX 671	PETERSBURG	AK	99833	Southeast
TATY Z	APICDA INC (CDQ)	234 GOLD ST	JUNEAU	AK	99801	Southeast
TSIU	OLNEY-MILLER BAE	622 MERRILL ST	SITKA	AK	99835	Southeast
VAGABOND QUEEN	WRIGHT FRANK	BOX 497	HOONAH	AK	99829	Southeast
VIKING SPIRIT	VIKING SPIRIT FISHERIES INC	24121 SW NEWLAND RD	WILSONVILLE	OR	97070	Southeast
VIS	SCHILE GEORGE	1807 4TH ST	BELLINGHAM	WA	98225	Southeast
VOSHTE LYNN	DEMMERT LAWRENCE	16136 41ST AVE NE	LAKE FOREST PARK	WA	98155	Southeast
VOYAGER	STROOSMA SVEN	18273 W BIG LAKE BLVD	MOUNT VERNON	WA	98274	Southeast
WARLOCK	WALLACE BRUCE	BOX 20209	JUNEAU	AK	99802	Southeast
WAVEDANCER	BACON JAMES	1410 TONGASS AVE	KETCHIKAN	AK	99901	Southeast
WESTERN QUEEN	WESTERN QUEEN LLC	21320 LAFAYETTE RD	SEDRO WOOLLEY	WA	98284	Southeast
XIP 50	MILLS PATRICK	BOX 301	HOONAH	AK	99829	Southeast
ODYSSEY	WALLACE BRUCE	BOX 20209	JUNEAU	AK	99802	Southeast

Vessel	Owner	Address	City	State	Zip	Area
PRIEST POINT	ERICKSON JEFF	BOX 53	PETERSBURG	AK	99833	Southeast
ADVERSITY	ADVERSITY FISHERIES INC	BOX 1144	PETERSBURG	AK	99833	Bristol Bay
CATCHER	HISAW EDMOND	BOX 241	PETERSBURG	AK	99833	Bristol Bay
CORSAIR	TRC INC	255 NW 17TH	NEWPORT	OR	97365	Bristol Bay
DAVID HENRY	HAVENS LARRY	BOX 769	CATHLAMET	WA	98612	Bristol Bay
EQUINOX	EID KIRK	349 W HEMMI RD	BELLINGHAM	WA	98226	Bristol Bay
FRAYED KNOT	PRITCHARD DAVE	10790 PETER ANDERSON RD	BURLINGTON	WA	98233	Bristol Bay
GODODDIN	HIGGINS GENE	109 DIGBY RD	MOUNT VERNON	WA	98273	Bristol Bay
GRATEFUL	BAKK DAVID	3700 W ARMOUR PL	SEATTLE	WA	98199	Bristol Bay
HANTA YO	ANDREWS CLINTON	9000 ASHLEY CIR	ANCHORAGE	AK	99502	Bristol Bay
INSATIABLE	BACKLUND CRAIG	601 HEVLY RD	ARLINGTON	WA	98223	Bristol Bay
JADE	HIGGINS LARRY	BOX 106	LA CONNER	WA	98257	Bristol Bay
JATEC	CHILLMAN FORREST	1410 FLETCHER DR	ABERDEEN	WA	98520	Bristol Bay
KAMI SEA	FRIIS-MIKKEL PAUL	13031 8TH AVE NW	SEATTLE	WA	98177	Bristol Bay
KIHAR	BB FISHERIES LLC	BOX 518	CORDOVA	AK	99574	Bristol Bay
LADY MINDY	HEYANO ROBERT	BOX 1409	DILLINGHAM	AK	99576	Bristol Bay
LORELLE RENEE	SIFSOF LAWRENCE	BOX 1250	DILLINGHAM	AK	99576	Bristol Bay
LORELLE RENEE	SIFSOF LINDSEY	BOX 1250	DILLINGHAM	AK	99576	Bristol Bay
MARIAM	OLSON DENNIS	BOX 537	DILLINGHAM	AK	99576	Bristol Bay
MISS ADRIANNE	CHRISTENSEN EMIL	BOX 49009	PORT HEIDEN	AK	99549	Bristol Bay
MISS ALISON	ELWELL DOUGLAS	4016 MERIDIAN AVE N	MARYSVILLE	WA	98271	Bristol Bay
MJOLNER	ANDERSON KEITH	2256 SOUNDVIEW DR	LANGLEY	WA	98260	Bristol Bay
MYSTERY GIRL	TRAN TAM	500 FOULKSTONE WAY	VALLEJO	CA	94591	Bristol Bay
OCEAN MAGIC	HART RON	4717 COLLEGE ST	BELLINGHAM	WA	98229	Bristol Bay
OPTIMA	BAYNE ERIC	1132 HOYT AVE	EVERETT	WA	98201	Bristol Bay
PAMELA JEAN	PRIMOZICH MARK	BOX 1981	ANACORTES	WA	98221	Bristol Bay
PREDATOR	PETERSON MARK	14250 130TH AVE NE	KIRKLAND	WA	98034	Bristol Bay
RAINBOW CHASER	BALCH PETER	BOX 80490	FAIRBANKS	AK	99708	Bristol Bay

Vessel	Owner	Address	City	State	Zip	Area
RAZOR'S EDGE	MOORE ROSELEEN	5140 KACHEMAK DR	HOMER	AK	99603	Bristol Bay
REEDER BEATER	TENNYSON RICHARD	BOX 167	DILLINGHAM	AK	99576	Bristol Bay
RIBA RIBA	RUZICH RANDY	3319 W 3RD ST	ANACORTES	WA	98221	Bristol Bay
ROBYN DARLEEN	SAMUELSEN HAROLD	BOX 412	DILLINGHAM	AK	99576	Bristol Bay
SANDMAN	MAGILL FREDERICK	BOX 1201	SITKA	AK	99835	Bristol Bay
TESSARA MORGAN	COUCH CAMERON	1216 RAYMOND	BELLINGHAM	WA	98229	Bristol Bay
TIGARA	COOK JODY	BOX 1472	PETERSBURG	AK	99833	Bristol Bay
CHRIS K	WAHL NICK	BOX 17	DILLINGHAM	AK	99576	Bristol Bay
COOL CHANGE	SELLERS HARLEY	77-6469 ALII #227	KAILUA KONA	HI	96740	Bristol Bay
CORAL	PARSONS DENNIS	BOX 204	CRAIG	AK	99921	Bristol Bay
GREYMIST	FULTON JOHN	BOX 920941	DUTCH HARBOR	AK	99692	Bristol Bay
IMMANUEL	CULMINE JOHN	804 PUGET ST	BELLINGHAM	WA	98229	Bristol Bay
JENNY O DAUN	KNUTSEN JOHN	BOX 134	NAKNEK	AK	99633	Bristol Bay
LADY TILLIE	LIBERATI VITO	BOX 236	NAKNEK	AK	99633	Bristol Bay
LORIJO	PULLEY EDWARD	11310 202ND AVE E	SUMNER	WA	98390	Bristol Bay
MISS JAEFV	MISS JAE LLC	BOX 1957	PRIEST RIVER	ID	83856	Bristol Bay
NEZZEN	NEZ GRIFF INC	133 BANGSBERG RD	PORT CHARLOTTE	FL	33952	Bristol Bay
NOAH	DICKINSON DAVID	BOX 37	LUMMI ISLAND	WA	98262	Bristol Bay
PAMELA RAE	HEIMBUCH MICHAEL	4540 ANDERSON ST	HOMER	AK	99603	Bristol Bay
PAMELA RAE	MARKUSEN ROB	8358 DELTA LINE RD	CUSTER	WA	98240	Bristol Bay
RISKY BUSINESS	LONT & SONS INC	BOX 298	QUILCENE	WA	98376	Bristol Bay
TANJENT	RIGGLE JAMES	16020 145TH NE ST	WOODINVILLE	WA	98072	Bristol Bay
AUKLET	JUDSON NORMAN	4915 WREN DR	JUNEAU	AK	99801	Bristol Bay
B G	ALBECKER WILLIAM	101 OLGA LN	UGASHIK	AK	99613	Bristol Bay
COMPROMISE	YOUNG BRIAN	BOX 806	KODIAK	AK	99615	Bristol Bay
EQUINOX	GORDON CHARLES	23307 VASHON HWY SW	VASHON	WA	98070	Bristol Bay
KRISSY MAE	GREEN OLIN	BOX 879	VANCOUVER	WA	98666	Bristol Bay

Vessel	Owner	Address	City	State	Zip	Area
KYLEA	HOLUM MARK	BOX 111932	ANCHORAGE	AK	99501	Bristol Bay
SKAGERRAK	FRIIS-MIKKEL PAUL	13031 8TH AVE NW	SEATTLE	WA	98177	Bristol Bay
VULCAN	WHITE CHRISTOPHER	953 JANISH DR	SANDPOINT	ID	83864	Bristol Bay
BERSERKER	GUSTAFSON GLENN	BOX 101962	ANCHORAGE	AK	99510	Bristol Bay
COLLEEN W	J & B FISHERIES	1302 W MUKILTEO BLVD	EVERETT	WA	98203	Bristol Bay
CORLISS III	FLENSBURG OSCAR	BOX 174	DILLINGHAM	AK	99576	Bristol Bay
FULL SCALE	TIMMERMAN JAMES	BOX 475	DILLINGHAM	AK	99576	Bristol Bay
JAZZ	JOHNSON FRITZ	BOX 1129	DILLINGHAM	AK	99576	Bristol Bay
KITTY LOUISE	WHITING BRUCE	1302 W MUKILTEO BLVD	EVERETT	WA	98203	Bristol Bay
LISA	SMALL STANLEY	BOX 1536	DILLINGHAM	AK	99576	Bristol Bay
LITTLE FISH	MORAN ANTHONY	BOX 1191	PETERSBURG	AK	99833	Bristol Bay
MIGHTY SON	HERZOG LEONARD	916 DELANEY ST	ANCHORAGE	AK	99501	Bristol Bay
NORTHERN FURY	SATHER MICHAEL	19014 32ND AVE NW	STANWOOD	WA	98292	Bristol Bay
ROXANNE	SMALL STANLEY	BOX 1536	DILLINGHAM	AK	99576	Bristol Bay
ROYALE ISLE	HENDRICKS RICHARD	3975 TUSTIN DR	PALMER	AK	99645	Bristol Bay
SERENITY	EDELMAN GREGORY	BOX 1870	KENAI	AK	99611	Bristol Bay
VIRGIE	SMALL STANLEY	BOX 1536	DILLINGHAM	AK	99576	Bristol Bay
WIDE LOAD	SMALL STANLEY	BOX 1536	DILLINGHAM	AK	99576	Bristol Bay
NEPTUNE	SMITH ROBERT	BOX 261	KASILOF	AK	99610	Chignik
JAMBO	BELLAMY, MARVIN & ANNETTE	BOX 6426	HALIBUT COVE	AK	99603	Cook Inlet
JR	BELLAMY, MARVIN & ANNETTE	BOX 6426	HALIBUT COVE	AK	99603	Cook Inlet
K-C	KEENE BRENTLEY	64765 PITZMAN AVE	HOMER	AK	99603	Cook Inlet
NEPENTHE	RAYMOND PAUL	BOX 2755	HOMER	AK	99603	Cook Inlet
SCEPTER	HALPIN KENNETH	BOX 2448	HOMER	AK	99603	Cook Inlet
ALASKA ADVENTRE	DUFFUS, DEA & KEN	20441 PTARMIGAN BLVD	EAGLE RIVER	AK	99577	Cook Inlet
CURRENCY	KUZMIN ILIA	BOX 3433	HOMER	AK	99603	Cook Inlet
DAPHNE S	PERSON WARD	BOX 1295	ANCHOR POINT	AK	99556	Cook Inlet
ENTERPRISE II	DUFFUS KENNETH	20441 PTARMIGAN BLVD	EAGLE RIVER	AK	99577	Cook Inlet

Vessel	Owner	Address	City	State	Zip	Area
FAMILY AFFAIR	CHALUP ELAINE	BOX 406	HOMER	AK	99603	Cook Inlet
HOLLY ANN	FINDLEY KEITH	805 NW BUCKEYE AVE	EARLHAM	IA	50072	Cook Inlet
KAGUYAK	MARTIN DAVID	BOX 468	CLAM GULCH	AK	99568	Cook Inlet
KAREN MARIE	MARTIN DAVID	BOX 468	CLAM GULCH	AK	99568	Cook Inlet
KELSEY	BELLAMY, MARVIN & ANNETTE	BOX 6426	HALIBUT COVE	AK	99603	Cook Inlet
LADY N	NORMAN WAYNE	BOX 5546	PORT GRAHAM	AK	99603	Cook Inlet
RASCAL	GARCIA CHRIS	BOX 203	KENAI	AK	99611	Cook Inlet
SMOKY BAY	HUGHES JACK	BOX 1401	CRESTED BUTTE	CO	81224	Cook Inlet
CAPTAIN COOK	MILNE GEORGE	BOX 1846	HOMER	AK	99603	Cook Inlet
KUSTATAN	HAKKINEN DANIEL	BOX 1398	KENAI	AK	99611	Cook Inlet
VINDSAGA	WEBB STEPHEN	BOX 1127	KASILOF	AK	99610	Cook Inlet
MARKAYLA-DAWN	CRAITY ALFRED	BOX 1	OLD HARBOR	AK	99643	Kodiak
SANDRA SUE	SCHMELZENBAC EVERT	920 REZANOF #B	KODIAK	AK	99615	Kodiak
CAPTAIN COOK	HERBERT JAMES	BOX 1461	SEWARD	AK	99664	Kodiak
CORA MARIA	HARRIS LEROY	BOX 262	CLAM GULCH	AK	99568	Kodiak
LUCKY STAR	PERRY CHRISTOPHER	BOX 1808	HOMER	AK	99603	Kodiak
FOUR WINDS	GOULD ROBERT	BOX 52	KING COVE	AK	99612	Peninsula/Aleutian Islands
KELLYS ROCK	SHURAVLOFF PETER	BOX 3	SAND POINT	AK	99661	Peninsula/Aleutian Islands
LINDA MARIE	DUSHKIN RUDY	8820 VERNON ST	ANCHORAGE	AK	99515	Peninsula/Aleutian Islands
MELANIE SUE	KOSO MELVIN	BOX 131	KING COVE	AK	99612	Peninsula/Aleutian Islands
PG1	GUNDERSEN GEORGE	BOX 51	SAND POINT	AK	99661	Peninsula/Aleutian Islands
RIVER DRAGGER	JOHNSON DANIEL	BOX 924	NELSON LAGOON	AK	99571	Peninsula/Aleutian Islands
TERI LYNN	FV TERI LYNN INC	4449 185TH AVE E	SUMNER	WA	98390	Peninsula/Aleutian Islands
CAPT'N ANDREW	WILSON COREY	BOX 267	KING COVE	AK	99612	Peninsula/Aleutian Islands
CASTLE CAPE	JOHNSON RYAN	1325 MISSION RD	KODIAK	AK	99615	Peninsula/Aleutian Islands
CELTIC	BERNTSEN LOUIS	1216 NW BLAKELY CT	SEATTLE	WA	98177	Peninsula/Aleutian Islands
LADY MARY	MOBECK BENJAMIN	BOX 11	SAND POINT	AK	99661	Peninsula/Aleutian Islands

Vessel	Owner	Address	City	State	Zip	Area
MARTHA MARIE	HENDRICKSON BRUCE	1060 MILLER LN	HOMER	AK	99603	Peninsula/Aleutian Islands
MYRNA DOLL	NORTHERN SEAS INC	BOX 26	KING COVE	AK	99612	Peninsula/Aleutian Islands
PRETENDER	LARSEN MELVIN	BOX 33	SAND POINT	AK	99661	Peninsula/Aleutian Islands
TAURUS	HOFF MARVIN	4800 KLONDIKE #2	ANCHORAGE	AK	99508	Peninsula/Aleutian Islands
WHITETAIL	NEWTON GRANT	BOX 51	KING COVE	AK	99612	Peninsula/Aleutian Islands
38 SPECIAL	GUNDERSEN GEORGE	BOX 51	SAND POINT	AK	99661	Peninsula/Aleutian Islands
ALEUT MISTRESS	NORTHERN SEAS INC	BOX 26	KING COVE	AK	99612	Peninsula/Aleutian Islands
AURORA DAWN	DONALD MCCALLUM & ASSOC INC	2431 W 70TH CIR	ANCHORAGE	AK	99502	Peninsula/Aleutian Islands
BUBBLES	HAYTER MERYLE	4038 W 88TH AVE	ANCHORAGE	AK	99502	Peninsula/Aleutian Islands
CONNIE LEE	BEAR RIVER FISHERIES LLC	3015 W 3RD PL	ANACORTES	WA	98221	Peninsula/Aleutian Islands
MELANIE JOANN	LUDVICK JOE	BOX 74	SAND POINT	AK	99661	Peninsula/Aleutian Islands
MERYLE M	DONALD MCCALLUM & ASSOC INC	2431 W 70TH CIR	ANCHORAGE	AK	99502	Peninsula/Aleutian Islands
RAVEN II	MCCALLUM DON	BOX 185	KING COVE	AK	99612	Peninsula/Aleutian Islands
ALJOTH	BERGQUIST DONALD	4922 S SMUGGLERS COVE RD	FREELAND	WA	98249	Prince William Sound
AMY	UJIOKA GLENN	BOX 932	CORDOVA	AK	99574	Prince William Sound
BIZZY DITCH	LAIRD SUSAN	BOX 1624	CORDOVA	AK	99574	Prince William Sound
CARLY JOE	MCLEAN JOHN	BOX 2191	HOMER	AK	99603	Prince William Sound
C-RUNNER	GROCOTT JOHN	BOX 59	ILWACO	WA	98624	Prince William Sound
DOUBLE TROUBLE	WIESE JOHN	BOX 1031	CORDOVA	AK	99574	Prince William Sound
ENGEDI	JENSEN SETH	BOX 2155	CORDOVA	AK	99574	Prince William Sound
HALBERD	DURTSCHI MICHAEL	BOX 1012	GIRDWOOD	AK	99587	Prince William Sound
JACQUELINE KAY	OLSEN JEFFREY	BOX 875524	WASILLA	AK	99687	Prince William Sound
JITNEY	BLAKE PETER	BOX 718	CORDOVA	AK	99574	Prince William Sound
JITNEY	CHESHIER ELMER	BOX 2264	CORDOVA	AK	99574	Prince William Sound
JITNEY	NOLAN PER	BOX 924	CORDOVA	AK	99574	Prince William Sound
KANAK	WIESE ROBERT	BOX 864	CORDOVA	AK	99574	Prince William Sound
LARC	DEVILLE CHARLES	BOX 529	CORDOVA	AK	99574	Prince William Sound
MEGAN VICTORIA	LARSON DAVID	BOX 581	CONWAY	WA	98238	Prince William Sound

215

Vessel	Owner	Address	City	State	Zip	Area
MS JENNIFER	KOMPKOFF MICHAEL	BOX 3733	VALDEZ	AK	99686	Prince William Sound
NORTHERNER	BERGQUIST RODGER	4816 SARATOGA RD	LANGLEY	WA	98260	Prince William Sound
OCTOPUS	TAYLOR GORDON	BOX 1841	VALDEZ	AK	99686	Prince William Sound
OLD FART	JONES VICTOR	BOX 1831	CORDOVA	AK	99574	Prince William Sound
PATRICIA DIANN	SMITH WAYNE	BOX 419	CORDOVA	AK	99574	Prince William Sound
PROCESSION	BERGQUIST RODGER	4816 SARATOGA RD	LANGLEY	WA	98260	Prince William Sound
PURSUIT	GARCIA CHRIS	BOX 203	KENAI	AK	99611	Prince William Sound
RELENTLESS	ADAMS MARK	8630 CAMBRIDGE LP	BLAINE	WA	98230	Prince William Sound
RYANS NICHE	THORNE GERALD	BOX 1192	CORDOVA	AK	99574	Prince William Sound
SUNSET	TOTEMOFF JAMES	BOX 811	CORDOVA	AK	99574	Prince William Sound
SWEET JUMPER	SMALLWOOD GERALD	BOX 453	CORDOVA	AK	99574	Prince William Sound
TIN CAN	WIESE JOHN	BOX 1031	CORDOVA	AK	99574	Prince William Sound
VIKING	ARVIDSON ALASKA LLC	BOX 1696	CORDOVA	AK	99574	Prince William Sound
WIHINE	ARVIDSON ALASKA LLC	BOX 1696	CORDOVA	AK	99574	Prince William Sound
HANNA ROSE	NOWICKI MITCHELL	BOX 2232	CORDOVA	AK	99574	Prince William Sound
PARAGON	CABANA LEROY	BOX 49	HOMER	AK	99603	Prince William Sound
AMY RAE	THORNE GERALD	BOX 1192	CORDOVA	AK	99574	Prince William Sound
FULL MOON	HENRICHS ROBERT	BOX 1000	CORDOVA	AK	99574	Prince William Sound
INLET SUNRISE	CABANA JEFFERY	BOX 26	HOMER	AK	99603	Prince William Sound
JAC OL BE	ADAMS, MARK & JULIE	8630 CAMBRIDGE LP	BLAINE	WA	98230	Prince William Sound
JENNIFER ROSE	SMITH ROBERT	BOX 251	CORDOVA	AK	99574	Prince William Sound
JITNEY	BLAKE RONALD	BOX 1236	CORDOVA	AK	99574	Prince William Sound
JULIANNE	ADAMS MARK	8630 CAMBRIDGE LP	BLAINE	WA	98230	Prince William Sound
KENNETH J	JONES VICTOR	BOX 1831	CORDOVA	AK	99574	Prince William Sound
KINGFISHER	MILLER, THANE & SHARRY	BOX 2961	VALDEZ	AK	99686	Prince William Sound
NORTHERN SPIRIT	GILDNES SWEN	498 SYMPHONY WAY	FREEPORT	FL	32439	Prince William Sound
O LETTA	LARSON JAMES	19003 COUNTY LINE RD	STANWOOD	WA	98292	Prince William Sound

Vessel	Owner	Address	City	State	Zip	Area
PRINCE WILLIAM	PHILLIPS BRITTANY	BOX 795	CORDOVA	AK	99574	Prince William Sound
SAM AN I	JONES KENNETH	BOX 1831	CORDOVA	AK	99574	Prince William Sound
SEDNA	WILSON RILEY	17701 SPAIN DR	ANCHORAGE	AK	99516	Prince William Sound
SHADOWFAX	ELESSAR ENTERPRISES INC	BOX 3476	HOMER	AK	99603	Prince William Sound
SILVER BEACH	CABANA LARRY	BOX 3388	HOMER	AK	99603	Prince William Sound
TEMPTATION	JENSEN HERBERT	BOX 294	CORDOVA	AK	99574	Prince William Sound
TINA	ADAMS KENNETH	BOX 1855	CORDOVA	AK	99574	Prince William Sound
TRI-K	BLAKE RONALD	BOX 1236	CORDOVA	AK	99574	Prince William Sound
C TREKS	HAGER KIM	BOX 1552	CORDOVA	AK	99574	Prince William Sound
CHELSEA DAWN	JONES VICTOR	BOX 1831	CORDOVA	AK	99574	Prince William Sound
J B	BABIC JACK	BOX 1208	CORDOVA	AK	99574	Prince William Sound
KNOTT E BOY	WIESE EARL	BOX 1981	CORDOVA	AK	99574	Prince William Sound
NAVIGATOR	KUZMIN EROS	BOX 1737	HOMER	AK	99603	Prince William Sound
SPINDRIFT III	MELOY BUCK	BOX 572	BELLINGHAM	WA	98227	Prince William Sound
SYLVIA ANN	ALLEN RUSSELL	BOX 1062	CORDOVA	AK	99574	Prince William Sound
VALKYRIE	JONES VICTOR	BOX 1831	CORDOVA	AK	99574	Prince William Sound
FINNEGAN	HASELTINE SHAUN	BOX 34856	JUNEAU	AK	99803	Southeast
HARDROCK	MAGILL FREDERICK	BOX 1201	SITKA	AK	99835	Southeast
MELANIE ANN	NEBL NIKOULAS	3828 EVERGREEN AVE	KETCHIKAN	AK	99901	Southeast
SPARTAN SUN	SILVER BAY SEAFOODS	4400 SAWMILL CREEK RD #B	SITKA	AK	99835	Southeast
VALERIE J	WALCOTT HOWARD	BOX 617	CRAIG	AK	99921	Southeast
ALEUTIAN SPIRIT	ALEUTIAN SPIRIT INC	BOX 1184	PETERSBURG	AK	99833	Southeast
CARLYNN	BECKER ROBERT	BOX 240238	DOUGLAS	AK	99824	Southeast
DARLIN MICHELE	LYNCH THEODORE	BOX 1232	HAINES	AK	99827	Southeast
LAVERN LYNN	GIBSON DAVE	BOX 210426	AUKE BAY	AK	99821	Southeast
MIGRATOR	MAY FRED	BOX 514	METLAKATLA	AK	99926	Southeast
RAGTIME	NELSON LESLIE	2164 MONTFORT AVE	BLAINE	WA	98230	Southeast

Vessel	Owner	Address	City	State	Zip	Area
SHILOH	MCDOWELL CHRIS	2207 RADCLIFFE RD	JUNEAU	AK	99801	Southeast
SIDNEY JEAN	OLSON CHARLES	3009 HALIBUT POINT RD	SITKA	AK	99835	Southeast
SNAKE DANCER	CROME DANIEL	BOX 1243	PETERSBURG	AK	99833	Southeast
SOUNDER	BRAYTON THOMAS	145 BEHRENDS AVE	JUNEAU	AK	99801	Southeast
SOUTHEASTERN	LYONS JACK	BOX 527	PETERSBURG	AK	99833	Southeast
STORMY	GIL JOSEPH	BOX 5	POINT BAKER	AK	99927	Southeast
TONKA	HOFSTAD ALBERT	BOX 1030	PETERSBURG	AK	99833	Southeast
EIGHT STARS	DAVIS NICHOLAS	BOX 234	KAKE	AK	99830	Southeast
ELEANOR S	BOYCE RICHARD	BOX 84	HAINES	AK	99827	Southeast
HANNAH POINT	KLEPSER DAVID	BOX 8946	KETCHIKAN	AK	99901	Southeast
JENNIFER LEE	SWANSON ROBERT	BOX 924	PETERSBURG	AK	99833	Southeast
KYRION	OCEAN HARVEST INC	730 PARK AVE	KETCHIKAN	AK	99901	Southeast
LARA LEE	CROME CARL	BOX 466	PETERSBURG	AK	99833	Southeast
NEW ADVENTURE	DE.MONTIGNY PAUL	BOX 1584	PETERSBURG	AK	99833	Southeast
SHELTER	MANN MICHAEL	BOX 32653	JUNEAU	AK	99803	Southeast
STAR OF THE SEA	NELSON NORVAL	1625 FRITZ COVE RD	JUNEAU	AK	99801	Southeast
STOMY	HASBROUCK TERRY	BOX 486	PETERSBURG	AK	99833	Southeast
TIA	MACDONALD CLIFFORD	BOX 575	PETERSBURG	AK	99833	Southeast

Vessel	Owner	Address	City	State	Zip	Area
CHRIS K	WAHL NICK	BOX 17	DILLINGHAM	AK	99576	Bristol Bay
COOL CHANGE	SELLERS HARLEY	77-6469 ALII #227	KAILUA KONA	HI	96740	Bristol Bay
CORAL	PARSONS DENNIS	BOX 204	CRAIG	AK	99921	Bristol Bay
GREYMIST	FULTON JOHN	BOX 920941	DUTCH HARBOR	AK	99692	Bristol Bay
IMMANUEL	CULMINE JOHN	804 PUGET ST	BELLINGHAM	WA	98229	Bristol Bay
JENNY O DAUN	KNUTSEN JOHN	BOX 134	NAKNEK	AK	99633	Bristol Bay
LADY TILLIE	LIBERATI VITO	BOX 236	NAKNEK	AK	99633	Bristol Bay
LORI JO	PULLEY EDWARD	11310 202ND AVE E	SUMNER	WA	98390	Bristol Bay
MISS JAEFV	MISS JAE LLC	BOX 1957	PRIEST RIVER	ID	83856	Bristol Bay
NEZZEN	NEZ GRIFF INC	133 BANGSBERG RD	PORT CHARLOTTE	FL	33952	Bristol Bay
NOAH	DICKINSON DAVID	BOX 37	LUMMI ISLAND	WA	98262	Bristol Bay
PAMELA RAE	HEIMBUCH MICHAEL	4540 ANDERSON ST	HOMER	AK	99603	Bristol Bay
PAMELA RAE	MARKUSEN ROB	8358 DELTA LINE RD	CUSTER	WA	98240	Bristol Bay
RISKY BUSINESS	LONT & SONS INC	BOX 298	QUILCENE	WA	98376	Bristol Bay
TANJENT	RIGGLE JAMES C	16020 145TH NE ST	WOODINVILLE	WA	98072	Bristol Bay
BERSERKER	GUSTAFSON GLENN	BOX 101962	ANCHORAGE	AK	99510	Bristol Bay
COLLEEN W	J & B FISHERIES	1302 W MUKILTEO BLVD	EVERETT	WA	98203	Bristol Bay
CORLISS III	FLENSBURG OSCAR	BOX 174	DILLINGHAM	AK	99576	Bristol Bay
FULL SCALE	TIMMERMAN JAMES	BOX 475	DILLINGHAM	AK	99576	Bristol Bay
JAZZ	JOHNSON FRITZ	BOX 1129	DILLINGHAM	AK	99576	Bristol Bay
KITTY LOUISE	WHITING BRUCE	1302 W MUKILTEO BLVD	EVERETT	WA	98203	Bristol Bay
LISA	SMALL STANLEY A	BOX 1536	DILLINGHAM	AK	99576	Bristol Bay
LITTLE FISH	MORAN ANTHONY	BOX 1191	PETERSBURG	AK	99833	Bristol Bay
MIGHTY SON	HERZOG LEONARD	916 DELANEY ST	ANCHORAGE	AK	99501	Bristol Bay
NORTHERN	FURYSATHER MICHAEL	19014 32ND AVE NW	STANWOOD	WA	98292	Bristol Bay
ROXANNE	SMALL STANLEY	BOX 1536	DILLINGHAM	AK	99576	Bristol Bay

Vessel	Owner	Address	City	State	Zip	Area
ROYALE ISLE	HENDRICKS RICHARD	3975 TUSTIN DR	PALMER	AK	99645	Bristol Bay
SERENITY	EDELMAN GREGORY	BOX 1870	KENAI	AK	99611	Bristol Bay
VIRGIE	SMALL STANLEY	BOX 1536	DILLINGHAM	AK	99576	Bristol Bay
WIDE LOAD	SMALL STANLEY	BOX 1536	DILLINGHAM	AK	99576	Bristol Bay
NEPTUNE	SMITH ROBERT	BOX 261	KASILOF	AK	99610	Chignik
CAPTAIN COOK	MILNE GEORGE	BOX 1846	HOMER	AK	99603	Cook Inlet
KUSTATAN	HAKKINEN DANIEL	BOX 1398	KENAI	AK	99611	Cook Inlet
VINDSAGA	WEBB STEPHEN	BOX 1127	KASILOF	AK	99610	Cook Inlet
CAPTAIN COOK	HERBERT JAMES	BOX 1461	SEWARD	AK	99664	Kodiak
CORA MARIA	HARRIS LEROY	BOX 262	CLAM GULCH	AK	99568	Kodiak
LUCKY STAR	PERRY CHRISTOPHER	BOX 1808	HOMER	AK	99603	Kodiak
38 SPECIAL	GUNDERSEN GEORGE	BOX 51	SAND POINT	AK	99661	Peninsula/Aleutian Islands
ALEUT MISTRESS	NORTHERN SEAS INC	BOX 26	KING COVE	AK	99612	Peninsula/Aleutian Islands
AURORA DAWN	DONALD MCCALLUM & ASSOC INC	2431 W 70TH CIR	ANCHORAGE	AK	99502	Peninsula/Aleutian Islands
BUBBLES	HAYTER MERYLE	4038 W 88TH AVE	ANCHORAGE	AK	99502	Peninsula/Aleutian Islands
CONNIE LEE	BEAR RIVER FISHERIES LLC	3015 W 3RD PL	ANACORTES	WA	98221	Peninsula/Aleutian Islands
MELANIE JOANN	LUDVICK JOE	BOX 74	SAND POINT	AK	99661	Peninsula/Aleutian Islands
MERYLE M	DONALD MCCALLUM & ASSOC INC	2431 W 70TH CIR	ANCHORAGE	AK	99502	Peninsula/Aleutian Islands
RAVEN II	MCCALLUM DON	BOX 185	KING COVE	AK	99612	Peninsula/Aleutian Islands

Purse Seiner & Drift Gill Net Salmon/Herring Boats

Vessel	Owner	Address	City	State	Zip	Area
HANNA ROSE	NOWICKI MITCHELL	BOX 2232	CORDOVA	AK	99574	Prince William Sound
PARAGON	CABANA LEROY	BOX 49	HOMER	AK	99603	Prince William Sound
C TREKS	HAGER KIM	BOX 1552	CORDOVA	AK	99574	Prince William Sound
CHELSEA DAWN	JONES VICTOR	BOX 1831	CORDOVA	AK	99574	Prince William Sound
J B	BABIC JACK	BOX 1208	CORDOVA	AK	99574	Prince William Sound
KNOTT E BOY	WIESE EARL	BOX 1981	CORDOVA	AK	99574	Prince William Sound
NAVIGATOR	KUZMIN EROS	BOX 1737	HOMER	AK	99603	Prince William Sound
SPINDRIFT III	MELOY BUCK	BOX 572	BELLINGHAM	WA	98227	Prince William Sound
SYLVIA ANN	ALLEN RUSSELL	BOX 1062	CORDOVA	AK	99574	Prince William Sound
VALKYRIE	JONES VICTOR	BOX 1831	CORDOVA	AK	99574	Prince William Sound
EIGHT STARS	DAVIS NICHOLAS	BOX 234	KAKE	AK	99830	Southeast
ELEANOR S	BOYCE RICHARD	BOX 84	HAINES	AK	99827	Southeast
HANNAH POINT	KLEPSER DAVID	BOX 8946	KETCHIKAN	AK	99901	Southeast
JENNIFER LEE	SWANSON ROBERT	BOX 924	PETERSBURG	AK	99833	Southeast
KYRION	OCEAN HARVEST INC	730 PARK AVE	KETCHIKAN	AK	99901	Southeast
LARA LEE	CROME CARL	BOX 466	PETERSBURG	AK	99833	Southeast
NEW ADVENTURE	DE MONTIGNY PAUL	BOX 1584	PETERSBURG	AK	99833	Southeast
SHELTER	MANN MICHAEL	BOX 32653	JUNEAU	AK	99803	Southeast
STAR OF THE SEA	NELSON NORVAL	1625 FRITZ COVE RD	JUNEAU	AK	99801	Southeast
STOMY	HASBROUCK TERRY	BOX 486	PETERSBURG	AK	99833	Southeast
TIA	MACDONALD, CLIFFORD	BOX 575	PETERSBURG	AK	99833	Southeast

Vessel	Owner	Address	City	State	Zip	Area
ADLER	STRUB ROBERT	BOX 1696	TONASKET	WA	98855	Bristol Bay
ALEUT PRINCESS	CHRISTENSEN JAMES	BOX 49090	PORT HEIDEN	AK	99549	Bristol Bay
AMY JANE	WASSILLIE WILLIE	BOX 28	TOGIAK	AK	99678	Bristol Bay
ANGELA A	CLARK ROBERT J	BOX 822	DILLINGHAM	AK	99576	Bristol Bay
ANNA MARIE	GIAMMANCO VINCE	129 A SAN BENANCIO RD	CORRAL DE TIERRA	CA	93908	Bristol Bay
ANNIE	MCALLISTER JOHN	2726 SUNSET DR	BELLINGHAM	WA	98225	Bristol Bay
ANUSKA T	TUGATUK WASSILLIE	BOX 189	MANOKOTAK	AK	99628	Bristol Bay
ARETE	SABO ERICK	3123 N SHIRLEY	TACOMA	WA	98407	Bristol Bay
ARTIC KNIGHT	NASH PETER J	1512 NW 58TH ST #4	SEATTLE	WA	98107	Bristol Bay
ARTIC SUN	INGHAM MIKE	3510 LANDAU CIR	ANCHORAGE	AK	99502	Bristol Bay
ATREVIDA	GRANGER TODD	2101 W SHORE DR	LUMMI ISLAND	WA	98262	Bristol Bay
AITU	WARFEL KRISTIAN	BOX 477	FRIDAY HARBOR	WA	98250	Bristol Bay
BABY KOKWOK	KAPATAK EDWARD	BOX 5002	KOLIGANEK	AK	99576	Bristol Bay
BELIEVER	WALDRON VINTON	3511 SW BALDA ST	OAK HARBOR	WA	98277	Bristol Bay
BIG EASY	SEGAL ROBERT J	BOX 583	KING SALMON	AK	99613	Bristol Bay
BOGART	BOGART INC	11 BEACH LN SW	LAKEWOOD	WA	98498	Bristol Bay
BRADLEY K	WILSON KENNY J	BOX 766	DILLINGHAM	AK	99576	Bristol Bay
BRISTOL BEAR	BINGMAN JAMES H	BOX 82	DILLINGHAM	AK	99576	Bristol Bay
BRISTOL STAR	SEABERG ERIC M	15632 VIRGINIA PT. RD.	POULSBO	WA	98370	Bristol Bay
BROWN DOG	GLASS TOM	4739 UNIVERSITY NE #1107	SEATTLE	WA	98105	Bristol Bay
BULLSEYE	LANDWEHR DOUGLAS	BOX 219	BAYVIEW	ID	83803	Bristol Bay
CANVAS BACK	MYERS JOHN R	270 SF GOLD CREEK RD	CARLTON	WA	98814	Bristol Bay
CAPELIN	MCGILL DAVID E	BOX 481	DILLINGHAM	AK	99576	Bristol Bay
CAPT CRUNCH	CLEMENT ROBERT	578 CLATSOP ST	ASTORIA	OR	97103	Bristol Bay

Vessel	Owner	Address	City	State	Zip	Area
CAROLYN MARIE	WASSILLIE WILLIE	BOX 28	TOGIAK	AK	99678	Bristol Bay
CARRIE ELIZABETH	PLEIER JUSTIN	BOX 294	DILLINGHAM	AK	99576	Bristol Bay
CASH FLOW	RAYMOND TYONE	BOX 2331	VASHON	WA	98070	Bristol Bay
CHARLIE	MARILLEY KEVIN P	7441 HANNEGAN RD	LYNDEN	WA	98264	Bristol Bay
CHISANA	COMPTON THEODORE	8811 CAROL AVE	LAKEWOOD	WA	98499	Bristol Bay
CINDY RAE	WOLLAN TOM	BOX 747	CONWAY	WA	98238	Bristol Bay
CLAUDE M BRISTOL	MARINKOVICH, M & M	BOX 2084	FRIDAY HARBOR	WA	98250	Bristol Bay
CORINTHIAN	ROEHL ADOLF JJ	BOX 41	DILLINGHAM	AK	99576	Bristol Bay
DARL	GROAT GUY C3	BOX 29	NAKNEK	AK	99633	Bristol Bay
DEAD RED	COOK TIM	3901 TAIGA DR	ANCHORAGE	AK	99516	Bristol Bay
DENISE C	STROOSMA ERWIN	1226 S 10TH ST	MOUNT VERNON	WA	98274	Bristol Bay
DEREK WADE	HAMMER DEREK W	BOX 43	CORDOVA	AK	99574	Bristol Bay
DEREK WADE	HAMMER WILLIAM	BOX 43	CORDOVA	AK	99574	Bristol Bay
DIANNE CAROL	JOHNSON DANIEL S	3820 GALACTICA	ANCHORAGE	AK	99517	Bristol Bay
DOLCE-VITA	RINAUDO DINO L	20244 PALOU DR	SALINAS	CA	93908	Bristol Bay
DR JACK	BOWSER GEOFFREY	14971 WILBUR RD	LA CONNER	WA	98257	Bristol Bay
DYLAN ROSS	SCHOLS MICHAEL	13211 WILSON DR	MOUNT VERNON	WA	98273	Bristol Bay
EARL	NICHOLSON WILLIAM	14439 TERRACE LN	EAGLE RIVER	AK	99577	Bristol Bay
EDEN	LUDWIG MARK	16300 38TH AVE NW	STANWOOD	WA	98292	Bristol Bay
EL NAYAR	SANCHEZ ELIZABETH	1713 MILL ST	BELLINGHAM	WA	98225	Bristol Bay
EL SALVATORE	MCDOUGALL JACK	915 W HERON	ABERDEEN	WA	98520	Bristol Bay
EMMA LYNN	CHYTHLOOK MOLLY	BOX 692	DILLINGHAM	AK	99576	Bristol Bay
EMMY C	CARLOS SEAN	BOX 195	TOGIAK	AK	99678	Bristol Bay
EXODUS	NIVER SCOT	BOX 2975	PALMER	AK	99645	Bristol Bay
FATSO	MORGAN MICHAEL	BOX 754	LANGLEY	WA	98260	Bristol Bay
FISHTALES	MOST CHARLES H	BOX 325	WESTPORT	WA	98595	Bristol Bay

Vessel	Owner	Address	City	State	Zip	Area
FRANCES ANNETTE	NELSON HERMAN	BOX 5023	KOLIGANEK	AK	99576	Bristol Bay
FRIEDA ANN	JOHNSON HERMAN	BOX 5010	KOLIGANEK	AK	99576	Bristol Bay
GALE FORCE	GALE FORCE INC	BOX 188	CHINOOK	WA	98614	Bristol Bay
GINNY K	KAPOTAK LENA	BOX 805	DILLINGHAM	AK	99576	Bristol Bay
GOLDEN GIRL	ZIMIN RALPH	BOX 242	KING SALMON	AK	99613	Bristol Bay
GOLDRUSH	MYERS DAVID	323 HOLOPUNI RD	MAUI	HI	96790	Bristol Bay
GOOD JUJU	WEBSTER CLAUDE	BOX 121	KING SALMON	AK	99613	Bristol Bay
HAGAR	PRATER MARK	24 ROY ST #296	SEATTLE	WA	98109	Bristol Bay
HAMMER TIME	FOX LEROY	BOX 136	TOGIAK	AK	99678	Bristol Bay
HARBOR LIGHTS	HILL PETE	BOX 269	NAKNEK	AK	99633	Bristol Bay
HARRIER	CLARK LELAND	167 PARPALA RD	NASELLE	WA	98638	Bristol Bay
HEIDI II	HESSELROTH ERIC	1001 DUCHESS RD	BOTHELL	WA	98012	Bristol Bay
HELENA RENE	WILSON VERNER	BOX 905	DILLINGHAM	AK	99576	Bristol Bay
HIGH OCTANE	VARDY TIM	BOX 129	LAKEWOOD	WA	98259	Bristol Bay
HIGHBALL	ARNESTAD PETER	2312 KENILWORTH PL	EVERETT	WA	98203	Bristol Bay
INTRUDER	MORGAN MICHAEL	BOX 754	LANGLEY	WA	98260	Bristol Bay
ISLA ANN	KNUTSEN AUGUST	706 COPPERBUSH CT	ANCHORAGE	AK	99504	Bristol Bay
JC	TINKER RANDY	BOX 31	ALEKNAGIK	AK	99555	Bristol Bay
JD	FV I INC	BOX 1170	HAILEY	ID	83333	Bristol Bay
JACI LYNN	QUASHNICK RICHARD	1645 SW 14TH ST	WARRENTON	OR	97146	Bristol Bay
JANICE M	HAUGEN EDDIE	632 N 201ST LN	SHORELINE	WA	98133	Bristol Bay
JEANNE MARIE	DERANJA IVO	1250 WESTERN AVE	GLENDALE	CA	91201	Bristol Bay
JESSE AND MERLE	CHYTHLOOK GUSTY	BOX 986	DILLINGHAM	AK	99576	Bristol Bay
JESSE N	HOIBY VINCE E	3121 WAVE DR	EVERETT	WA	98203	Bristol Bay
JOHNNY JOE	ANDREW JOSEPH	BOX 102	TOGIAK	AK	99678	Bristol Bay
JOHNNY K III	JOHN RALPH A	BOX 37061	TOKSOOK BAY	AK	99637	Bristol Bay
JWG 1	GAMECHUK TERENCE	BOX 66	MANOKOTAK	AK	99628	Bristol Bay

Vessel	Owner	Address	City	State	Zip	Area
K-4 PICKENS	MARDESICH ANTHONY	5101 GUEMES ISLAND RD	ANACORTES	WA	98221	Bristol Bay
KABOUTER	ARMSTRONG JOHN	78687 S 3RD	ATHENA	OR	97813	Bristol Bay
KAREN II	MONTECUCCO JOHN	BOX 2938	VASHON	WA	98070	Bristol Bay
KASANDRA FAYE	KOHLER STEVEN J	BOX 83	ALEKNAGIK	AK	99555	Bristol Bay
KATHRYN ANN	MUNSON GREGORY	1670757TH AVE SE	SNOHOMISH	WA	98296	Bristol Bay
KATHY ANN	OCONNELL MATHIAS	BOX 331	DILLINGHAM	AK	99576	Bristol Bay
KING OSCAR	SJODIN KARL	714 148TH ST NE	ARLINGTON	WA	98223	Bristol Bay
KIRA	ANDERSON BRUCE	BOX 70045	SOUTH NAKNEK AK	AK	99670	Bristol Bay
KIRRA B	SCHMIDT FAMILY TRUST	561 LA MARINA DR	SANTA BARBARA CA	CA	93109	Bristol Bay
KIRSTEN MARIE	SEYBERT MITCHELL	705 PALO VERDE ST	BAKERSFIELD	CA	93309	Bristol Bay
KO LEA	SELITSCH QUINN	19415 HIGH BLUFF DR	EAGLE RIVER	AK	99577	Bristol Bay
KRISTI	MEDHAUG JAN O	1328 NW 201ST	SHORELINE	WA	98177	Bristol Bay
KULUKAK CHIEF	STRUB ROBERT	BOX 1696	TONASKET	WA	98855	Bristol Bay
LADY BEA II	BONANNO JOE	348 HANNON AVE	MONTEREY	CA	93940	Bristol Bay
LADY COLLEEN	ADAMS CARL	BOX 241	KING SALMON	AK	99613	Bristol Bay
LADY K	BYAYUK DARREN	BOX 171	TOGIAK	AK	99678	Bristol Bay
LADY PATRICIA	CARSCALLEN VERN	BOX 398	DILLINGHAM	AK	99576	Bristol Bay
LILLY ANN	CHUCKWUK GEORGE	BOX 124	KIPNUK	AK	99614	Bristol Bay
LISA III	ILUTSIK WASSILLIE	BOX 914	DILLINGHAM	AK	99576	Bristol Bay
LISA J	BARBER BRAD S	7703 137TH AVE SE	SNOHOMISH	WA	98290	Bristol Bay
LITTLE ANGEL	JAMES FRANK	BOX 25	PLATINUM	AK	99651	Bristol Bay
LITTLE BOOBOO	PAPETTI DOMINIC J	1410 WILSON AVE	BELLINGHAM	WA	98225	Bristol Bay
LITTLE MOOSE	SPEAK MARTIN B	15439 85TH AVE NE	KENSMORE	WA	98028	Bristol Bay
LOU & MOE	CHYTHLOOK MOSES	BOX 15	ALEKNAGIK	AK	99555	Bristol Bay
LUCY LEWIS	ANAVER JONES	BOX 2	KWIGILLINGOK AK	AK	99622	Bristol Bay
LYRA	CHRISTENSEN LARRY	1487 OLYMPIC HEIGHTS LN	FREELAND	WA	98249	Bristol Bay
MAGGOT	HEYANO PETER K	BOX 730	DILLINGHAM	AK	99576	Bristol Bay

Vessel	Owner			Address	City	State	Zip	Area
MAI THAI	DRISCOLL	DAVID		BOX 385	KING SALMON	AK	99613	Bristol Bay
MARIA	WYAGON	BOBBY		BOX 123	NEW STUYAHOK	AK	99636	Bristol Bay
MELODY	POTTER	COREY	R	BOX 1192	QUECHEE	VT	5059	Bristol Bay
MICHAEL LEE	SWIFT	ALLEN		BOX 368	DILLINGHAM	AK	99576	Bristol Bay
MIMI	HANSEN	PAUL	J	BOX 82	NAKNEK	AK	99633	Bristol Bay
MISS MOLLY	CHYTHLOOK	JOSEPH		BOX 692	DILLINGHAM	AK	99576	Bristol Bay
MISTRAL	STRICKLAND	LUKAS		5992 N NODDING AVE	PALMER	AK	99645	Bristol Bay
MOLLY V	PAUK	WILLIAM	J	BOX 36	MANOKOTAK	AK	99628	Bristol Bay
MONSTER	ANTTILA	RODNEY	D	825 ISLAND VIEW DR NE	BEMIDJI	MN	56601	Bristol Bay
MY GIRLS	MARTIN	SAMUEL		BOX 66	GOODNEWS BAY	AK	99589	Bristol Bay
N 12	HUFF	ROBERT	D	2610 FRANKLIN ST	BELLINGHAM	WA	98225	Bristol Bay
N 3	BRIGHT	GENEVA		BOX 100116	ANCHORAGE	AK	99510	Bristol Bay
N 9	LIMBACHER	RON		BOX 3275	FERNDALE	WA	98248	Bristol Bay
NATASHA N	TOYUKAK	MOSES		BOX 30	MANOKOTAK	AK	99628	Bristol Bay
NATIVE DANCER	WONHOLA	EVAN		BOX 51	NEW STUYAHOK	AK	99636	Bristol Bay
NEW ALASKAN	RUSSO	ANTHONY		BOX 502	MOSS LANDING	CA	95039	Bristol Bay
NEW ST JUDE	BARTLETT	WALLACE		3762 GLACIER DR	PITTSBURG	CA	94565	Bristol Bay
NORRIN RADD	FERRIS	BRYAN	S	3408 HARLEQUIN CT	KODIAK	AK	99615	Bristol Bay
ONE ARMNICK	ANGASAN	FRED		BOX 70069	SOUTH NAKNEK	AK	99670	Bristol Bay
ONE CAPTAIN	LAWLER	DAVID		BOX 6533	KETCHIKAN	AK	99901	Bristol Bay
ORA	HALL	DANIEL	R	BOX 1164	PALMER	AK	99645	Bristol Bay
PACIFIC DRIFTER	AGEN	DANIEL	J	14145 AVON ALLEN	MOUNT VERNON	WA	98273	Bristol Bay
PANDEMONIUM IV	NEESE	MICHAEL		BOX 2947	HOMER	AK	99603	Bristol Bay
PAT-DE-J	HUNT	ROBERT		BOX 772181	EAGLE RIVER	AK	99577	Bristol Bay
PAULINE MARIE	JORDAN	LINDA		BOX 98	MANOKOTAK	AK	99628	Bristol Bay
PETER	SUAREZ	ROBERTO		16039 TILLER TRAIL HWY	DAYS CREEK	OR	97429	Bristol Bay
PRELUDE	KALUGIN	ALEXANDER		BOX 4282	HOMER	AK	99603	Bristol Bay

Purse Seiner & Drift Gill Net Salmon/Herring Boats

Vessel	Owner	Address	City	State	Zip	Area
PROVIDENCE	KANDOLL BRIAN	BOX 1363	PETERSBURG	AK	99833	Bristol Bay
QUANTUM LEAP	GARDNER LUKE	BOX 62	NASELLE	WA	98638	Bristol Bay
QUEEN ANN	CHRISTENSEN JOHN	1001 TRAPPER HILL RD	PORT HEIDEN	AK	99549	Bristol Bay
QUESTAR	TORGERSON ROLF	5118 167TH AVE CT KPS	LONGBRANCH	WA	98351	Bristol Bay
RAINI MARIE	THORSON RAYMOND	BOX 1130	DILLINGHAM	AK	99576	Bristol Bay
RASCAL	CARL SAMUEL	BOX 001	KIPNUK	AK	99614	Bristol Bay
RATSO	ROGOTZKE ROGER	27090 320TH ST	SLEEPY EYE	MN	56085	Bristol Bay
RAVEN	WHITTLESEY PATRICK	16121 PENINSULA RD	STANWOOD	WA	98292	Bristol Bay
RECOVERY	ENGBRETSON VINCENT	35622 TUCKER CREEK LN	ASTORIA	OR	97103	Bristol Bay
RED BLUFF	MULHOLLAND MARTIN	4978 HIGHLAND DR	BLAINE	WA	98230	Bristol Bay
RED INERTIA	FRANKS MICHAEL	3565 SAILBOARD CIR	ANCHORAGE	AK	99516	Bristol Bay
RED MAGIC	WHITE TARAN	1910 SW 18TH AVE #23	PORTLAND	OR	97201	Bristol Bay
RED ZONE	WILLIS VICTOR R	444 FREDRICKS DR	ANCHORAGE	AK	99504	Bristol Bay
RIMROCK	FITZGERALD JANE	BOX 3088	KODIAK	AK	99615	Bristol Bay
ROGUE	BAY BOAT FISHERIES INC/FYECK	75-678 NANI OHAI PL #9	KAILUA KONA	HI	96740	Bristol Bay
ROLAND D	TUFTE PAUL	7529 BOWSER CT	CRANE LAKE	MN	55725	Bristol Bay
RYAN A	ANDREW ROY	BOX 137	TOGIAK	AK	99678	Bristol Bay
SABOTAGE	WILLIS VICTOR	444 FREDRICKS DR	ANCHORAGE	AK	99504	Bristol Bay
SAPPHIRE	LARSEN BRADLEY	BOX 2914	WASILLA	AK	99654	Bristol Bay
SHANNON	BELL MICHAEL E	BOX 849	CRAIG	AK	99921	Bristol Bay
SHARON A	FOX STEVEN	7034 DIBBLE AVE NW	SEATTLE	WA	98117	Bristol Bay
SHERRY SEA	CHRISTENSEN NICK	BOX 203	DILLINGHAM	AK	99576	Bristol Bay
SHOWDOWN	MARTUSHEV SERGEI	BOX 1299	HOMER	AK	99603	Bristol Bay
SIGNE LIND	FV I INC	BOX 1170	HAILEY	ID	83333	Bristol Bay
SIVIA	NOSTE SEAN	2167 W BEACH RD	OAK HARBOR	WA	98277	Bristol Bay
SOCKEYE SUMMERS II	FRANULOVIC ADRIAN	1129 SAN ANDRES ST	SANTA BARBARA	CA	93101	Bristol Bay
SOPHIA MARIE	MORGAN MICHAEL	BOX 754	LANGLEY	WA	98260	Bristol Bay

Vessel	Owner	Address	City	State	Zip	Area
STAR OF ICELAND	SPANGLER JOHN	3111 S 273RD ST	AUBURN	WA	98001	Bristol Bay
STELLA MARINA	LOGRANDE BENIDETTO	2700 CAHUENGA BLVD E #4216	LOS ANGELES	CA	90068	Bristol Bay
STEPHANIE M	TARABOCHIA FRANK	872 15TH ST	ASTORIA	OR	97103	Bristol Bay
STORMIN' NORMAN	JAMES FRANK	BOX 25	PLATINUM	AK	99651	Bristol Bay
STORMY	MACH PAUL	8257 16TH AVE NUE	SEATTLE	WA	98115	Bristol Bay
SUMMER GOLD	CABANILLA CHARLIE	14857 PIERCE RD	BYRON	MI	48418	Bristol Bay
SUNLIGHT	WILSON MIKE	181 KEVINA RD	ELLENSBURG	WA	98926	Bristol Bay
SYDNEY GRACE	CLEVELAND DARREN	BOX 88	QUINHAGAK	AK	99655	Bristol Bay
TEODORO	PAUK DAN	BOX 82	MANOKOTAK	AK	99628	Bristol Bay
TERRI LYNN	ALBRIGHT DUANE	BOX 132	EGEGIK	AK	99579	Bristol Bay
TERRIE	HANEY STEVEN	7691 N NAN LN	PALMER	AK	99645	Bristol Bay
THERESA LEE	PEPER DEAN	1406 19TH AVE	SEATTLE	WA	98122	Bristol Bay
THUMPER	THAYER RAYMOND	626 VAN WYCK RD	BELLINGHAM	WA	98226	Bristol Bay
TIBURON	WHITE RAYMOND	BOX 28	EEK	AK	99578	Bristol Bay
TILLKEN	KROON LOREN	1131 MCADOO WY	WASILLA	AK	99654	Bristol Bay
TIMOTHY	DYASUK ANDREW	BOX 12	TOGIAK	AK	99678	Bristol Bay
TOMMIE O	BURNFIELD SCOTT	561 E EAGLE RIDGE DR	SHELTON	WA	98584	Bristol Bay
TOONCES	BUCHMAYR ROBERT	18770 RIDGEFIELD RD NW	SHORELINE	WA	98177	Bristol Bay
TRC	WASSILY STEVE	BOX 458	DILLINGHAM	AK	99576	Bristol Bay
TRIPLE P	MATHEWS ALLEN	3450 CATHEDRAL ROCK RD	MALAGA	WA	98828	Bristol Bay
TRISHA E	SWANSON ROBERT	BOX 924	PETERSBURG	AK	99833	Bristol Bay
VALERIE ANN	LARSON ALBERT	BOX 702	DILLINGHAM	AK	99576	Bristol Bay
VITUS	WHITTERN C. KEITH	7490 W 350 N	SHIPSHEWANA	IN	46565	Bristol Bay
WAVE DANCER	MARTIN MAX	BOX 994	DILLINGHAM	AK	99576	Bristol Bay
WICKERSHAM	WALKER RONALD	9820 W SOLOMA CT	WASILLA	AK	99654	Bristol Bay
WIGEON	RYAN MATT	5145 GRAVELINE RD	BELLINGHAM	WA	98226	Bristol Bay
WILLOW	SQUALICUM MOUNTAIN INC	1808 ACADEMY RD	BELLINGHAM	WA	98226	Bristol Bay

Vessel	Owner	Address	City	State	Zip	Area
WOOSTER	JONROWE MICHAEL	BOX 272	WILLOW	AK	99688	Bristol Bay
XS	XS LLC	BOX 1230	DILLINGHAM	AK	99576	Bristol Bay
YOYO	ETUCKMELRA MIKE	BOX 3	ALEKNAGIK	AK	99555	Bristol Bay
ALEUT	ANGASAN MARK	BOX 532	KING SALMON	AK	99613	Bristol Bay
AMBER MONIQUE	THORSON THOMAS	BOX 1130	DILLINGHAM	AK	99576	Bristol Bay
ANDI	LOCKUK PETER	BOX 88	TOGIAK	AK	99678	Bristol Bay
AYHAN	AYHAN AFANASI	12499 HOWELL PRAIRIE RD NE	GERVAIS	OR	97026	Bristol Bay
BEER BOTTLE MAMA	PEDERSEN DAVID	BOX 1332	DILLINGHAM	AK	99576	Bristol Bay
BRADEN	WILLIAMS ABE	BOX 105	KING SALMON	AK	99613	Bristol Bay
BRIANNA MARIE	BRANDON EDWARD	BOX 1016	DILLINGHAM	AK	99576	Bristol Bay
BRISTOL BREEZE	BROYLES KELLY	BOX 759	FIRST HILL	CA	95631	Bristol Bay
BUPBUP	FLENSBURG GEORGE	BOX 77	DILLINGHAM	AK	99576	Bristol Bay
CAPE CLEARE	PILLING MICHAEL	14245 OTTER WAY	JUNEAU	AK	99801	Bristol Bay
CAPE MENSHIKOF	KINGSLEY DANIEL	BOX 463	PILOT POINT	AK	99649	Bristol Bay
CHAOS	BASARGIN ANDREAN	BOX 1393	HOMER	AK	99603	Bristol Bay
CHULYEN	THOMPSON EVERETT	BOX 151	NAKNEK	AK	99633	Bristol Bay
CINDY B	BAVILLA HENRY	BOX 111	TOGIAK	AK	99678	Bristol Bay
DOLPHIN	TARABOCHIA DANIEL	7613 ELM CT SE	OLYMPIA	WA	98503	Bristol Bay
DREAM BOAT	GERVAIS TIMOTHY	BOX 7	RUBY	AK	99768	Bristol Bay
DUES PAYER II	THOMPSON PETER	BOX 3037	KODIAK	AK	99615	Bristol Bay
EAGLE II	JOHNSON WILLIAM	BOX 1178	DILLINGHAM	AK	99576	Bristol Bay
FAIR WIN	JOHNSON DENNIS	BOX 757	DILLINGHAM	AK	99576	Bristol Bay
FREE SPIRIT	TIMMERMAN JAMES	BOX 475	DILLINGHAM	AK	99576	Bristol Bay
GARFIELD	SHARP MICKEY	BOX TWA	TWIN HILLS	AK	99576	Bristol Bay
ISLANDIA	HANDY TRAVIS	BOX 55	DILLINGHAM	AK	99576	Bristol Bay

Vessel	Owner	Address	City	State	Zip	Area
JENNIFER LYNN	NICHOLSON HANS	5301 SHENNUM DR	WASILLA	AK	99654	Bristol Bay
JIMMY JOHN	ECHUCK RICHARD	BOX 213	TOGIAK	AK	99678	Bristol Bay
JOAN W	WHITING STEPHEN	1302 W MUKILTEO BLVD	EVERETT	WA	98203	Bristol Bay
KAHUNA	MATHIEU STEVEN	1721 MISSION RD	KODIAK	AK	99615	Bristol Bay
KRIAD	HELLBERG KARL	900 SE ANCHOR AVE	WARRENTON	OR	97146	Bristol Bay
KRISTIN KAY	TOLBERT WITHERS	BOX 324	KING SALMON	AK	99613	Bristol Bay
LAURA LEE	ZIMIN CARL	BOX 387	NAKNEK	AK	99633	Bristol Bay
LISA K	KOETJE JEFFREY	18180 DUNBAR RD	MOUNT VERNON	WA	98273	Bristol Bay
LITTLE ONE II	PAVIAN SAMUEL	BOX 208	TOGIAK	AK	99678	Bristol Bay
LUND	ANDREW JOSEPH	BOX 102	TOGIAK	AK	99678	Bristol Bay
MIRANDA	ALEXIE, MOSES & MARY	BOX 103	TULUKSAK	AK	99679	Bristol Bay
MISS DEBI	SPANGLER JOHN	3111 S 273RD ST	AUBURN	WA	98001	Bristol Bay
NEXUS	VUKICH DANISLAV	BOX 177	NAKNEK	AK	99633	Bristol Bay
NICKIO	NICKIO	BOX 1266	DILLINGHAM	AK	99576	Bristol Bay
NO POINT	KWACHKA ALEXUS	326 COPE ST	KODIAK	AK	99615	Bristol Bay
ORION	SOMERVILLE DAVID	BOX 163	PETERSBURG	AK	99833	Bristol Bay
PATRICK JASON	LOCKUK PETER	BOX 88	TOGIAK	AK	99678	Bristol Bay
PEGASUS	DERANJA BOZHO	2667 DUNDEE PL	LOS ANGELES	CA	90027	Bristol Bay
PERRY L	MCWILLIAMS TATSURO	BOX 921377	DUTCH HARBOR	AK	99692	Bristol Bay
PHANTOM	KIRK GEORGE	BOX 2796	KODIAK	AK	99615	Bristol Bay
PROFIT	ANDREAS FISHERIES	BOX 506	KODIAK	AK	99615	Bristol Bay
PROWLER	MYERS DALE	BOX 433	KING SALMON	AK	99613	Bristol Bay
QUICKIE	NELSON WILLIAM	BOX 33	EKWOK	AK	99580	Bristol Bay
RAINY DAWN	BLOOM LINDSEY	1114 SLIM WILLIAMS WY	JUNEAU	AK	99801	Bristol Bay
RED RIDER	YEOMAN FAMILY FISHERIES	51053 E END RD	HOMER	AK	99603	Bristol Bay
SALLY-O II	OLSEN THOMAS	BOX 856	DILLINGHAM	AK	99576	Bristol Bay
SAMSON II	GAMECHUK TERENCE	BOX 66	MANOKOTAK	AK	99628	Bristol Bay

Vessel	Owner	Address	City	State	Zip	Area
SEA KING	GERVIAS, MEGHAN & TIMO	BOX 7	RUBY	AK	99768	Bristol Bay
SEA RACER	BASARGIN NIKITA	BOX 1788	HOMER	AK	99603	Bristol Bay
SPIKE	PIKE FRED	BOX 5	NAKNEK	AK	99633	Bristol Bay
STARGAZER	THOMPSON CHARLES	BOX 2193	KODIAK	AK	99615	Bristol Bay
SURRENDER	REUTOV TRIFILYI	BOX 793	HOMER	AK	99603	Bristol Bay
SUSAN ANN	POULSEN ANTHONY	BOX 154	TOGIAK	AK	99678	Bristol Bay
TASHA ANN	ECHUCK RICHARD	BOX 213	TOGIAK	AK	99678	Bristol Bay
TEAL	NOSTE MARK	2167 W BEACH RD	OAK HARBOR	WA	98236	Bristol Bay
ULU	TILDEN THOMAS	BOX 786	DILLINGHAM	AK	99576	Bristol Bay
VESTIGE	URE DAVID	BOX 1950	KODIAK	AK	99615	Bristol Bay
WEBBSLINGER II	WEBB JOHN	92615 ASTOR RD	ASTORIA	OR	97103	Bristol Bay
WIND N SEA	BELSON ROGER	6700 EILEEN CIR	ANCHORAGE	AK	99507	Bristol Bay
YELLIN MAN	EGBERT HARRY	BOX 114	CLARKS POINT	AK	99569	Bristol Bay
BLUE ICE	JACKINSKY BRENDA	BOX 39127	NINILCHIK	AK	99639	Cook Inlet
HYUS	VANDEVERE DYER	BOX 504	KASILOF	AK	99610	Cook Inlet
KAKNU	SHOWALTER JAMES	BOX 352	SOLDOTNA	AK	99669	Cook Inlet
MO	WESTERN TONY	53320 LINDGREN CT	KASILOF	AK	99610	Cook Inlet
OLD FACEFULL	FV INDEPENDENCE INC	BOX 273	SELDOVIA	AK	99663	Cook Inlet
RISKY BUSINESS	DAVIS LLOYD	BOX 2253	KENAI	AK	99611	Cook Inlet
SNOW BREEZE	KIVI GARY	BOX 7208	NIKISKI	AK	99635	Cook Inlet
TEKTITE	BUCKMEIER DARRELL	BOX 222116	ANCHORAGE	AK	99522	Cook Inlet
YABUTT	JACKINSKY GARY	BOX 39127	NINILCHIK	AK	99639	Cook Inlet
AGHILEEN	WOLFE ROBERT	BOX 1125	GIRDWOOD	AK	99587	Cook Inlet
ANGARA	KALUGIN KONDRATY	6098 TOPAZ ST NE	SALEM	OR	97305	Cook Inlet
ANGARA	KALUGIN MARIA	6098 TOPAZ ST NE	SALEM	OR	97305	Cook Inlet

Vessel	Owner	Address	City	State	Zip	Area
ANNIE Q	PERRY CHRISTOPHER	BOX 1808	HOMER	AK	99603	Cook Inlet
ARCTIC VIKING	OLSGARD DALE	BOX 999	HOMER	AK	99603	Cook Inlet
ARIZONA	KUZMIN VASILY	BOX 1599	DELTA JUNCTION	AK	99737	Cook Inlet
BALLAD	CHAPMAN BRYAN	BOX 31	SOLDOTNA	AK	99669	Cook Inlet
BARON	SELF RICHARD	BOX 805	STERLING	AK	99672	Cook Inlet
BUCKWHEAT	RUSSELL JUSTIN	BOX 795	WASILLA	AK	99654	Cook Inlet
BUENA VIDA	DOLCHOK RONALD	BOX 83	KENAI	AK	99611	Cook Inlet
CHIPPEWA	MEEHAN RONALD	BOX 1670	SOLDOTNA	AK	99669	Cook Inlet
COMMITMENT	PIPER CHARLES	BOX 15233	FRITZ CREEK	AK	99603	Cook Inlet
COPA	JONES ROLAND	250 PHILLIPS DR	KENAI	AK	99611	Cook Inlet
CYGNET	MARTUSHEV ANDREI	BOX 805	HOMER	AK	99603	Cook Inlet
DANCING SKY	THOMPSON ERIC	1241 DENALI #205	ANCHORAGE	AK	99501	Cook Inlet
GRETA LYNN	EIDEM JERALD	331 PAMELA PL #1	ANCHORAGE	AK	99504	Cook Inlet
HOOLIGAN	LORAN KEVIN	5536 KENNY HILL DR	ANCHORAGE	AK	99504	Cook Inlet
KAHUNA	MAHAN MARK	BOX 110316	ANCHORAGE	AK	99511	Cook Inlet
KENAITZE	WILSON WAYNE	212 LINWOOD LN	KENAI	AK	99611	Cook Inlet
LADY LEE	SPARLIN DREW	37020 CANNERY RD	KENAI	AK	99611	Cook Inlet
LEOPARD	ROGERSS JERRY	605 CEDAR DR	KENAI	AK	99611	Cook Inlet
LOUJON	HOLT WILLIAM	BOX 794	KASILOF	AK	99610	Cook Inlet
MARIA LYNN	SALTZ EDWIN	BOX 747	SOLDOTNA	AK	99669	Cook Inlet
NAVIGATOR	WATKINS ERICK	BOX 2536	SOLDOTNA	AK	99669	Cook Inlet
NO FEAR	IVANOV SAVIN	802 STARK ST	SILVERTON	OR	97381	Cook Inlet
OTTER WOMAN	VANEK RION	BOX 39251	NINILCHIK	AK	99639	Cook Inlet
PANTHER	SUBLETT REUBEN	29557 STERLING HWY	STERLING	AK	99672	Cook Inlet
PREDATOR	WESTERN TONY	53320 LINDGREN CT	KASILOF	AK	99610	Cook Inlet
RD-73	TEPP ROBERT	2715 WATERGATE WY	KENAI	AK	99611	Cook Inlet
ROGUE	VANDEVERE DYER	BOX 504	KASILOF	AK	99610	Cook Inlet

Vessel	Owner	Address	City	State	Zip	Area
ROULETTE	WESTERN BRENT	2500 AUTUMN DR	ANCHORAGE	AK	99516	Cook Inlet
ROY	PERRY CHRISTOPHER	BOX 1808	HOMER	AK	99603	Cook Inlet
RUTH ANN	TAURIAINEN A.CARL	46850 TAURIAINEN TRAIL	KENAI	AK	99611	Cook Inlet
SHADOW LINE	KLINKER THOMAS	408 NO VIEW AVE	HOMER	AK	99603	Cook Inlet
SHERRY	RUSSELL RONALD	BOX 2	CLAM GULCH	AK	99568	Cook Inlet
SHOGUN	CLARK STEVEN	BOX C	NEWMAN GROVE	NE	68758	Cook Inlet
SIRRAH	HARRIS ROGER	BOX 7013	NIKISKI	AK	99635	Cook Inlet
STA SEA	GUERTIN MARK	6327 STATE ST	GARDEN	MI	49835	Cook Inlet
STACY JO	CORREIA ROBERT	BOX 227	KASILOF	AK	99610	Cook Inlet
STARSHINE	BRIDGES DONALD	BOX 963	KENAI	AK	99611	Cook Inlet
SWIFT ARROW	VANDEVERE DYER	BOX 504	KASILOF	AK	99610	Cook Inlet
TEMPEST	SYLCE CHRIS	BOX 1238	HOMER	AK	99603	Cook Inlet
VOLGA	KUZMIN FADEY	BOX 3009	HOMER	AK	99603	Cook Inlet
ZIMA	KUZMIN PAVEL	BOX 1669	KODIAK	AK	99615	Cook Inlet
ARLENE ROSE	GALILA HOMER	BOX 85	GOODNEWS BAY	AK	99589	Kuskokwim
DAUGHTER	FOX ESTHER	BOX 70	GOODNEWS BAY	AK	99589	Kuskokwim
TRISTAN J	JOHN NORMAN	BOX 68	KWIGILLINGOK	AK	99622	Kuskokwim
ONEY	AMIK DAVID	BOX 1033	BETHEL	AK	99559	Lower Yukon
SILVER DAWN	LAMONT JOHN	BOX 32248	MOUNTAIN VILLAGE	AK	99632	Lower Yukon
ISADORE T II	KELLY ELIAS	BOX 5093	PILOT STATION	AK	99650	Lower Yukon

Vessel	Owner	Address	City	State	Zip	Area
STACY ANNA	DUNLAP WILLIAM	6209 RIVERSIDE DR	YANKEETOWN	FL	34498	Peninsula/Aleutian Islands
GIDEON	BROWN LEO	35717 WALKABOUT RD	HOMER	AK	99603	Peninsula/Aleutian Islands
BAR TENDER	MERRITT JAMES	BOX 386	CORDOVA	AK	99574	Prince William Sound
BELEN C	COOK JOE	BOX 215	CORDOVA	AK	99574	Prince William Sound
DOG MATIC	WIESE ROBERT	BOX 864	CORDOVA	AK	99574	Prince William Sound
ESTER C	CABANA HILARY	BOX 612	HOMER	AK	99603	Prince William Sound
JAMM'N SALM'N	HARRINGTON MARK	BOX 1450	PALISADE	CO	81526	Prince William Sound
KARI JEAN	GILMAN INC	BOX 223	CORDOVA	AK	99574	Prince William Sound
PENTIUM	PHILLIPS GARY	BOX 3041	VALDEZ	AK	99686	Prince William Sound
SLO LEARNER	SAUNDERS PAUL	BOX 451	CORDOVA	AK	99574	Prince William Sound
SPIKE ISLAND	HARVILL JOHN	BOX 1569	CORDOVA	AK	99574	Prince William Sound
SURVIVOR	BABIC RUSSELL	BOX 1833	CORDOVA	AK	99574	Prince William Sound
TAYLOR MAID	BARNES STEPHEN	BOX 332	CORDOVA	AK	99574	Prince William Sound
WITS END	BABIC JACK	BOX 1208	CORDOVA	AK	99574	Prince William Sound
CANVAS BACK	BOCCI JOHN	BOX 1312	CORDOVA	AK	99574	Prince William Sound
CORACLE	WIESE HENRY	BOX 1708	CORDOVA	AK	99574	Prince William Sound
DRIFTER	JENSEN JACK	BOX 1265	CORDOVA	AK	99574	Prince William Sound
EAGLE	KRITCHEN KENNETH	BOX 1255	CORDOVA	AK	99574	Prince William Sound
INDIAN SUMMER	FLEMING JOSEPH	BOX 231746	ANCHORAGE	AK	99523	Prince William Sound
INVESTOR	FEFELOV IVAN	BOX 684	HOMER	AK	99603	Prince William Sound
JENNA MARIE	BOWEN MICHAEL	BOX 203	PALMER	AK	99645	Prince William Sound
KARINA NICHOLE	PHILLIPS GLENN	BOX 1165	CORDOVA	AK	99574	Prince William Sound
MISS STEPHANIE	LIPSCOMB GORDON	BOX 1311	CORDOVA	AK	99574	Prince William Sound
NORTHERN STAR	ANDREWS JON	BOX 1034	SEWARD	AK	99664	Prince William Sound
POINT AFTER	TAYLOR GARY	BOX 112241	ANCHORAGE	AK	99511	Prince William Sound
PROSPERITY	CARROLL KIP	3746 27TH PL S	FEDERAL WAY	WA	98003	Prince William Sound

Vessel	Owner	Address	City	State	Zip	Area
PROSPERITY	HAISMAN KEVIN	BOX 174	CORDOVA	AK	99574	Prince William Sound
SEA DANCER	REUTOV EFERY	BOX 283	WILLOW	AK	99688	Prince William Sound
SOPHISTICATED LADY	REID WILLIAM	BOX 1234	CORDOVA	AK	99574	Prince William Sound
TWIN SISTERS	DEBRULER DAN	BOX 1892	CORDOVA	AK	99574	Prince William Sound
AMERICANEXPRESS	HANSON BRET	2916 ST CLAIR ST	BELLINGHAM	WA	98226	Southeast
ARCTIC DREAM	GREGG RICHARD	BOX 20669	JUNEAU	AK	99802	Southeast
CAROL LOUISE	NILSEN MICHAEL	BOX 2069	PETERSBURG	AK	99833	Southeast
CLANCY	LEACH LEONARD	BOX 6017	KETCHIKAN	AK	99901	Southeast
CORSAIR	JOHNSON CHRISTOPHER	BOX 2183	WRANGELL	AK	99929	Southeast
HOLLY RAE	LEASK JOHN	BOX 331	METLAKATLA	AK	99926	Southeast
HOT ROD	KLEPSER DONALD	1108 DUNTON ST	KETCHIKAN	AK	99901	Southeast
MISS TREE	MILLER JOSHUA	BOX 252	PETERSBURG	AK	99833	Southeast
MONICA ANN	HUDSON RICHARD	BOX 194	METLAKATLA	AK	99926	Southeast
NINA MARIE	MCCAY CALEY	BOX 2142	PETERSBURG	AK	99833	Southeast
NO PROBLEM	KLEPSER, DAVID & MELISSA	BOX 8946	KETCHIKAN	AK	99901	Southeast
PACIFIC DON	HAMILTON JAMES	BOX 3082	KODIAK	AK	99615	Southeast
PISCES	FREDERICK JAMES	2007 COVE PL	ANACORTES	WA	98221	Southeast
SALTY	BEZENEK CLAY	1617 WATER ST	KETCHIKAN	AK	99901	Southeast
TENACIOUS	DICKINSON ROBERT	1175 MOUNT BAKER HWY	BELLINGHAM	WA	98226	Southeast
WHISTLER	THYNES STEVEN	BOX 193	PETERSBURG	AK	99833	Southeast
AMBER TIDE	STROMDAHL JAMES	BOX 1326	PETERSBURG	AK	99833	Southeast
ARVILLA ANN	MAVES SHELTON	BOX 117	CRAIG	AK	99921	Southeast
BIDARKA	LARSON ERIC	BOX 301	PETERSBURG	AK	99833	Southeast
BIG SHOOTER	COTTRELL MIKE	BOX 2010	PETERSBURG	AK	99833	Southeast
CHRISDAHL I	CHRISTENSEN CHARLES	BOX 824	PETERSBURG	AK	99833	Southeast

Vessel	Owner	Address	City	State	Zip	Area
CONDOR	MARTIN DAVID	BOX 88	PETERSBURG	AK	99833	Southeast
DAYSPRING	MATTSON BRIAN	BOX 1168	PETERSBURG	AK	99833	Southeast
DEJA VU	ATKINSON ELDON	BOX 279	METLAKATLA	AK	99926	Southeast
DENAE MARIE	THYNES DEREK	BOX 1624	PETERSBURG	AK	99833	Southeast
ECLIPSE	KLEPSER KEVIN	1108 DUNTON ST	KETCHIKAN	AK	99901	Southeast
ELENA MARIE	SALDI MARK	BOX 287	SKAGWAY	AK	99840	Southeast
FIN	MARTIN JOHN	BOX 825	PETERSBURG	AK	99833	Southeast
KIRSTEN ANNA	SHELTON JEV	1670 EVERGREEN AVE	JUNEAU	AK	99801	Southeast
LADY LISA	HUDSON RICHARD	BOX 194	METLAKATLA	AK	99926	Southeast
LASER	THOMPSON RICHARD	443 WINDWARD WAY	DAVENPORT	FL	33837	Southeast
LESLEY ANN	BOSWORTH DALE	BOX 45	PETERSBURG	AK	99833	Southeast
MOONSHADOW	ENGE ARNOLD	BOX 2113	PETERSBURG	AK	99833	Southeast
OCEAN PEARL	JACKSON WAYNE	BOX 8395	KETCHIKAN	AK	99901	Southeast
PENNOCK	ODMARK TED	BOX 23027	KETCHIKAN	AK	99901	Southeast
RED HEAD	COOK KARL	BOX 492	METLAKATLA	AK	99926	Southeast
REVERIE	ALMQUIST ALLAN	308 DEERMOUNT	KETCHIKAN	AK	99901	Southeast
RUNAWAY I	SALTY SEA FISHERIES	2417 TONGASS AVE #111-114	KETCHIKAN	AK	99901	Southeast
RYLEY DAWN	BOOTH CHRISTOPHER	BOX 576	METLAKATLA	AK	99926	Southeast
SAKINA	WILLIS JOE	BOX 43	PETERSBURG	AK	99833	Southeast
SILVERDAWN	ODEGAARD JAMES	2309 CEDAR CT	MOUNT VERNON	WA	98273	Southeast
SOPHIA NICOLE	SCUDERO JERRY	955 FOREST AVE	KETCHIKAN	AK	99901	Southeast
STAR SHIP	WRIGHT ANDY	BOX 1432	PETERSBURG	AK	99833	Southeast
WAVE RYDER	ARRINGTON PAUL	BOX 252	WRANGELL	AK	99929	Southeast
YASHA	BOSWORTH DALE	BOX 45	PETERSBURG	AK	99833	Southeast

About the Author

Captain Jonathan Allen graduated in 1980 from California Maritime Academy with an Unlimited Third Mates License, a naval commission, and, in his words, a deep distrust of anyone wearing khaki.

During the first nine years of his maritime career Capt. Allen worked aboard many types of vessels—dry cargo ships, tankers, and research ships—reaching the rank of chief mate. In 1989 he discovered fishing. He tried them all: trawling, crabbing, & longlining. He ran the *Unimak Enterprise, Lilli Ann, Arctic V, Blue North,* and others. After an extremely exciting and successful fishing career, realizing that fishing is a young man's gig and having become a proud father of three children over the years, he finally relented and returned to cargo shipping, where he remains today.

Throughout the years, Capt. Allen has attended the most comprehensive theoretical and practical training offered to seafarers through Maritime Institute of Technology and Graduate Studies / Pacific Maritime Institute (MITAGS-PMI). In July of 1998, Capt. Allen became a member of the International Organization of Masters Mates and Pilots. Capt. Allen's qualifications include an Unlimited Masters License and several Alaskan pilotages. He is conversational in Spanish as a second language.

Capt. Allen currently lives in Idaho with his wife, Tammy, and children, Benjamin, Shaelyn and Daegan. He currently works as a Chief Officer for APL Maritime Ltd. He and his wife, Tammy own and operate Prodigious Press LLC.

Capt. Allen, the published author of *The Big Bucks Guide to Commercial Fishing in Alaska,* is presently working on writing his second book, *The Big Bucks Guide to Merchant Shipping*—that is, when he and his family are not off hunting the Big Holes, or fishing the Snake River.